THE IMPACT OF ARMED CONFLICTS ON WOMEN IN SOUTH ASIA

The Regional Centre for Strategic Studies (RCSS) is an independent, non-profit and non-governmental organization for collaborative research, networking and interaction on strategic and international issues pertaining to South Asia. Set up in 1992, the RCSS is based in Colombo, Sri Lanka.

The RCSS is a South Asian forum for studies, training and multi-track dialogue and deliberation on issues of regional interest. All activities of RCSS are designed with a South Asia focus and are usually participated by experts from all South Asian countries. The Centre is envisaged as a forum for advancing the cause of cooperation, security, conflict resolution, confidence building, peace and development in the countries of the South Asian region.

The RCSS serves its South Asian and international constituency by: (a) networking programmes that promote interaction, communication and exchange between institutions and individuals within and outside the region engaged in South Asian strategic studies; (b) organizing regional workshops and seminars and sponsoring and coordinating collaborative research, and (c) disseminating output of the research through publications which include books, monographs and a quarterly newsletter. The RCSS facilitates scholars and other professionals of South Asia to address, mutually and collectively, problems and, issues of topical interest for all countries of the region.

Queries may be addressed to:

Regional Centre for Strategic Studies
2 Elibank Road
Colombo 5
SRI LANKA
Tel: (94-11) 2599734, 599735
Fax: 2599993; e-mail: edrcss@sri.lanka.net
RCSS website: http://www.rcss.org

THE IMPACT OF ARMED CONFLICTS ON WOMEN IN SOUTH ASIA

Edited by
AVA DARSHAN SHRESTHA
RITA THAPA

REGIONAL CENTRE FOR STRATEGIC STUDIES
COLOMBO

MANOHAR
2007

First published 2007

ISBN 81-7304-724-3

Published by

Ajay Kumar Jain for
Manohar Publishers & Distributors
4753/23 Ansari Road, Daryaganj
New Delhi 110 002

Typeset at

Digigrafics
New Delhi 110 049

Printed at

Lordson Publishers Pvt. Ltd.
Delhi 110 007

Contents

RCSS is grateful to the Ford Foundation
for its generous support for the project on
Understanding and Combating Terrorism in South Asia
under Regional Collaborative Research Initiatives
on Non-Traditional Security in South Asia.

Preface

This book is a direct outcome of the Regional Centre for Strategic Studies (RCSS) workshop on 'Conceptualization & Planning Conference on Understanding and Combating Terrorism in South Asia' that was held in Sri Lanka on 5–6 July 2003. All along, it has been a fascinating and a challenging journey in putting together this study. The value and the use of this book has been in engaging some of the most outstanding women activists and academics in the region. Their commitment to the issues that are underlined throughout this book made it a possibility. Using the most suitable approach, the writers culled out and built on the lifelong work some of them have done in this area. Amena Mohsin was caught in the crossfire doing this work, Anuradha Chenoy engaged her students in the collection of data and materials, and Saba Gul Khattak had to bring 'time' on her side. It was very lucky for us to have Sunila Abeysekera's take on the Sri Lanka paper. In Nepal, during the height of the conflict, research of this nature brought with it many challenges, and we were lucky to strengthen our Nepal team with the inclusion of Chandra Bhadra. Rita personally led the research in the Far Western District during the time of state-declared emergency. This research volume often and to varying degrees involved costs at the personal level for the writers. We are thankful that this book was possible without any mishap. Jennifer Hales, a doctoral student from the University of Toronto volunteering with Nagarik Aawaz assisted in putting the papers together and providing external and additional insights.

Although it was our responsibility to facilitate the outcome of this book, the authors were involved in the design and processing of this book. Anuradha Chenoy and Amena Mohsin provided invaluable guidance and helped shape the original framework for this book, while Sunila Abeysekera helped us weave together some of the key points of the study in the introduction. Being new to this kind of work, we greatly valued their inputs, though we feel that they gave precedence to a feminist approach in doing this work. Communications across country-borders in this region were always thoughtful, caring and respectful, making this difficult work pleasurable and our learning immeasurable in this process. We feel the book is done, but the connections and work have only begun, not only for the writers but for all who will engage in the issues highlighted in this book.

From the inception until the end of this work, we have been inspired and have felt completely supported by the Executive Director of the RCSS, Professor Sridhar Khatri. We are glad that he felt that this was an important area to single out, explore and highlight while we talk of terrorism and ensuing/existing conflicts. During this process, we feel we could not have managed to fulfil our tasks in the given time without his wholehearted support, understanding, and valuable inputs.

Though we have not been surprised by the similarities of the implications of the conflict on the women of the region despite their geographic and cultural diversity, viewing the unfolding narrative post-research has been personally difficult and painful. We also recognize that though this study focused on women, there is a need to look into the impacts of conflicts on men separately for a holistic understanding of its gendered impact. Finally, we hope this book will shake up the complacency and the 'take it for granted' attitude of all responsible parties, primarily the nation states of our region for the apparent negligence and systemic abuse that women of the region have borne, particularly in situations of conflict. This book no longer allows for any excuse for lack of empirical evidence to act seriously and promptly.

We are very thankful for having been given this opportunity to be authors as well as editors in this important endeavour.

AVA DARSHAN SHRESTHA AND RITA THAPA

1. Introduction
Historical Background: The Nature of Conflict in Modern South Asia

Ava Darshan Shrestha and Rita Thapa

The history of post-colonial South Asia is riven with a variety of conflicts based on the diverse identities of the region, which have often manifested themselves in extremely brutal and violent ways. The consequences of this violence and its impact on ordinary civilians, and, in particular, its impact on women, forms the focus of this study of five South Asian countries: India, Pakistan, Bangladesh, Nepal, and Sri Lanka.

As all the papers in the volume point out, violent conflict in South Asia has arisen due to many different reasons. This diversity is in part because of the differences in the historical evolution of each of these countries as independent nation states. There are also geopolitical, economic, social, ethnic, religious and linguistic differences and disadvantages in these societies. In most of the cases under discussion here, the conflicts primarily tend to be located in the remotest, poorest and least developed parts of the countries. It is these experiences of discrimination and disadvantage that have led to the emergence of various identity-based political groups that have taken up the cause of their immediate community. In the form of diverse struggles for independence, nationhood, self-determination, autonomy, secession, and separation.

The various struggles discussed in these papers bear witness to these differences. In her paper on Bangladesh, Amena Mohsin describes the struggle for autonomy launched by the indigenous people of the Chittagong Hill Tracts (CHT). They hope that, this will give them the right to govern the regions they inhabit and control over its resources. Writing about Sri Lanka, Sunila Abeysekera focuses on the insurgencies in both the south and north of the island, driven by an extreme form of nationalism in the south and by a separatist demand in the north. Chandra Bhadra, Ava Darshan Shrestha and Rita Thapa study the situation in Nepal brought about by the Maoist insurgency and their struggles for social and economic justice and equitable distribution of wealth and resources. Saba Gul Khattak, writing on Pakistan, references her paper on the post-9/11 scenario and writes of the suppression of all those communities identified as 'terrorists' or as 'terrorist supporters' on the borders between Pakistan and Afghanistan. The conflict-ridden regions of Nagaland, Manipur and Kashmir provide the backdrop to Anuradha Chenoy's exposition of violent conflict in India.

In all five countries, armed conflict and insurgency seem to have regional and international ramifications. Often neighbouring states provide moral and material support to militant and insurgent groups at one point in time, and then extend support to the state at other times. The conflicts also have an impact on the economic and political structures of neighbouring states, through the transfer of extremist political ideologies by various communication media, and, for example, the illegal trafficking of persons, drugs and arms that is facilitated by the conflict. While all conflicts seem to have a geopolitical impact and influence, as well as transnational and international linkages, the physical violence of conflict remains very much an internal issue in each country, often in one geographic region.

The main focus of these papers is on the different ways in which a violent conflict increases patriarchal controls on women and on the impact of militarization on women and men, on masculinities and femininities. Anuradha Chenoy describes it as a situation in which 'women's identities are constructed to intersect with the needs of militarized nationalism'. In all societies and communities under discussion in the five countries, the writers point to the different ways in which women react and respond to conflict, becoming victims of various acts of repression and abuse, as well as armed militants who choose to respond to violence with violence, and militant's mothers who respond to violence with non-violent means of political agitation.

WOMEN, MEN AND GENDER RELATIONS IN A CONFLICT SITUATION

Although the duration, nature and root causes for the conflicts vary across the five countries, the papers reveal the ways in which both men and women are affected by the conflict, focusing on the specific manner in which existing norms of masculine/feminine and patterns of gender relations influence and shape the impact of the conflict on women. All the chapters are written from the perspective of the changing roles of women—and men—in insurgencies and internal armed conflicts. They all explore, in different ways, the tensions that arise between notions of nationhood, citizenship, and gender relations rooted in centuries of patriarchal practice. As the writers look at the ways in which contemporary processes of democratization and militarization are located within specific historical and political contexts, they also look again at the role played by women as cultural signifiers, and at the constantly vacillating duality of victimhood and agency of women in conflict situations in general.

While the papers stress the point that the 'women' they are writing about do not constitute á homogeneous category, they nevertheless do draw some general conclusions on the basis of the patriarchal norms that are prevalent in each of the societies under study. Taking into consideration the difference among women on the basis of factors such as caste, class, religion, ethnicity, age, education level, marital status, nationality, and region of residence, the authors argue that different women are affected differently by conflict. However, they also point to the specific cultural norms imposed on women and men in South Asian societies in general, which enable some generalizations regarding the impact of the conflict on women in South Asia.

As all the country studies show, women living in conflict situations are directly subject to a range of human rights violations such as rape and other forms of physical and sexual violence. Conflict also generates waves of migration away from conflict-affected areas; it is often male family members who undertake the journey from village to town and city, and sometimes even out of the country. High levels of frustration among men due to unemployment and political tensions lead to increased levels of consumption of alcohol and drugs, which often result in sexual abuse and violence against women.

Describing the various situations they have researched and analysed, the chapters all point to the mainstream definition of women in conflict situations by both external and internal observers as being appendages of male actors. This is what, for example, leads to the different treatment of women who are victimized during a conflict situation depending on the status of their male relative, on whether he was a member of the security forces or of a militant group.

Women are also indirectly affected through abuses inflicted on members of their families, such as arrest, arbitrary execution, disappearance, and torture. In many of the communities under study, many women living in the conflict-affected areas are widows or 'half-widows'; they are breadwinners and heads of households.[1] Women are also among the largest number of those rendered homeless in a conflict; they are the world's largest number of refugees and internally displaced persons.

The papers all comment on the fact that female-headed households are increasing day by day due to the conflict—through abandonment and desertion by men as well as through the deaths of men. Although women are thrust into these new decision-making roles and their responsibilities increase, they remain largely invisible in the eyes of society. While this situation undoubtedly adds to the stressful situation faced by women in a conflict situation, there is also no doubt that this phenomenon challenges traditional assumptions of family and of women's role within the family. Thus, this factor plays a role in slowly transforming the societal perceptions towards women.

Motherhood is seen as a symbol of nation in most South Asian countries. In the papers, the authors explore the ways in which in situations of armed conflict and militarization, mothers are glorified as bearers of sons/martyrs who sacrifice their children for greater national or ideological causes. In spite of historical glorification, mothers suffer physically and psychologically due to 'foetal bereavement' when they lose their offspring in armed conflict. They perceive the loss of their children in armed conflicts as being futile and something that is unasked for.

The papers all focus on the specific impact of armed conflicts and insurgencies on adolescent girls. Among the most critical are the loss of educational opportunities, the high vulnerability to being trafficked and/or forced into prostitution. In addition, from both Nepal and Sri Lanka, there have been reports of forced recruitments of young girls and boys by militant groups. Soha Gul Khattak, writing about women in the conflict zones on the border between Pakistan and Afghanistan, refers in particular to hasty arranged marriages of young girls because of anxious fathers and family members seeking protection for them. Early marriages arranged for young girls are also referred to in Nepal and Sri Lanka, due to fears of their being abducted or violated by the 'enemies'. In some cases, young girls too have agreed to marriages with members of militant groups or of the state security forces, which seem to be politically motivated. Khattak, for example, points out that 'many young girls were convinced that they were serving their cause by marrying "wanted" men'.

Many of these marriages contracted in haste in a conflict situation seem doomed to fail; there are many reports of young girls made pregnant, deserted, and widowed. Thapa and others make the point that in Nepal, strangely enough, parents seem to be more willing to send their daughters to join the insurgent groups, while protecting sons; the authors attribute this to the lower value placed on girls in Nepali society.

Political Economy of Conflict: Structural Violence

The papers all analyse the impact of a range of anti-terrorist and counter-insurgency methods of warfare on civilian populations, including women, in situations in which the military regards an entire geographic area as a conflict region and makes no distinction between public and private space, attacking homes and schools as well as roads and public places and rendering every citizen a terrorist 'suspect'.

The analysis also includes a perspective of the economic impact of violent conflict, the losses to production caused by strikes, curfews, and extortion by militant groups as well as by others who simply take advantage of the instability, and loss of livelihoods due to actions by the army and by militants. The absence of economic opportunities and resulting high unemployment, specially in sectors which rely on daily wages for their livelihood create many problems for ordinary people. The tendency to 'feminize' agriculture and the growth of the number of 'poor' women is exacerbated by conflict due to the absence of men's contribution to family income.[2] There are also, in each country, certain social groups which benefit economically and politically from conflict. They act to protect their own interests; this is a factor that hinders and delays processes of conflict resolution and peace-building processes.

Expansion in military spending is also commonplace during a conflict and results in the diversion of funds earmarked for development programmes to military budgets. Cuts in social spending on health, education and infrastructure such as transport and communication have a tremendous impact on the lives of ordinary people caught up in a conflict. Decreased attention on and resources for women-focused programmes by the state become the norm as the state is embroiled more and more in conflict and military activities.

Military actions destroy the physical infrastructure and cripple the economy. In countries where tourism is a key economic activity, lack of peace and security hinder tourist inflows, with a severe impact on the tourism industry, and a skillover into the overall national economy. In countries where export-oriented industrial and agricultural production are key sectors of the economy, heightened risk and denial of access to markets and transport can sound a death-knell for those engaged in these areas of economic activity as well as for national production as a whole.

Militarization of the State and Masculinization of Society

Women who have joined the insurgency speak through interviews, addressing the dilemmas inherent in their situation. On the one hand is their genuine desire to bring about social justice, to transform their lives and the lives of their communities. On the other is the framing of the extremist discourse within which they must play out their role as a woman militant and activist, accepting a framework that is patriarchal in method, ideology, and leadership.

A clear link is made between conflicts and militarism, arising out of the patriarchal definition of nationalism that legitimizes armed conflict. In all five countries, conflicts have arisen because of struggles for power between dominant political structures that have in-built prejudices and majoritarian tendencies. The most striking commonality among the five countries is the way in which each society is rooted in patriarchy, which lead to a masculinization of the definition of nationalism and patriotism, creating a political context in which democratic norms fail to prevail and all dissent is subject to brutal repression. In the process, the daily subsistence and survival of ordinary citizens, specially women, is subsumed by the overarching masculinist and militarist ideological framework that easily transforms conflict into a form that can only be expressed through the use of violence. In such situations, even the state, which is usually perceived as the 'protector' of its citizens becomes an entity which unleashes violence against its civilian population in the name of national security.

The masculine nature of militarization is remarked upon by all the authors. Most of the actors involved in a conflict are male, whether they belong to liberation or anti-state groups or to state or government security or intelligence forces. Even when women form a significant part of the structure of the insurgent/militant group, their military roles tend not to be as significant as those of men. Civilians in general, and women in particular, suffer the most in these conflicts, since most often they are caught between the warring factions and face the consequences of social fragmentation and disruption of homes, social networks, and livelihoods. In the civilian sector, women's agency is most apparent in those situations in which they become active initiators of peace-building processes, within their own communities and in the public arena. Their primary motivation seems to be the dire need of addressing and mitigating sufferings of women and other vulnerable social groups affected by the violent armed conflict. However, it is often also clear that women perceive themselves to be more capable of effecting dialogues and discussions among warring parties due to their long-standing experiences of dispute resolution and conflict management at the domestic and family levels.

The Women Left Behind

Widows and Half-Widows

Given that widowhood in South Asia is perceived as a misfortune, and a widow as an inauspicious person, all those women who are left without a husband or male partner in a conflict situation find themselves at the receiving end of society and face isolation, social stigma, and loss of individual identity and dignity. They also experience psychological and emotional stress due to the denial of their inheritance rights and property rights by their husbands' relatives, sexual harassment by men in the vicinity, a sense of physical/sexual insecurity, and loss of control over children as a single parent. They are slotted into positions of powerlessness and are left at the mercy of relatives, and have very little autonomous social standing.

Even in cases where widows receive support from an extended family, they suffer from loneliness and have few avenues for dealing with the psychological aspects of their situation. In spite of all the negative consequences attached to widowhood, the verifiable death of a husband helps women to come to terms with their loss and status. The situation is far worse for the 'half-widows', whose husbands are 'missing' or have 'disappeared'. These women live in constant grief and uncertainty, and have fewer rights and lower status than widows.

In many situations of conflict, researchers and observers remark on the increase in the number of women in sex work in place of other employment opportunities, especially when women are forced to fend for their families in the absence of men. These high-risk occupations place women in further jeopardy in terms of their vulnerability to sexual harassment, abuse, and health risk. In addition, the papers point to the ways in which women living in a conflict area have to bear the burden of traumatized and alienated youth, and a range of problems created by excessive dependence on drugs and alcohol.

The breakdown of the rule of law and militarization of society have a major impact on women's lives and on their sense of security and well-being, creating feelings of constant fear, alienation, and despair. There is a wide range of psycho-social effects of conflict on women and girls which has a grievous impact on their capacity to lead full and dignified lives.

THE INTERNALLY DISPLACED

In all the countries under study, the conflicts have resulted in large-scale 'displacement' of populations, due to villages and communities becoming part of the battlegrounds. Fleeing their original places of residence, women, men and children find themselves seeking shelter in temporary locations, some run by state agencies, others organized by non-governmental organizations (NGO). Saba Gul Khattak refers in her paper to the centrality of home and its connections with security, of the traditional concept of 'home' as a 'safe' place and a site for affirmation of one's identity. In this context, she looks at the deliberate destruction of homes during the Wana Operations as a collective punishment meted out to the community for not handing over 'wanted terrorists' to the military, through which a situation of mass displacement due to forced eviction by the military was generated.

Many of the authors refer to the ways in which the disruption of the social fabric places an especially heavy burden on women who must care for children and the elderly. The loss of women's domains within their homes and communities leads to a sense of lack of control over their circumstances. Many women who are displaced find themselves marginalized and often ignored due to the lack of gender sensitivity among officials who run camps and welfare centres. The living conditions in these camps are most often not conducive to giving women a sense of security and stability. In her paper, Amena Mohsin focuses on the need to adopt a human rights approach to issues of internal displacement, and, in particular, to the situation of women refugees, referring to the importance of basing responses to internal displacement within a framework of already-existing international human rights and humanitarian standards.

WOMEN'S BODIES AS BATTLEGROUNDS

The papers in this volume all address the notion of the nation state as it establishes and sustains a dichotomy between the public and private realms, and inscribes gender roles on men and women. Anuradha Chenoy points to the consequences of shifting the battleground from nation state borders to villages, communities, and homes. As she describes, modern conflicts are waged with no distinction being made by the combatants between the private and public domains. A common experience of all the authors is the targeting of innocent villagers and civilians by the state security forces after they have been attacked.

Women are valued for their symbolic role of being biological and cultural reproducers, which emphasizes the importance of their sexual purity. Women, thus, become symbols of both the continuity of the community, and the honour of the family/community. Women and girls are, therefore, particularly vulnerable to violence and sexual abuse from 'outsiders'. This vulnerability is heightened during times of conflict, and the battle is mostly fought over women's bodies. On the one hand, victories over enemies are reinforced by violating their women's bodies, and on the other, in attempts to protect a community's honour, its men can impose severe restrictions on women's freedom of mobility and choice. Women also become victims of genocide by their own men when they are perceived to bring shame and dishonour to the family/community through having been 'polluted' by the enemies. At the other extreme, this very shame and pain of women are used by nationalist leaders, through demonstrating and publicizing women survivors as the nation's sacrifices to gain sympathy for the advancement of their cause and legitimize the politics of revenge. However, the papers also speak of the lack of concern shown by the state for women victims, and the various acts of silencing and denying human rights abuses against women, such as rape and molestation, whether committed by the state forces or by militant groups. As their analysis shows, the manner in which the entire society and the families of the women are complicit in this process is also rooted in the ideology of women as bearers of the community's/nation's honour.

Anuradha Chenoy describes how, in Kashmir women's bodies determine their value and undermine their roles, with women being considered worthy of respect only if they conform to the community's regulations. The imposition of dress codes by militants in Manipur (indigenous dress instead of jeans and T-shirts) and Kashmir (*hijab* and other forms of purdah prescribed by other Islamic countries), opposition to sterilization and abortion in Kashmir, are all ways in which Chenoy understands the role played by women through their bodies in a conflict situation.

Thus, women become subjects of militarized politics as 'victims'. Victimization ultimately leads to loss of agency and being 'covered up', symbolically and physically. Women also perceive the world outside from their experiences of the private sphere of the family/household and reproductive tasks associated with home and family. Hence, in their understanding and explanations of armed conflict, women identify themselves not as independent entities, but through their relationships to men engaged in the warring factions.

WOMEN AS COMBATANTS

In the South Asian context, where the public-private divide strictly adheres to gender lines, women joining armed militant movements raises many questions. To what extent is their participation a matter of free choice? Is recruitment based on gender equality (i.e. strategic), or on the need for a greater recruitment base (i.e. circumstantial)? Is the rupture of the public-private divide and the gains women make as combatants truly empowering for women? Or is this a case of 'ambivalent empowerment'? Are women equally represented in the decision-making process in the nexus of insurgency, counter-insurgency, militarization and armed conflicts, or are they just participating in 'men's wars'? These questions form the core inquiry around which all the papers in this volume are structured.

In each country, women living in the conflict zone face the duality of their situation, as members of specific communities subject to discrimination and marginalization, and as women who bear reproductive and productive responsibilities while at the same time being cultural and symbolic signifiers of the nation and of the community. Some women break away from the traditional bonds and move into militancy, facing many personal and political challenges. However, the evidence from the research that constitutes the various papers in this volume and many other sources goes to show that the empowerment and advances women gain from joining militant movements tend to be short-lived. When the conflict moves into a moment of transition, conflict transformation, dialogue and reconciliation through formal and informal peace processes, the positions women have reached during the conflict are most often not taken into consideration. Women are generally absent in political negotiations between the combatant parties.

Part of the analysis of the authors in this volume is based on an understanding that women's engagement with militant politics is often not integrated into the ideological constructions of the movement. Patriarchal norms and frameworks of culture and tradition that are insensitive to women's autonomy and dignity are not challenged. This is why, in case after case, women's position in decision-making and active participation in the daily life and struggles of any movement are not sustained during times of peace or during transitional periods such as peace talks.

Women in movements and in political positions are quoted by the authors as often saying they want gender equality and are working towards it. Yet, as the authors point out, many accept patriarchal ideologies, and, therefore, remain non-confrontational regarding the manner in which the 'woman question' tends to be subsumed by the 'nationalist question', which is always framed within a patriarchal framework. Some women within movements accept this framework of male superiority themselves, and do not question either the patriarchal ideology or the masculinist nature of their movements.

Yet, the tensions between tradition and modern ideological positions are manifest in situations such as those that have arisen in Nepal, Sri Lanka, and Kashmir, when young girls recruited by militant groups are not accepted back into their own homes and are not considered eligible for marriage even by their own combatant male colleagues.

The contradictions that are found between the rhetoric of militant movements which claim to foster women's emancipation, and their practice that, in fact, reproduces and reinforces traditional, patriarchal practices create many dilemmas for the women within these movements. They are often on the sidelines in terms of actual leadership and decision-making, and are, in fact, assigned tasks that are very much in line with their domestic caretaking responsibilities in civilian life, such as nursing, providing support networks, and focusing on the younger members of the movements.

The papers address the many different dilemmas faced by women in militant movements in the five countries under study. In Nepal, the authors say that according to the women they interviewed, many of them joined the insurgency because they perceived themselves as fighters for the liberation of their people. As women, they also raised issues of gender-based discrimination in the areas of education, property rights, and citizenship. Within the movement, women cadres could make some choices in terms of personal relationships, marriage and motherhood 'as long as it did not harm the organization'. In other situations, for example, in Sri Lanka, for many years the militant movements prohibited any relationships among cadres, imposing sanctions on their young membership from an extremely moralistic perspective. In the case of Kashmir, the women within the various militant movements are mostly confined to secondary roles such as nursing and carrying messages.

WOMEN AS PEACE-BUILDERS

The chapters all address women's involvement in militancy and in peace from the perspective of a new construction of citizenship and of security, with an emphasis on a definition of human security that includes peace with justice, rights, and equality. Using secondary material, both published and unpublished, as well as referring to interviews and first-hand impressions of the experiences of women in conflict situations, the authors provide invaluable and unique perspectives on the diverse forms of engagement with conflict which women in South Asian countries experience at the present juncture. Describing the different ways in which women face the daily overt violence of militancy and counter-militancy of the state, and the structural violence that comes with poverty, unemployment and loss of livelihood, the authors frame a new understanding of the gendered nature of the political economy of conflict.

Analysing the ways in which conflicts have a negative impact on women, the papers focus on the strategies used by women to confront and combat these negative impacts. This analysis is set within the context of the shrinking spaces for civil society activism and the erosion of democratic institutions, which combine to decrease the chances of activism and advocacy for women's human rights. The papers all reflect the diverse attitudes of women on either side of the conflict: women civilians and family members of the military caught in the web of nationhood, patriotism, and national security, and women within the militant movements who perceive themselves as fighters for the liberation of their people.

In each country-study, the authors look at the diverse movements for peace-building, reconciliation and conflict transformation that have emerged in the past decades against the background of the conflict. In spite of the intense victimization of women within armed conflict situations, women have also been key actors in organizing and mobilizing for an end to the conflict from different standpoints: as civilians, and as members of militant groups. Women from all spheres of life have come together to participate in peace-building initiatives and used various means, the media, and also demonstrations and meetings. Women have used motherhood as a means of negotiating space to protest against the violence of conflict in Nagaland, Manipur, and Sri Lanka. In the case of Sri Lanka, one sees the coming together of diverse groups of women who have been affected by the conflict. A good example is the organization of parents of soldiers missing in action as also an organization of parents whose children have been detained by and/or disappeared through the agency of the military. This identification and sympathy between women of both sides provides a unique opportunity for moving forward to processes of healing and reconciliation. The unique feature of all these individual or collective actions has been their emphasis on non-violent means of political expression.

However, as the authors conclude, the gendered nature of politics—which seems to be the norm in South Asian countries—means that women's issues tend not to be included in negotiations for peace or in peace accords. Women are almost never present or represented in the decision-making and policy-making processes regarding conflict transformation. Even in cases where women have taken active roles in peace initiatives, they have given up their rights to be negotiators and/or have remained in the background.

THE WAY FORWARD

Through their analysis of the historical contexts of nation building in South Asia, the authors describe the exclusion of women from consideration in this process and call for a rejection of all political projects that are patriarchal in method, ideology, and leadership. As Anuradha Chenoy posits, if the symbolic 'woman' becomes the mother of the nation who pleads for justice on behalf of herself and the nation and gives up her sons for the nation, in this patriarchal 'bargain' she can 'either ask for peace or sustain the nationalism necessary for war'. As the papers show, more and more women are choosing the first option.

All the authors ground their analysis in the different forms in which nationalism emerged in response to colonialism in the subcontinent. Describing the post-colonial period in Pakistan, Saba Gul Khattak refers to the absence of modern state structures in certain parts of the country that she argues permitted religion to gain a far greater foothold than would have been possible if other institutions existed in the area. She also speaks of this period as 'placing women within the overall racist discourse inherited from the British that the Pakistanis reproduce unintentionally'. In her turn, Amena Mohsin describes the background to the movement for autonomy among the indigenous communities of the CHT region as a consequence of which Bangladesh adopted a hegemonic and homogenizing attitude to the CHT.

The conclusions articulate a general position on the need to redefine democracy within the South Asian context, in a way that recognizes minority rights and acknowledges the nature of all South Asian states as multicultural and multinational. Within this overarching framework, the authors see women's involvement in militancy and in peace-building as enabling a new construction of democracy, human rights and citizenship and a reconceptualization of security to mean human security and peace with justice and rights and equality. In this process, they address the need to begin a deconstruction of the exercise of masculinist power in its different forms, and especially as played out in war and conflict.

Manifesto for Support of Women's Concerns in Conflict Situations

Describing and analysing the impact of armed conflict on women in South Asia necessitates the following actions:

- Immediate response to conflict: There should be an immediate ceasefire and provision of immediate relief and rehabilitation to victims of conflict. Recognize and acknowledge the victimization of women, and seek justice for crimes committed against women.
- Short-term: Sustaining the rupture of the public-private divide experienced during insurgency, remove discriminatory policies and demolish discriminatory societal practices. Simultaneously, incorporate a gender/feminist perspective in all policies, legislation, programmes, and accords. This would include supporting women's rights groups and strengthening women's participation in decision- and policy-making bodies, and ensuring adequate financial support for women's initiatives and agencies.
- Long-term: Demasculinize and demilitarize the state and society through structural adjustment, gender sensitization, and changes to the education system to inculcate a culture of peace for future generations and lasting peace.

In addition, the authors focus on the ways in which conflicts and their impact are gendered, such as internal displacement, sexual violation, widowhood, foetal bereavement, among other things which are discussed in detail.

NOTES

1. A term coined to describe women whose husbands are 'missing' or have 'disappeared', leaving them in a state of uncertainty as to their civil status—married or widowed.
2. By international standards, those earning less than US $1 a day.

2. For Her the War Continues: Women, Insurgency and the Chittagong Hill Tracts, Bangladesh

Amena Mohsin

> What kind of future do you think there is for my children in this land, why did we make so much sacrifices [*sic*], what kind of education do you think I can give my children over here?
>
> Noni Chakma
> Khagrachari, 20 March 2004

> Today I am an independent woman, but at what cost? I do not want any other woman to buy her independence at this cost. See, I stayed on only for my daughter.
>
> Shushoma Chakma
> Rangamati, 23 March 2004

The situation in the Chittagong Hill Tracts (CHT) is qualitatively somewhat different from the other conflict scenarios of South Asia. A peace accord was signed on 2 December 1997 between the Government of Bangladesh (GoB) and the Parbattya Chattagram Jono Shonghoti Samity (PCJSS), the party that had carried on the movement for autonomy of the CHT. The accord brought to an end more than two decades of armed insurgency in the region. Though more than six years have passed since the signing of the accord, peace remains a chimera in the south-eastern hills of Bangladesh, with the PCJSS often threatening to take up arms again. The conflict, though now in a different form, continues to affect the people in general and women in particular in the CHT.

While war, conflicts, insurgency, and violence impact on women in ways very different from those of men for reasons discussed later in this paper, it needs to be emphasized that it impacts on women also variously. Women, as will be argued in this paper, are a social construction with deep political implications and are not a homogeneous category. Their voices and social make-up vary according to class, race, religion, culture, education, age, and so on. Any attempt to homogenize them as woman only silences other aspects in the voices, thereby marginalizing them. The two quotations in the beginning of the paper have been selected consciously to emphasize the differentiations based on sufferings. Despite the differentiations, their voices come together through common concerns: the acute sense of insecurity, concern for home and children are evident.

This paper is an attempt to examine the impact of insurgency upon women in the CHT. The paper is divided into five sections. The first engages in a critical examination of the conceptual, wherein the notions of state, nation, and citizenship are examined. The second details the contextual, wherein the CHT problem has been discussed. The third section discusses the political economy of war. It suggests that conflict scenarios create their own dynamics, which give rise to an informal sector of the economy with negative and long-term implications for the polity. This makes peace quite an improbability in the region. In the fourth section, the impact of insurgency upon women and their roles during the period have been examined. Finally, the fifth section makes certain suggestions in an attempt to move beyond the situation.

METHODOLOGY

The paper is based on an extensive review of the existing literature on the CHT, as well as literature on women, war, and conflict. Besides this, select in-depth interviews have been conducted in the Rangamati and Khagrachari districts of the CHT in March 2003. The unpredictable security situation did not permit a questionnaire survey. Extreme difficulties were faced in carrying out the interviews. Given the politically charged and insecure situation prevailing in the Hills, the field trip was undertaken under risky conditions. Then, the women did not want to speak out at all. They were concerned about their security, and except for Kalashona, Jorita and Kabita, all the rest wanted their identities to be concealed. Consequently, except for the above three, the rest are fictitious names and their places of residence also could not be mentioned. Apart from the problem of accessing the interviewees, the research also raised many ethical questions for me, especially my right to invade their world and privacy. A major limitation of this study is the selective nature of interviews. In view of the total reluctance of the women to talk and also the prevailing political climate, there was no option other than to restrict myself to those who came forward willingly. The study, therefore, is by no means an exhaustive one. However, one came back with the conclusion that there was no way to examine or measure the impact of insurgency on human lives; one lives with it for the rest of her/his life.

THE CONCEPTUAL: NATION, STATE AND WOMEN

The notions of nation and state have a distinct gender bias and operate within a masculine paradigm that marginalizes and peripheralizes women. The nation state predicates itself upon the conception of a collective homogeneous identity that is the nation. This collective identity sets it apart from the other collectives. This supposedly homogeneous nation interacts with the external world through a political system called the state. This state is again sovereign, independent, and autonomous—attributes associated with masculinity. The sovereign, however, legitimizes its power through the nation. Hence nation and state are often used interchangeably. This nation or collective in the discourse of nationalism has been likened to a clan or kinship. Authenticity of the clan members is, therefore, imperative. In order to maintain the purity and authenticity of the nation, women become the biological as well as cultural bearers of that nation. They also become the property and symbols of honour of that nation. Arguably, if women were integral to the process of nation construction, then one would associate tremendous power and authority with them as well.

This, however, has been curtailed through the construction of the dichotomies between public and private. This divide has its origins in the Greek states, which are looked upon as conceptual models for the Western state. The formation of the state depended on a sexual division of labour which established and reinforced the economic and political structures. Two sets of social relations were established. Female roles revolved around the work of the home and the family; and male social roles extended to the duties of citizens and war and to relations with other city states. The process of distinction began at the level of the family.[1] It is argued here that the private or the domestic, though supposedly the realm of women is not in actuality a realm where the woman reigns. Due to the construction of gendered roles and attributes of masculinity and femininity, the latter is characterized by submissiveness, politeness, emotion, irrationality, dependency and weakness, and the former, as suggested earlier is associated with independence, rationality, autonomy, and so on.

In the name of protecting the honour of the nation, time and again women's freedom has been curtailed. As the bearer of culture, she has to carry the burden of being a 'proper woman', which again is a construction. This more often than not puts her in an inferior position to man. This construction of women's image as the honour of a nation, it is argued here, has largely contributed to the adoption of rape as a systematic war strategy. Raping a woman is equated with dishonouring the enemy's property and honour. Wars have often been fought in the name of protecting women and children, who are considered weak and vulnerable. In conventional understatement and the parlance of dominant mainstream state and nationalist discourse, men appear as the protectors and women the protected. This, it is suggested here, is a myth—as will be abundantly clear from the CHT case—created to perpetuate the hegemony of men over women and keep the latter out of state or public discourse. To further discuss this, the concept of citizenship is analysed below.

Women and Citizenship

Citizenship is the agency through which an individual becomes the member of a state. It supposedly ensures certain basic rights for the individual in return for taxes, obedience to law, and loyalty and patriotism in times of war. The individual citizen's rights to life, security and liberty are to be guaranteed by the state. The notion of individual citizenship was centred on the idea of individualism. It was expected that such a person would be rational, independent and autonomous, that is, a citizen with agency. Historically, however, the above notions were associated with maleness, while subjectivity, personal care, dependence and emotionality were associated with femininity. Hence, initially, the notion of a citizen was premised on masculinity and extended only to men. Women were excluded from citizenship and were considered to be part of the private sphere. They did not have the right to vote, to stand for election, or to hold public office. However, with time, the notion of universal franchise developed. At present, nearly every state recognizes the equality of all citizens before law and does not differentiate—at least in theory.[2] This, however, is not to suggest that women have full access to citizenship rights. Culture and religion have often been used to curtail women's citizenship rights. The citizenship laws are mostly gendered. For instance, in Bangladesh, citizenship is determined through paternity; in other words it is mediated through a male.

The sacrifice of one's life for the sake of the nation is considered to be the highest form or duty of citizenship. A patriot is the most revered citizen. This again is a masculine notion, for in conventional wisdom war is men's domain, while women are associated with peace. The association of women with peace is an essentialist one. The language of compromise, flexibility, and accommodation is usually associated with women, and femininity is, in effect, the language of the marginalized, of those who have been kept outside the structures of power, and whose lives have been a struggle both within and without. Wars are considered to be games of men, hence, their roles and sacrifices appear in the pages of history. Women appear as footnotes, as supporters or symbols. Such constructions and conceptualizations not only fail to recognize and acknowledge the active roles played by women during war and conflict situations, but also relegate them as inferior, in need of protection, thus strengthening the gender bias in the state and nationalist discourse. It needs to be emphasized that the above discourse has reinforced the asymmetrical gender-power position in which women have been structurally subordinated. Thus, despite taking the worst brunt of war, their roles and sacrifices continue to be peripheralized.

Women in the CHT, which has witnessed more than two decades of armed violence as a consequence of insurgency and state military action, have also taken the worst brunt of this violence. But their sacrifices and sufferings have not been acknowledged, the peace accord is extremely gendered, with no reference whatsoever to the woman question.[3] However, before discussing the impact of the insurgency on women in the CHT, the context of the conflict is detailed below.

The Context

The CHT, located on the south-eastern part of Bangladesh, has about 10 per cent of the total land area of Bangladesh (143,998 sq. km.). The region comprises three districts: Rangamati, Khagrachari, and Banderban. It is surrounded by the Indian states of Tripura on the north and Mizoram on the east, Myanmar on the south and east, and Chittagong district on the west. Its population according to the last census held in 1991 was approximately 974,000.[4] Of this, the Hill people constituted 500,000 and the Bengalis 470,000. Eleven ethnic groups populate the CHT: Bawm, Chak, Chakma, Khami, Kheyang, Lushai, Marma, Mrung, Pankho, Tanchangya, and Tripura. They closely resemble the people of North-East India, Myanmar, and Thailand rather than the predominantly Bengali population of Bangladesh.

The process of alienation of the Hill people from the Bangladesh state is rooted in the nation and state building process of the state. Subsequently, the Hill people constructed an identity and formulated a set of demands for themselves within a nationalist framework to realize autonomy within the state of Bangladesh. The following is a discussion of the above.

Political

Bangladesh attained independence from Pakistan on 16 December 1971 after nine months of a war of liberation. It was an intensely nationalist war that had its genesis in the fractured space for the culture and language of the Bengalis within the state of Pakistan. The Bangladesh nationalist movement and also the liberation war were predicated on the ideals of Bengali nationalism. This left the Hill people out of the Bangladesh nationalist movement, for they could not identify themselves with Bengali language or culture. The Bengali political elite also never made any attempts to incorporate the Hill people within the fold of this movement. Consequently, the Hill people felt it necessary to demand constitutional safeguards for their protection and recognition as a separate community within the new state. As the country was moving ahead with the framing of its Constitution, a Hill people's delegation led by Manobendra Narayan Larma (Larma) called on the Prime Minister and Father of the Nation, Sheikh Mujibur Rahman (Mujib), and placed the following demands:

(a) autonomy for the CHT with its own legislature;
(b) retention of the 1900 CHT Manual[5] in the Constitution of Bangladesh;
(c) continuation of the tribal chiefs' offices;
(d) constitutional provisions restricting the amendment of the Manual, and imposition of a ban on the influx of non-tribal people into the CHT.[6]

Mujib rejected the above demands. He asked the Hill people to give up their separate identity and become 'Bengalis'. The Constitution of Bangladesh adopted on 4 November 1972 indeed consolidated the ideals of Bengali nationalism and gave no recognition to the non-Bengali population of the state. The Constitution, in its Preamble, Para 2, accepted 'nationalism', 'socialism', 'democracy' and 'secularism' as state principles. Article 8, Clause 1 reiterated these. Article 9 defined the basis of state nationalism as Bengali nationalism. Bengali nationalism was itself based on the Bengali language and culture. Larma, thus, refused to endorse the Constitution.

Larma's contentions, however, failed to make any impact on the Bengali policy-makers. Article 1, Part 1 of the Constitution declared Bangladesh to be a unitary state. Through Article 3, Part 1, Bengali was adopted as the state language and Article 6, Part 1 declared that the citizens of Bangladesh were to be known as Bengalis. The unitary system ruled out any possibility of having a separate legislature or autonomy for the CHT as was demanded by the CHT delegation. The new state thereby turned into a hegemonic and majoritarian state.

On 15 August 1975, Sheikh Mujib was assassinated along with other family members in a coup engineered by a group of disgruntled young army Majors. From 1975 till 1991 the country was under military/quasi-military (military Generals turned civilians) rule. During this period, fundamental changes were brought about in the Constitution. Secularism, was dropped from the Constitution. It was substituted by the principle of absolute trust and faith in the Almighty, Allah.[7] Article 9, which stressed the lingual and cultural unity of Bengali nationalism, was also replaced with Bangladeshi nationalism. Through Article 6, Clause 2, the citizens of Bangladesh were to be known as 'Bangladeshis' in place of 'Bengalis'. Bangladeshi nationalism, while retaining the linguistic and cultural connotations of the Bengali people, incorporated Islamic ideals within its fold. The above construction was a Bengali plus Islamic construction of nationality. The Hill people, neither Bengalis nor Muslims could not identify themselves either with the Bengali or Bangladeshi constructions of nationhood. The nationalist constructions in Bangladesh, therefore, failed to accommodate the Hill people and they perceived their cultural identities threatened within the state. The failure of the state to integrate the Hill people had its ramifications on the economic lives of these people as well, since the state pursued its development paradigms in the Hills to the exclusion of the indigenous population. The following is a discussion of this.

DEVELOPMENT

Development in the Hills has meant destruction, displacement, and despair for the Hill people. The state has exploited the resources of the Hills by alienating the local population from resources that they had traditionally been using as common property. The first major development project in the Hills was undertaken by the then Pakistan government in the early 1960s. In order to accelerate the process of industrialization in the then East Pakistan, the decision was taken to harness the water resources of CHT. To this end, a hydroelectric project was constructed on the Karnafuli River in Rangamati. The construction of the dam had far-reaching consequences for the Hill people. No study of the social impact of the project had been done prior to its construction. The dam submerged an area of about 400 sq. miles, including 54,000 acres of cultivable land which was 40 per cent of the district's total acreage. The dam made about 100,000 people homeless. About half of them crossed over to India as refugees where many of them are still living as stateless persons. The Hill people did not benefit at all from the dam. The employment opportunities created by this project were taken up by the Bengalis. The Hill people allege that they were promised free electricity. Today, very few areas in the Hills have electricity and that too is not free of cost. The Hill people still regard the Kaptai, otherwise an attractive tourist spot and a source of revenue earner for the state, as their teardrop. Their experiences within the state of Bangladesh have been quite the same: an examination of the state's appropriation of the forest and land resources of the Hills in the name of development will make this clear.

FORESTS

Forests constitute an integral part of the Hill people's lives. Their interaction with forests is rooted within their economic and cultural mores. These were considered as common property and utmost care was taken for their conservation. These were not only their vital sources of livelihood, but they also considered the forests to be the abode of their ancestors' spirits. The first attack on their customary rights over the forests and their resources, however, came during British colonial rule when, in 1865, the Indian Forest Reserve Act was passed. The notion of social forestry was changed into commercial forestry. The local people were barred from entering and using the resources of the forests in an attempt to 'protect' those resources. But in actuality it was to meet the requirements of the imperial railway companies.

In 1875, the British classified forests into two types, Reserve Forests (RF), and District Forests (DF). The RF were put entirely under the management of the Forest Department. *Jhum* (slash and burn) cultivation and any kind of use of forest resources was totally prohibited. The DFs were put under the direct control of the district collector (DC). In the DF, *jhum* cultivation and the use of forest produce for domestic purposes were allowed with certain restrictions as the DC might impose from time to time.[8] The state also gave away high-quality land to European entrepreneurs for plantation. The state's forest policy was, thus, informed by its profit motive. The Hill people, however, were marginalized as the state did not provide them with any alternative livelihood opportunity.

This exclusion of the local population from the forest resources continued in the post-colonial state of Pakistan as well. The forest resources were used for the production of paper and pulp in the Karnafuli Paper Mill, built in Rangamati in 1953. Predictably, out of its total workforce, only 1 per cent were Hill people, and those too did the lower rung jobs. The state also took away more land as RF for plantation. In Bangladesh today there are three categories of forests in the CHT. These are: RF, the Protected Forests (PF, formerly DF), and the Unclassed State Forests (USF). The last are village common forests. The taking over of land as RF has marginalized the Hill people in various ways since the state did not provide them with any viable alternate sources of income generation. It has resulted in their displacement, loss of rights, increased criminalization, and environmental degradation. It also impacted upon the women negatively, since they were dependent upon forest resources and in *jhum* cultivation (which the state had banned) they had an equal status with men.

LAND

The Hill people have been alienated from their land and its resources through various forms of state intervention. The process started with the British colonial state. The latter claimed ownership of all lands in the Hills in 1868, whereas land was considered to be communal property by the Hill people: individual families had the right to usufruct only. Two types of land tenure were introduced into the CHT by the British.

(1) Private rights: From 1868 onwards these rights were given to people who took to plough cultivation. This land was subject to acquisition by the government on payment of monetary compensation. (2) Usufruct: This meant the right to use the land over which the state retained proprietary rights. This right belonged to anyone who cleared the forest and occupied it first and then got it registered with the local headman. These rights were based upon customs and usage that dated centuries back. The colonial administration, thus, took the ownership of land away from the community and vested it with the state, an institution in which the Hill people had no representation or participation. The DC was given absolute powers over land matters.

The process of land alienation of the Hill people accelerated in the new state of Bangladesh due to state-sponsored plans of settlement of Bengalis. In 1979, the government, through an amendment to Rule 34 of the CHT Manual, did away with the restrictions against settlements of CHT lands by non-residents. According to one estimate, between 1980 and 1984, around 400,000 Bengalis were said to have been settled in the CHT.[9] The land alienation of the Hill people through Bengali settlement has had far-reaching implications for the Hill people and Bengali-Hill People relations as a whole. It resulted in the displacement and pauperization of the Hill people and violated their traditional rights. The state also refuses to recognize the indigenous view of land and claims that Bengalis have been settled on *khas* lands, i.e. government-owned lands. What the government regards as *khas* land, the Hill people regard as common property.

The indigenous people of the CHT believe that through Bengali settlement the government aims to 'colonize' the Hill Tracts by bringing about a demographic shift in the region. A demographic shift has indeed taken place in the Hill Tracts. In 1947, the Hill people constituted more than 98 per cent of the CHT population, but by 1991 Bengalis constituted 50 per cent of the total population of the region.[10] This change in the demographic composition of the region is viewed with alarm by the local populace, which they regard as a government policy of ethnocide. This perception strengthens their solidarity and deepens their alienation from the state.

THE JUMMAS

The refusal of the Bangladesh state to recognize the cultural distinctiveness of the Hill people and their subsequent political and economic marginalization gave rise to a sub-nationalist movement in the Hills. On 7 March 1972, the PCJSS, a political platform for the Hill people was formed by Manobendra Narayan Larma. Soon, a military wing, the Shanti Bahini (SB, Peace Force) was added to it. The PCJSS, however, started its major activities after the assassination of Sheikh Mujib on 15 August 1975. Till then, Larma had hoped that he could carry on his bargaining at the political level with Mujib. But the military takeover on 15 August dashed those hopes.

Apart from changes in the domestic scenario, external factors were also critical in the crystallization of the Hill people's movement. Many of the sub-nationalist movements are dependent upon an external safe haven or sanctuary for political, and more importantly, military support to carry on their struggle. Prior to 1975, Larma had sought Indian help, but owing to very close relations between the Mujib regime and the Indian government the requests were turned down. However, the equation changed with Mujib's assassination. In Bangladesh, though initially there was an element of gratitude towards India because of its role and support for the Bangladesh liberation movement, the economic crisis facing the country in the post-Independence period was largely blamed on India. Mujib was blamed for selling out to India. In fact, during the later part of his life, Mujib was getting closer to the Muslim countries for economic and political reasons. The Bangladesh military also bore much resentment against India.[11] In this backdrop, India probably made its own calculations and decided to support the Hill people's movement. On 16 August 1975, that is a day after Mujib's assassination, the Research and Analysis Wing (RAW), the Indian intelligence agency, contacted Larma. The latter crossed over to India. ASB Headquarters was set up in Tripura, India. SB men were trained and given arms by India.[12] Apart from giving assistance to the SB, India also got involved in the CHT issue through the flow of refugees from the CHT to Tripura. By the early 1980s, the PCJSS sought to unify the Hill people under a nationalist framework through the construction of the Jumma identity for the eleven communities in the CHT.

Around this time, the CHT underwent full-scale militarization. The General Officer Commanding (GOC) of the Chittagong division was put in charge of the CHT administration. The military controlled the political and economic lives of the Hill people. In the name of counter-insurgency and national security, massive violations of human rights took place, which impacted upon the entire population adversely, women being the worst sufferers on gender and ethnic grounds. Women also suffered due to certain measures undertaken by the military in the name of counter-insurgency. Jungles were cleared in search of the SB. In the CHT, women collected many of their household essentials from the forests, and many resources from the forests were sold by them in the market. Women, thus, were deprived of their traditional means of livelihood.

A peace accord signed between the Government of Bangladesh (GoB) and the PCJSS on 2 December 1997 brought armed hostilities to an end. But there is no abrupt break between war, conflict, and peace. Accords are no guarantee to sustainable peace unless they address the genuine and actual grievances of the aggrieved, which this paper suggests the CHT peace accord largely failed to do. The accord has polarized the Hill community into pro-accord and anti-accord groups. This, along with the extremely slow pace of accord implementation has created a situation of uneasy peace in the region. Exchange of gunfire between the anti-accord United Peoples Democratic Front (UPDF) and the pro-accord PCJSS are quite common.[13] Besides taking advantage of the ongoing conflict in the region, a vested interest group has emerged in the Hills whose interest is to keep the conflict going. Strong economic interests dictate them; there is, thus, a political economy of conflict which further marginalizes the chances of peace. It is to a discussion of this that the paper now turns.

The Political Economy of Conflict

It has been suggested earlier that there is no abrupt break between war, conflict, and peace. War creates many dimensions and the creation of a war economy is one of them. This war economy helps to sustain the conflicts since certain powerful vested interest groups are created by it. More than two decades of insurgency created a vested interest group in the CHT. The region allegedly became a conduit for small arms and drugs. The Hill people allege that Bengali security personnel along with the civil administration officials were involved in the extraction of forest resources. The military officials, however, deny the involvement of the military in such activities, but concede that a certain degree of pilferage of resources might have taken place.[14]

Following the accord, the security scenario in the region has become further complicated due to the emergence of unidentified armed groups. These groups are involved in collecting tolls from vehicles plying the roads. It is alleged that Myanmar rebels have joined forces with these groups in Banderban, providing them guns in exchange for shelter. Extortion and toll collection are also on the rise in the region. People allege that formerly they had to pay toll only to the PCJSS, which they could justify since they were fighting for their rights. But now there are several groups and they collect tolls under different pretexts. The PCJSS and the UPDF are also active in this. The people find it difficult to justify the toll collection in the post-accord situation.

The use of drugs and small arms is also on the rise in the region. Two decades of armed violence and the continued instability in the region have turned the CHT into a violence-prone society and a safe haven for trafficking arms and drugs, particularly given the region's close proximity to Myanmar. The effects of such trafficking on the Hill youth could be disastrous. The Hill people argue that their children have grown up witnessing violence, which has resulted in the erosion of many of their traditional values. This erosion itself is a form of violence because the society has lost its harmony and traditional balance. During the autonomy movement, they could still justify the violence: it was expected to bring about social justice, political equality, in other words, rights for which they were fighting. So they had some hope. But in the post-accord situation, the continued protracted violence has been most frustrating and is unacceptable to them.

Many of the PCJSS men have not been rehabilitated, and this coupled with the lack of employment opportunities have created an acute sense of frustration among them. The UPDF members too are frustrated and discontented with the accord, which they look upon as a compromise formula. An acute sense of frustration and uncertainty grips the Hills. Under such a scenario drugs provide an easy refuge to the youth, and guns provide the youth of the two groups with a sense of power.

The Hill people also allege that the opening up of the Hills for tourism following the accord has opened the Hills for vices associated with a tourist culture. For the first time, they are witnessing the phenomenon of prostitution in the region. This, they allege, is mostly taking place in Rangamati, which is a popular tourist resort. Along with this, they fear the rise of a heroin culture and the spread of HIV/AIDS. The Hill people accuse the state of abetting these activities. They point to the heavy presence of the military in the region and charge that the trafficking of arms and drugs cannot go unnoticed by them. They regard the above as a form of ethnic cleansing.

The gendered dimensions of the conflict are evident from the above. The circumstances leading to the insurgency and the post-accord scenario point to the dominance of factors associated with masculinity. It was most blatant in the nationalist agenda of the state, both of which, as argued earlier, are gendered categories. The conflict and its impact too have gendered dimensions. While in no way deprecating the sufferings of men, this paper argues that women suffer more and differently during conflict situations. They suffer due to their 'otherness', in both ethnic and gender terms. The following section based on selected case studies from the Hills is an exposition of this.

Women and Insurgency

When war begins, the homes and children are left to the women to protect. The men either flee for fear of being taken away, or join the war. Thus, women are left to face the enemy, yet in the dominant war and security discourse men are looked upon as the 'protectors' and women the 'protected'. One can, however, argue that wars are fought in the battlefield between men in uniform, so civilians (of whom the women constitute the majority) do not face the brunt of war. But recent wars, and, in particular, insurgencies, have broken this dichotomy between battlefields and civilian fields. Also, wars are no longer military wars: civilians were half the casualties in the Second World War, while they are almost 90 per cent in recent wars. Since men are mostly mobilized, civilians are constituted overwhelmingly of women and children.[15]

As homemakers, wives, mothers, sisters, lovers, daughters, and, above all, women, they suffer variously. This suffering, commonly characterized as victimization, categorizes women as objects bereft of agency. This author's research in the CHT amply demonstrated the inexorable link between victimization and agency. Through each case or instance of victimization, women strategized different channels of coping with adversity. Indeed, there were moments of rupture and breakdown, but the agency was always there. The interviews also revealed that notions of empowerment and the public-private divide need to be placed within cultural and socio-economic contexts and cannot be universalized. Violence and victimization also took different forms.

It was indeed very difficult for Priyolata Chakma, now aged 67, a schoolteacher and widow to narrate to me her experience of becoming an internally displaced person in 1987. The most traumatizing part of it was that she had to hire people to break down her own house because the military had ordered the people living in that locality to break their houses. SB men used to come to that locality and Priyolata's husband was the *karbari* (manager) of that village so he was taken away and severely tortured by the army on suspicion of supporting the SB. They had earlier sent their only son away lest he be taken away by the army. Priyolata was left alone with her three daughters. Every day, she would go and plead with the army to release her husband. She felt helpless but never gave up; her only solace was God. Then, to protect themselves, she hired people to break their home. She was left with no place to live. So she moved into a different locality and took refuge in a relative's house. She supported the family with her small income from the school. The family with which she was residing soon decided to leave for India, since things were becoming intolerable. Then Priyolata moved to another relative's house with her daughters. She told me quite emphatically that she could not leave her husband behind: she had to protect him and plead for his release. Though those were extremely difficult times, yet she feels that she emerged a stronger and more independent person out of that trauma. She nursed her husband after his release as his hand was fractured due to torture by the army. He was mentally shattered, and never recovered fully from the trauma of torture in the army camp till his death. Today, they live in a different locality. They could never return to their old locality.

Maloti Chakma, 55, became an internally displaced person too in 1987. Since 1985, the army had started serious offensives and assaults against civilians. Every day, different localities were raided in search of the SB. Nobody felt secure. They too had sent their son away. Her husband used to sleep in the jungles nearby and rarely came home for fear of being arrested. Maloti used to carry food for him to the jungles. This was extremely difficult for her but she risked it every day. For two years she slept along with her three daughters with a big knife by her side. During the day too, she would hide her daughters and guard the house with a big knife in her hand whenever there were rumours of the military coming to their locality. At times, she felt that she would not survive this ordeal, but carried on for the sake of her husband and children. The army came to their house several times and took away their valuables and also poultry and food, but did not dare touch her or look for the daughters. Very proudly, she told me that she always carried the knife with her, and her face showed that she would not hesitate to use it if required. After two years, they left the place because by that time most of the people had left for India. The family also decided to take refuge in India, but after having reached the border she decided to come back and live with a relative. At the border, she felt that she could not leave her homeland. Her husband accepted her decision, since she had been looking after the family for two long years. They stayed with a relative. Those were days of extreme mental and economic hardships. However, she continued the education of her children and through raising poultry and weaving at home started a small business. Later, they moved into a new locality and bought a small house there. She continues to look upon herself as an internally displaced person and considers her old home to be her home, to which she could never go back again since it was dismantled by the military.

Home, it appeared, is the most crucial and integral part of these women's lives. They associated it with their children and family. But in the cultural and socio-economic context of the Hill society (as discussed below), the modernist-feminist public-private dichotomy did not hold. 'Refugeehood' experiences were most traumatizing for the Hill women, the more so because it totally disrupted the security of their children. The rupture of the public-private sphere, both Nonita Chakma and Noni Chakma said, was not an issue for them, since in their societies women normally go to the marketplaces to sell their products and they also work with the men in the fields; rather, it is the men who stay at home after finishing their daily chores in the fields or office.

'Refugee' is a term having legal status with important political and legal implications. In this matrix, one often loses sight of the fact that it is, above all, a human rights issue. From this perspective, an individual does not become a refugee by the host country's conference of this status upon her/him: rather, the moment an individual leaves the security of home and undertakes the journey to refugeehood, she/he becomes a refugee. For both Nonita and Noni, the road to refugeehood was brutalizing and traumatizing. Neither could recall the dates and details, except that they joined the ranks of the stateless in 1986. It was a long journey; there was an ocean of people undertaking this ordeal. They hid in jungles, took refuge in villages, and went without food for days.

Nonita, along with her two daughters, husband and a few fellow travellers, was arrested by the army. They were interrogated and the men tortured. The women were threatened but not physically assaulted. But her daughter was beaten up for she would not stop crying. Very sadly, Nonita told me that she had to leave home because the settler Bengalis aided by the military were killing the locals in their locality. She does not recall how long they stayed in army custody. The food was inadequate, and the uncertainty and fear had numbed and paralysed her mind. Then the local chairman came and got them released. The journey started again. She could not recall after how many days they reached Tripura. They had to stay under the open sky for many days in the local bazaar; during the day they used to hide in different places. Then they were taken to Shilachuri refugee camp and provided with ration, which was most inadequate. The family crowded into one small makeshift room barely adequate for two persons. Her husband used to do all kinds of odd jobs and she worked as a housemaid. As she narrated this, she broke into tears and kept on repeating that it was very disturbing and painful for her as she had never done this before. Back home, they were quite well off. She heard of much violence against the women by their folks in the camp. The men vented their frustration upon the women, though she was never a victim of this. Then, one day, thinking of the education and future of her children, she decided to flee from the camp. They fled one night: the Indian Border Security Force (BSF) and the SB did not allow the inmates to leave the camps. They were used as political tools by the Indian government and the SB to carry on the movement and portray their cause at the international level.

Noni's experience is not much different from Nonita's. They took refuge in the Thakumbari camp. The ration was most inadequate and housing unbearable. About 75–100 women had to use one latrine. The water crisis was unbearable. Every day, she had to queue up for hours to fetch drinking water. Her husband did not work at all, which put extra pressure on her. She would collect straws from the jungles and make small sitting stools. She carried these to the markets and sold them. Often, she had to pay toll to the local goons for the refugees were not allowed to sell their products in the market. The market was not alien to her. As she candidly put it to me, that unlike Bengali society, it was traditionally common for Hill women to go to the *hats* (local markets) to sell their produce and products. Many women faced violence from their men in the camp, though she denied having experienced it herself. Like Nonita, she took the decision to run away from the camp along with her children. Their education had become her primary concern. Refugees had set up schools in the camps; this happened in Shilachuri camp as well. But they did not have the resources to buy Indian textbooks from the market. Besides, education was imparted by the refugee inmates themselves. One night a group of about 60–70 women and children slipped out of the camp in batches. Her husband did not accompany them; he was too scared to return. They began their journey back home. No men accompanied them. All the women felt they had to go back because of the future and education of their children. Her husband joined them after a month.

Both Nonita and Noni feel traumatized by their experiences of refugeehood. The most traumatizing part was the loss of control over their lives; they had lost their space and autonomy as human beings and were confined within the categorization of refugeehood. Extreme tension and insecurity gripped them. They get nightmares even now. Nonita pointed out that she could not recall things and often suffered from amnesia. But Noni feels that those days have made her more independent and equipped her to face the challenges of life. Both of them, however, contested the notion of empowerment. They felt that in their society the women are empowered, since they are more independent and go to the marketplaces. They also argued that the decision to return was taken by them, and in family matters, decisions were taken together. Lack of property rights for the women did not appear to be an issue for them, but they pointed out that both the PCJSS and the UPDF have this in their political reforms programme.

Within the social and cultural context of the Hills, 'widowhood' is not looked down upon. The extended family provides them with a safety net and niche to fall back upon. There is no bar to the kind of work that they might undertake, or inhibitions and taboo upon food intake. But widowhood itself is a life of loneliness, pain, and struggle. Both Arti and Anuja became widows very early in their lives. They lost their husbands while only in their mid-twenties. Arti had gone to the paddy field, while her husband, along with their two sons aged 5 and 2, was at home. Their two daughters were in the neighbour's house. She recalled that it was 1 May 1986. Suddenly, the military encircled their village in Panchari. The inmates were asked to come out. Men and women were segregated. The houses were set on fire and men were killed. Women, along with the children, began to flee to the jungle. Arti too fled to the jungle, where she met some of the villagers who told her that her husband along with her two sons had been killed. She did not know where her daughters were. That was the longest night of her life: she does not even recall what happened to her after that. Early next morning, she went to the village but nothing was left. She searched for the bodies of her husband and sons, but an old man from the neighbouring village told her that the military had called the people from his village and asked them to burn the bodies, then dump the charred bodies in a big grave that the villagers were told to dig. Arti did not know what to do, or where to look for her daughters. She returned to the jungle in search of her daughters: late in the afternoon, she found them along with her neighbour.

Then began her life of struggle. She went to stay with her brother. Her only concern was her daughters and their education. She used to work in the fields of her brother and other people to support herself and her two daughters. Though her brother was very supportive, she did not want to be a burden on him. Today, her daughters have graduated and are working: they have built a small house and live separately. But long years of struggle and pain have taken their toll on her. At the age of fifty, she looks as if she is sixty. She suffers from various diseases, especially insomnia.

Anuja's village in Panchari was often raided by the military in search of SB men. This began in early 1984. Then one day the military arrested the men on charges of aiding the SB. The women went to the army camps and pleaded for the release of their husbands. They were released after three days, but ordered to report to the military headquarters every Tuesday. Anuja's husband did it most religiously for a full one year, for they had three small sons and he did not want to invoke the wrath of the military. One Wednesday, the military surrounded the village: everybody ran for their lives. But Anuja's husband consoled her and said that he had reported to the military camp the day before, the commanding officer knew him, so they would not hurt them. The military, however, took him along with 10–12 other men. Anuja again went to the camp but was not allowed to go in. She went continuously for three days. The third day, her husband's dead body was handed over to her. An army guard told her that he was kept in a big hole without any food and water. There, he was tortured and died out of shock. With tears in her eyes, she told me that he had wanted water before he passed away.

After burying him, she went to meet the commanding officer to ask about her husband's offence. She was seized with anger and rage. The officer was polite and offered her a job. Though she hated the military, but, thinking of her sons, she took up the job of a family welfare assistant. Her in-laws also helped her. Today, her sons have grown up: two of them are working, and the youngest is in college.

Arti and Anuja did not face any societal pressure for re-marriage. Though their families had wanted them to get remarried, they resisted it. Both told me that their society respected widows and eve teasing or sexual harassment by the Hill men of Hill women was unheard of. But they asked me sadly why they had to live this life of loneliness, why their children were deprived of the love of their father. Arti kept asking repeatedly why her two sons were killed, and how they could possibly have aided the SB. She was still breastfeeding the youngest one. Indeed, the traumas of war continue and haunt their victims for the rest of their lives: for them, the war never ends. This writer left wondering whether the impact could at all be measured or even examined.

'Rape' is the most brutal, masculinized, and commonly practised means of brutalizing and hurting the enemy. The woman's body is turned into a battleground, since she is considered to be the cultural and biological bearer of the nation. By polluting her, the nation is polluted. It is also a form of genocide. Change in demographic composition can be brought about through mass rape. It boosts the masculine ego of the aggressor, while the masculinity of the aggrieved is hurt. Society, however, silences the voice of women for it is considered a shame for the entire community. Yet, the nationalist leaders continue to flog the issue of rape to demonstrate the sacrifices that the nation had to make for a nationalist cause, while the actual victims remain faceless and voiceless. This, however, is not the case when deaths are documented: there, the faces of martyrs—mostly men—appear. War, after all, is an affair of men, and sacrifice of one's life is the highest form of patriotism. Of course, the rape victims continue to live lives of the dead.

Talking to the rape victims was the most difficult part of this research project. They refused to talk or even be identified. However, Shushoma, now 45, came forward. She told me categorically that she had nothing more to lose, and she did not want any more wars, referring to the continuous fighting between the PCJSS and the UPDF. That was why, for the sake of her people, she was telling her story after twenty years of silence. She did not want any other woman to suffer like her. Shushoma was a family planning worker. Her husband was a government servant. In 1984, there were often raids in their village. The military would come, beat up the men, take away the food, and accuse the villagers of helping the SB. The men mostly used to spend the nights outside, either in relatively safe localities or hide in jungles. Shushoma used to be alone in the house with her 2-year-old daughter. One night, when the military entered the village, everybody ran for their lives. But Shushoma could not, as her daughter had high fever. The Bengali settlers also arrived with the military. They entered her house, damaged everything, then shouted at her, accusing her of supporting the SB secretly. They enquired about her husband. By that time she had almost lost her senses: she thought that she would die out of sheer fear. She could not say a single word, her daughter was crying. Next, she remembers that two Bengali settlers were over her. She regained her senses the next morning. Her daughter was lying near her, fast asleep. The house was in a mess and the village was almost deserted. Her neighbours consoled her and took care of her. She could realize that people knew about it, but nobody said anything to her. Her husband did not return for many days, and when he came, he refused to even look at her. This hurt her the most. The village elders talked to him and tried to make him understand. But Shushoma could never go back to her husband. With tears in her eyes, she told me that she lived on only for her daughter's sake. She blamed her husband for not being there that fateful night, and treating her like dirt after his return. She never talked about it, but within herself, she had changed. She could not trust any man anymore, or even the institution of marriage. She believes that we are all lonely in this world, and one needs to accept this. After all, she has lived a life of loneliness and trauma. Her daughter is a schoolteacher. She wants her to be independent and take her own decisions in life. Before winding up with this writer, she said, 'Look, I am an independent woman today, but at what cost? I don't want any other woman to buy her independence at this cost.'

Shushoma's dreams are, however, far from being achieved. Even today in the post-accord CHT, women continue to be raped as a result of the Bengali–Hill people divide. Kalashona, 45, hails from Mohalchhari, where, as a consequence of a Bengali settler's and Hill people's dispute, the former killed a man, wounded 25 others, raped 9 women, and torched about 400 houses in 12 villages rendering 2,000 Hill people homeless on 26 August 2003.[16] Kalashona is one of those unfortunate rape victims. As she saw this writer, she broke into tears. Seizing the writer's hands, she kept on repeating that she could not stay in her house, the military was looking for her, and she had sneaked out to see the writer. Sobbing, she said that on that fateful day she was working in the field when she saw fire in the neighbouring villages. People began to run in fear. At first, she thought that the Bengali settlers would not come to their village, but they did. People got on boats or ran for their lives. She too accompanied them. Her 20-year-old daughter and 9-month-old granddaughter were also with her. The settlers and the army got hold of the boats and took them to the cremation ground in the mountains. They were beating up people mercilessly. The settlers had got hold of her daughter, who was shouting for help. Kalashona snatched the baby from her daughter and asked her to run. Then the army men attacked her: there were eight of them, and two of them raped her. They strangled the baby to death. Many people saw this and they were talking about it. They brought the body of the baby back and buried her. Many other young girls were raped but they don't talk about it, since they are young and have their futures before them, but Kalashona, despite all the risks, wants the world to know. She claims that the military is looking for her to shut her mouth, her husband is angry with her, yet, as a woman, she feels that she has this obligation to other women. Her daughter is quite like an insane person today after the loss of her daughter and the fate of her mother. But Kalashona, despite all her traumas, miseries, and fear, is holding on. She does not want any compensation in return. As she put it, 'You cannot compensate for certain things in life, but you can fight it, and opening up is my mode of fighting back.' One could not but be impressed by her agency, will to resist and to fight back.

Women in the CHT have also actively supported the insurgency. The armed resistance of the SB actually began in 1973. The combatant men had gone into hiding. Their families too had to go into hiding. In order to organize these women-headed households and to inspire them as well as the women of the CHT towards the movement, the Parbattya Chattagram Mohila Samity (CHT Women's Association) was formed in 1975. The female members among the armed combatants formed the core of the Mohila Samity. They were given armed self-defence training by the SB men in order to protect themselves. But there was no armed women's battalion, or women combatants in the SB. The Mohila Samity has wings in all the villages of the CHT, and it is still a part of the PCJSS. The latter has members in the central committee, but there are no women members in the executive committee.[17]

Jorita Chakma, wife of an ex-SB combatant, is one such active supporter who had received armed self-defence training. Currently, she is the organizing secretary of the Mohila Samity. She narrated to this writer the dual role that she had to play. She was in hiding with her children. The party maintained very strict discipline. The men could only visit the families once in one and a half years. She was the head of the household and had to take all decisions by herself and also provide for the family economically. They would hide in deep jungles, where she did *jhum* cultivation to provide for the family. She also had to educate her children at home. There was a *gono* (people's line) of informers. They would inform her if the military was coming. Then her family would have to move again to a new place, which usually used to be in deep jungle. The military was aware that the SB families were in deep jungles but did not know the exact location. At times, the villagers also used to hide them. It was a very difficult time, and from 1977 when she got married till 1997, when the peace accord was signed, that is, for twenty years, she led a life of hiding. She had to move thirteen days before her youngest son was born, and she had to move again the day her son was born. Those were the most traumatizing and fearful days. On the one hand, she used to remain tense and worried about her husband; on the other, the family had to be taken care of. But she was imbued with the ideals of the movement, and these carried her through.

As for the ideology of the Mohila Samity, she argued that they were fighting for the cause and rights of the Hill women, which she believed could be fulfilled through the nationalist agenda of the PCJSS. The women's question is, thus, subsumed under the national question. This became most evident when she spoke about the women's forum—the Hill Women's Federation (HWF) of the anti-accord UPDF, and the settler Bengali women. The Mohila Samity, she pointed out, was working with the Adivasi Bengali women,[18] but not the HWF and the settler Bengali women. The latter two, she argued, were working against the national cause of the Hill people.

Though women have actively supported the movement, yet it is argued here that this has not given them equality. No women were represented in the peace process, nor did the woman question figure in the peace accord. On this, Jorita (prompted by her husband) said that there was no need to incorporate women within the peace process. Though the woman question did not figure in the peace process, the PCJSS publications do talk about women's repression during the insurgency. When asked if women were part of the decision-making body of the PCJSS, instead of her, her husband responded that women were not capable of taking party decisions, which were issues of high politics, and that the family was the domain of women. Jorita seemed to agree with her husband. The gendered dimension of nationalism became most evident in this instance.

It had been suggested earlier that Hill women who were homemakers had contested the notion of empowerment and also the public-private divide, but in the case of Jorita and her husband, both of whom were actively involved in the nationalist movement, the public-private divide and the masculine paradigm of the nationalist discourse appeared in full form. It is also important to note that despite repeated efforts, none of the other women who had actively supported the movement and now had settled down into family lives agreed to talk to this writer. They pointed out that security considerations did not allow them to talk. It has been mentioned earlier that the post-accord CHT presents a very complicated security scenario. These women did not want to be identified by the army, the Bengali settlers, and also the UPDF. This is indicative of the militarization that the society has undergone.

This writer spoke to Kabita Chakma, former president of the now-dissident HWF. Kabita had been an active member of the HWF and had been in the forefront of the movement since 1989, when she was a college student. The HWF was formed in 1988 in Chittagong University to protest army repression against women in the CHT. It used to work in association with the Pahari Chatra Parishad (PCP) and the Pahari Gono Parishad (PGP). While the PCJSS had gone into hiding, these three organizations were in the open and carried on the Hill people's cause through democratic means. In 1995, the HWF held its first independent procession in Khagrachari to protest the sexual assault on Shumita Chakma, a class V student. From there, Kabita contends, women's uprisings began in the Hills. They used to protest, hold meetings, bring out publications on women's repression in the CHT by the military and Bengali settlers. They used to support the PCJSS movement, but were totally frustrated with the provisions of the peace accord. Terming it a compromise accord, the PCP, PGP and the HWF disassociated themselves from the PCJSS cause and formed the UPDF in 1998. Factions of these three bodies have joined the PCJSS. As an activist, life has not been easy for Kabita: formerly, she was hunted by the army, so she spent most of the time in Dhaka. Now, the PCJSS is also after her. She pointed out that she was scandalized: obscene posters had appeared in her name in the CHT. She never went to the Khagrachari market, her hometown, nor did she spend any night in her house when she did go to Khagrachari. Her family was being harassed, and her mother remained worried about her. Like Jorita, Kabita also believed that once national emancipation was achieved, women's issues and problems would also be resolved, but for her the national question was the main issue. She refused to see the patriarchy inherent in nationalism. She too drew a line between Bengali women, PCJSS women, and the Hill women. She was quite militant in her attitude, and did not see any problem in resorting to arms to attain one's objectives.

The above suggests that insurgency in the CHT and the continued conflict in the region has resulted in the militarization, and consequently masculinization of the society. The Bengali–Hill people divide has deepened, but more significantly, the Hill society and polity has become polarized. In such a scenario, human security is the first casualty. Women and children suffer most in these circumstances. As homemakers, home and children were the most important elements of women's lives; their security and protection kept them most traumatized. At the same time, their protection became their source of inspiration and power and gave them the will and strength to fight and live on. They constantly talked of food and water insecurity and scarcity. It was common knowledge that under such circumstances they ate less or even went without food. Their priorities were their children and husbands. Loneliness and the fear of being uprooted haunted them. Psychologically, all of them were shattered. Bodily too, they had been brutalized and humiliated. All of them had suffered economically as well, but the psychological impact was the most severe. It had displaced and dislocated them as individuals: many of them pointed out that the sight of the military froze them. They had nightmares and suffered from insomnia and amnesia. Women also suffered from violence from their own men: this became evident in the rape cases and also in the refugee camps. One might refer to this form of violence as 'hurt masculinity', when men vent their frustrations upon women. Women's battles, thus, are fought both within and without.

But contradictorily enough, despite the acute trauma and fear, most of them felt that they had become more independent and were capable of facing any situation now. This is indicative of the enormous inner resilience, strength, and agencies that women carry. The interviews also suggest that in tremendous adversity, women were capable of taking independent decisions. They are fully conscious of the injustices done to them and want a better future for their posterity and do not want other women to suffer like them, which is why many of them, specially the rape victims, spoke out. Victimization and agency, thus, go hand in hand.

The dominant notions of empowerment and the public–private divide were also contested by the interviewees. As pointed out earlier, women suggested that their society allowed them space in the public sphere. This, however, did not appear to be the case with Jorita once she had settled down to a normal family life. Being the wife of a front-ranking nationalist leader might be the reason behind this. One can, thus, suggest that the public-private divide is a modernist intrusion in an otherwise traditional and more equitable society. This intrusion, however, is a gendered one, bound to have a marginalizing impact upon women.

A dominant and common theme that came through the interviews was the concern for home and children, the resilience and will to fight back and survive for the sake of a better world for posterity. Peace and security seemed to be their major concerns. Except for the active supporters, none of the other interviewees had any space for violence in their lives. Though they all appeared to be conscious of the political ideas of nation and statehood, they stressed the commonalities that we as human beings shared, and wanted these to be the bases of a polity that they dreamed of and aspired for. Based on their lived experiences of trauma, fear, loneliness, and, above all, insecurity, and their aspirations and dreams for the future, the paper in its final section makes a case for re-imagining the polity.

RE-IMAGINING THE POLITY

The study identifies structural and systemic factors to be at the root of the maladies. The patriarchy/hegemony inherent in the construction of the modern state cuts across ethnic, class, and gender lines. Within these matrices, however, women remain most marginalized, though the level or degree of marginalization may vary. It has further been observed that with the growing use of drugs and arms the fabric of the society is collapsing. The society is increasingly being militarized and masculinized. A re-imagining, therefore, entails change at very fundamental levels. This involves strategizing on various fronts. The following are suggested in this vein.

EDUCATION AND BRIDGES

A major concern of most of the interviewees was the future of their children. Special emphasis was put on education. Women braved the (in)security system of the refugee camps and returned for the sake of education of their children. Education and schooling, thus, can be important tools for healing and bridging the divides between communities. This, however, begs the question of the nature and content of education. The present academic curriculum, if one may say so, is quite soulless, devoid of emancipatory spirit and philosophy. It only reinforces the culture of hegemony through the imparting of a knowledge that glorifies the Bengali nation, its culture and history. The Hill people—or for that matter the non-Bengalis—find themselves totally missing from the canvas of the land, of which they are supposedly equal citizens, as proclaimed by the state Constitution. This culture of hegemony sustained by the education system produces a counter-hegemonic culture, which deepens the divides. It is, therefore, important to recast the education system through inculcating the values of critical thinking and consciousness, build up a culture of tolerance, dialogue, harmony, and emancipation. This is not a tall order: these are rooted in our culture and values. We only need to rediscover and relocate it.[19]

Humanizing and Feminizing the Refugee Regime

Women in refugee situations face tremendous hardships. The interviews reveal that apart from the psychological traumas, they also faced bodily insecurity. Violence against women prevailed in the camps. The women had to face extreme hardship in procuring necessities like water, for which they had to stand in queues for hours. The living conditions were inhuman, and about 75–100 women used a common latrine. Women require more privacy, and during menstruation they require more time and hygienic conditions. Yet, no separate regime exists for women in refugee situations. A major factor for this is the definition of refugees contained in the 1951 Convention Relating to the Status of Refugees which omits the category of sex as a ground upon which refugee status may be determined.

There is a need to free the refugees from the legalistic frame and treat it as a human rights issue. Women refugee issues ought to be treated as women's rights. Women ought to be included in the management and decision-making bodies of refugee camps and also during the framing of the refugee regimes. Adequate attention ought to be given to reproductive health concerns and the provision of maternal health services, sanitary supplies, and family planning methods. The integrity of women refugees as women ought to be protected.[20]

Rooting Social Justice

A just and sustainable security and social system cannot be established unless the injustices and crimes are taken cognizance of, recognized, and acknowledged. Women have suffered and continue to suffer immeasurably due to the continual conflict scenario in the CHT. The CHT peace accord—supposedly the foundation for peace in the region—is totally silent on the questions of justice and women. It is, therefore, not surprising that Hill women continue to be raped by the Bengali settlers and the military. It is imperative that the injustices and crimes committed during the insurgency and afterwards be acknowledged and justice meted out to the victims. Bangladesh is a signatory to the Convention on the Elimination of all forms of Discrimination Against Women (CEDAW), and also to the convention on the International Criminal Court (ICC), which declares rape as a crime against humanity. It is, therefore, legally binding upon the state to fulfil its treaty obligations. The civil society at the national and international levels can make forceful interventions in this regard.

Another important point to be emphasized here is that justice cannot be blind. It is time it opened its eyes and treated women from the women's rights perspective on the basis of equity, not equality.

Re-Imagining the Nation State

Women in the CHT, while discussing the notions of nation and state, were very categorical in drawing the line between the two. Nation, according to them, is a cultural category, while state is political. Despite the differences in culture, language and religion, they stressed upon the commonalities of human beings. A common statement was that they all shared the same colour of blood, their basic needs and wants were the same, like food, shelter, security. The divisiveness created by the ideology of nationalism was considered by them to be a construction of the politicians for their own vested interests, not by the people in general. They considered themselves to be citizens of Bangladesh, but identified their nationhood as Chakma, Marma, or Tripura. Pluralism and multiculturalism was at the heart of how they saw themselves.

Yet, the nation state of Bangladesh is predicated and premised on a hegemonic, homogenizing mode, which gave birth to the nationalist movement in the CHT. It is time we put the concepts of nation, state and citizenship in their proper perspective, which, indeed, the Hill women have. Feminism idealizes the culture of sharing, collective empowerment, pluralism, and contextuality. These ideals need to infused in the concept of nation state and Bangladesh being recognized as a multicultural and multinational state. Human security and the means towards sustainable security should be incorporated as the main security agenda. The concept of citizenship ought to be engendered, and in light of the experiences of the Hill women, there is a need to re-examine the notions of war, patriotism, protector, and protected. It has been amply demonstrated that women fought the war for the protection of their children, homes and families: the tools were different, but the objective was the same.

The above are not difficult propositions. Apart from a vested interest group, as so rightly pointed out by the Hill women, these are the dreams and aspirations of the people in general. It is the people—both men and women—that this paper pins its hope upon to bring about the transformation towards a humane society imbued with the ideals and institutions of tolerance, dialogue, and respect for diversity in all its forms.

NOTES

1. Rebecca Grant and Kathleen Newland, eds., *Gender and International Relations*, Buckinghan: Open University Press, 1991, pp. 11–12.
2. Rubina Saigol, 'Women and Citizenship in South Asia', Working Note presented at the workshop on Women Building Peace, South Asian Forum for Human Rights (SAFHR), Kathmandu, 22–28 June 2001.

3. For details, see Amena Mohsin, 'Gendered Nation, Gendered Peace', *Indian Journal of Gender Studies*, vol. 11, no. 1, 2004, pp. 43–64.
4. Bangladesh Bureau of Statistics (BBS), *Statistical Pocket Book of Bangladesh*, Dhaka: Government of the People's Republic of Bangladesh, Ministry of Planning, Statistics Division, 1993, p. 33.
5. This manual was promulgated by the British colonial power for the administration of the CHT. It sought to disaggregate the CHT from the administrative system of Bengal and set up special political, economic, and security provisions for the region that, the Hill people argue, protected them from competition with Bengalis. The CHT was declared a Backward Area and the District Commissioner (DC) was given extraordinary powers. For details, see Amena Mohsin, *Politics of Nationalism: The Case of the CHT, Bangladesh*, Dhaka: University Press, 1997.
6. Selina Haq and Ehsanul Haque, *Disintegration Process in Action: The Case of South Asia*, Dhaka: BILIA, 1990, pp. 44–6.
7. Ministry of Law and Parliamentary Affairs, *The Constitution of the People's Republic of Bangladesh [as modified up to 30th June 1994]*, Dhaka: Government of Bangladesh, 1994, p. 10.
8. Government of Bengal, *Selections from the Correspondence on the Revenue Administration of the Chittagong Hill Tracts, 1862–1927*, Calcutta [now Kolkata]: Government of Bengal Press, 1929, pp. 202–4.
9. *Guardian*, 6 March 1984.
10. Md. Nurul Amin, 'Bangladesher Jatishottar Shomossha O Shangbidhanik Shomadhaner Onushandhan' (Problems of National Identity in Bangladesh and the Quest for a Constitutional Solution), in *Bangladesher Shongshodiya Gonotantra: Prashangik Chinta Bhabna* (Parliamentary Democracy in Bangladesh: Some Reflections and Thoughts), ed. Emajuddin Ahamed, Dhaka: Karim Books, 1992, p. 118.
11. For details, see Amena Mohsin, 'Bangladesh–India Relations: Limitations and Options in an Evolving Relationship', in *Bangladesh, South Asia and the World*, ed. Emajuddin Ahamed and Abul Kalam, Dhaka: Academic Publishers, 1992.
12. For details, see Subir Bhaumik, *Insurgent Crossfire: North-East India*, New Delhi: Lancer Publishers, 1996.
13. For details of the post-accord CHT, see Amena Mohsin, *The Chittagong Hill Tracts, Bangladesh: On the Difficult Road to Peace*, Boulder, CO: Lynne Rienner, 2003.
14. Author's interview with Brig. Shahed Anam (retd.) on 28 March 2003. The latter had served in the CHT as Commanding Officer.
15. Cynthia Cockburn, 'The Gendered Dynamics of Armed Conflict and Political Violence', in *Victims, Perpetrators or Actors? Gender, Armed*

Conflict and Political Violence, ed. Caroline O.N. Moser and Fiona C. Clark, London: Zed Books, 2001, p. 21.

16. *Daily Star* (Dhaka), 19 March 2004.
17. Author's interview with Dhiru Kumar, former President of PCJSS Khagrachari Zilla Samity on 21 March 2003 in Khagrachari.
18. The Hill people make a distinction between the Bengalis who came naturally to the Hills till 1971, and those who were settled by the state. The former are called 'Adivasi Bengalis' and the latter 'settlers'.
19. For a good critique of education and schooling, see Avijit Pathak, *Social Implications of Schooling: Knowledge, Pedagogy and Consciousness*, New Delhi: Rainbow Publishers, 2002.
20. Chaloka Beyani, 'The Needs of Refugee Women: A Human-Rights Perspective', *Gender and Development*, vol. 3, no. 2, June 1995, pp. 29–35.

3. Implications of Insurgency on Women: The Sri Lankan Experience

Sunila Abeysekera

Gender Ideology and Conflict: An Overview

The emergence of social formations and political organizations that challenge discrimination, exploitation, and marginalization on the basis of a specific identity based on minority status, language, religion, or ethnicity has been a key factor in facilitating social change in the modern world. As communities strive to create a collective identity that confronts their marginalization, they re-create their community, rewrite its history, and reinvent traditions and customs in order to draw the community together.[1] This process provides symbolic and imaginary meaning to the cohesion that is called for in order to establish a shared identity and shared goals. It is an essentially patriarchal process, strengthening existing divisions in society and ascribing different roles to men and women, in relation to one another, as well as to social and political formations, including the state. The division between the public and the private worlds prevails, keeping women within the confines of the home, domesticity, and the family. The emphasis is on women as biological and social reproducers, with little or no space allotted to them in the public arena. The fact that the level of participation of women in structures of governance throughout the region is much lower than that of men is a reflection of this phenomenon.[2] In the same way, the role played by women in the leadership of social and political movements is often marginal, except for a few exceptions.[3] The arenas of diplomacy, international relations and security have been ones in which patriarchal control has been most marked. The participation of women regarding questions of 'security', specially in active combat as well as in the decision-making bodies of security studies institutions, is very low.[4]

In the South Asian context, anti-colonial social movements positioned themselves against the colonizers; their nationalism enabled large crowds of otherwise disempowered indigenous citizens to engage in widespread acts of civil disobedience that challenged the might of the British empire. The work of many scholars on the nationalist movement in South Asia have pointed to the dynamic relationship between nationalism and patriarchy, that created an image of the 'modern' post-colonial indigenous woman that, in fact, contained within it the seeds of her subordination.[5] Neloufer de Mel states that:

> Despite repeatedly affirming the centrality of women to nationalist projects—whether as signifying modernization or for their allegorical value as mothers of the nation—women have in this respect been primarily a discursive terrain on which significant socio-cultural tenets of the nation are produced. Women are constructed as the nation's subjects—not only as citizens but also as members of ethnic, class and caste groups—differently to men.[6]

The 'Indian' identity that was constructed in opposition to colonialism disintegrated in the face of tensions within that identity grouping as issues of power-sharing came to the fore. 'Independence' was accompanied by the partition of India and Pakistan in 1947. We have seen this process continue within the modern nation states of the subcontinent: in 1971, East Pakistan became Bangladesh after the Bangladeshis fought a War of Liberation against the West Pakistan government. As the years went by, the grievances and prejudices experienced by a specific community within a state—for example, the ethnic minority Tamils in Sri Lanka, the tribal communities of the north-east of India, the indigenous peoples of the Chittagong Hill Tracts (CHT) region in Bangladesh, the mohajirs of Karachi, the rural poor of Nepal—led them to seek a transformation in their own situation which often manifest as political struggles, including armed and militant struggles for self-determination and autonomy. Some of these conflicts remain at the level of internal conflicts, or civil wars, while others cross borders and become transnational in nature. Some of them are resolved through non-violent political means: sadly, however, many of them become violent, and the violence of those who challenge state power is responded to by the state in extremely brutal and undemocratic ways. All identified conflicts have arisen because of struggles for power among male actors, male-dominated political structures, and patriarchal ideologies. These struggles are classified as 'insurgencies', as attempts to overthrow legitimate governments; those engaging in these struggles are 'subversives', 'insurgents', and 'terrorists'.

The language of 'insurgency' and 'counter-insurgency', 'subversion' and 'counter-subversion' is inherently patriarchal. The state, and the groups that oppose the state, are male-dominated. The power that is fought for is formulated in terms of the ability to control resources, including human resources, and to use coercion and violence in order to win assent and support for their aims. A conflict situation in itself allows for a lack of accountability and the impunity of those engaged in actual fighting, state and non-state. Many of the legal and infrastructural frameworks that are set in place as a response to a conflict in society, such as prevention of terrorism legislation, provide for the widespread 'normalization' of the use of violence as a means of silencing dissent and maintaining social and political stability. In such a situation, democratic norms fail to prevail, and all opposition and dissent, even when it is non-violent, is subject to brutal repression. On the part of the state, all acts that question and challenge the anti-democratic actions of the state security forces in waging war and the breakdown of normal law and order processes are 'subversive' and a part of a 'conspiracy to overthrow the state'. On the part of non-state actors engaging in the armed conflict, all acts that question their power and capacity to represent the interests of their community are seen as treacherous and divisive.

The process of militarization pervades the entire society and transforms struggles for daily subsistence and survival into conflicts of life and death. Anuradha Chenoy describes militarization as a process which implies 'the growing dominance of the military over civilian institutions with a simultaneous decline in democratic institutions and the freedoms and rights of citizens'.[7] This process of militarization has a tremendous impact on the lives of ordinary people, specially women.

On the basis of the different experiences that men and women go through in life, Cynthia Cockburn argues for an understanding of what she refers to as a 'sexual division of war',[8] through which we can see the 'connection between violence, militarism and certain masculine cultures in which men learn violence and bond together as men in an atmosphere of disrespect for women. The close link between nationalism, militarism, and patriarchy creates a pattern of gender and power relations that enable conflict, and much feminist analysis of violence calls for an understanding of the continuum between violence against women and children within the family and the violence of wars. The analysis of war and power/gender relations that has been developed by practitioners of participatory conflict transformation processes such as Diana Francis builds on these linkages between patriarchy and militarism, in order to examine the constructions of masculinity that are so closely related to the institution of war, for example, through the creation of the archetype of the male warrior/hero.[9]

The Specific Impact of the Conflict on Women

The various ways in which violent conflicts in the South Asian region have an impact on women's rights and dignity have been documented and analysed by many feminist activists and scholars over the past years.[10] Building on the work of feminist scholars and academics such as Nira Yuval Davis[11] and Cynthia Enloe,[12] they have examined the role of women within armed conflict as members of armies and fighting forces; at the same time they have observed the changing role of women in society as the conflict challenges and transforms many traditional norms and social/cultural practices.

As any social group begins to base its sense of belonging, community, and identity on factors of ethnicity and ethnic origin, religion, membership in a tribal or indigenous community, a special role is ascribed to women in the construction and maintenance of this identity. Within the community, women are perceived as the biological and social reproducers of the community. Especially in situations in which a particular group is in the minority, the focus on biological reproduction as critical to the survival of the group places great pressure on women and men to marry within the community and to bear children, as many of them as possible. In their role as social reproducers, women bear the responsibility of preserving and passing on the traditions and culture of the community to the next generation. Because of their reproductive capacity, women become symbolic of the community, and of its 'honour': this renders them vulnerable to all forms of violence and sexual abuse at the hands of those who seek to 'dishonour' their community. This, in turn, enables the community, specially male elders, to impose restrictions on women's mobility and choice, and to prescribe appropriate behaviour and practices for women, including sometimes the imposition of a dress code. Such a process of affirmation of identity can also result in a resurrection of stereotypes of women from traditional folklore and myths; most often, these women are identified by virtues of self-sacrifice and dignity in the face of adversity. In the Indian context, Sita from the *Ramayana* is one such figure. These figures begin to reappear in both traditional and modern guise in songs, stories, and television serials and create a role model for women in contemporary society.

In addition, in conflict situations, women are told that since the pursuit of the community's rights and dignity is the most critical issue at that moment, they should refrain from raising issues that would 'divide' the community from within. Thus, issues such as domestic violence, incest, and denial of equal rights to women in traditional law are perceived as 'divisive'. Women who raise these issues are labelled as 'traitors' or agents of 'alien' interests. As Urvashi Butalia points out, 'In the hierarchy of violence . . . the "external" violence of conflict somehow comes to acquire much greater significance than the "internal" violence of domestic strife . . . to everyone, the male is the hero, whether as an army man, or a militant, or simply someone caught in conflict.'[13]

Rape and sexual violation of women has been a strategy of war and conflict through the ages. The experiences of women in the former Yugoslavia and in Rwanda during conflicts in those countries for the first time raised the issue of the wide range of sexual violence and abuse of women in conflict situations—not only rape, but sexual harassment, sexualized methods of torture, forced pregnancy, forced abortion, enslavement, and sexual slavery were all a part of the gross violations of human rights perpetrated against women in the course of those wars and conflicts. In modern South Asia too there is a terrible history of the use of sexual violence against women in times of conflict, from Partition in 1947 to the war of liberation in Bangladesh in 1971, from checkpoint rapes of Tamil women in Sri Lanka to anti-Muslim violence in Gujarat in 2002. It is only with the intense campaigning by women around these issues in the creation of the International Criminal Court that public attention has been drawn to the tendency to render these crimes against women 'invisible'. Yet, the inability of activists to seek justice for women victims of sexual violence and assault accompanied by murder in Gujarat, India, has once more raised a host of issues relating to the gender-blind and gender-insensitive construction of the structures of justice and jurisprudence.

The Impact of Conflict on Women in Sri Lanka

The period of conflict in Sri Lanka sharply demonstrates the continuum of violence that women face in modern society. Sexual violence in the context of the conflict has been the focus of many women's rights and human rights groups. The environment of impunity that has prevailed during this period has, in particular, led to several cases of rape, and of rape and murder of women while in the custody of the Armed Forces and the police. Among the cases that attracted international outcry were the rape and murder of Krishanthy Kumarasamy in Jaffna (Northern Province) in 1996, the murders of Koneswary Murugesupillai in Amparai (Eastern Province) and of Sarathambal in Mannar (Northern Province) in 1999. Only in the Kumarasamy case had a trial proceeded to a conclusion and the perpetrators (at least some of them), sentenced to death and imprisonment.[14]

The impunity with which sexual violence is perpetrated against women who are in custody has also extended to the areas of the island that are technically outside the conflict. The rape of Nandani Herath in Wariyapola in 2001 is but one example. Thus, the normalization of violence and impunity, both of which are critical components of a process of militarization, have come to apply throughout the island of Sri Lanka, despite the 'actual war' being fought only in the north and east. The high levels of post-traumatic stress disorder among members of the security forces that have been commented on by counsellors working in organizations assisting women victims and survivors of violence point to the high incidence of domestic violence within families of Armed Forces personnel. The presence of large numbers of armed army deserters engaging in petty crimes has led to an increase in crimes against women, while some researchers and journalists have also commented on the increase in the numbers of women engaging in sex work in and around areas in which there is a large army presence.

Many women in conflict situations face the trauma and tragedy of the loss of loved ones, often mostly male relatives, through death, disappearance, or migration. Sri Lankan women were no exception. The use of the symbol of 'mother' to draw attention to their loss and to demand public accountability is not something that is specific to Sri Lanka alone. Resorting to traditional rituals and other methods of easing their pain and grief has also been a strategy used by women throughout Sri Lanka. In 1991, the southern Mothers' Front organized a ritual of appeals to the Goddess Kali, calling on her to wreak vengeance on those who were responsible for the disappearances and deaths of their children. In Colombo in 2002, women from the Theatre Action Group, which works with the 'ritual for healing' form of theatre in the north and east, held a public march and performance by women affected by the war. This practice has continued to be a contentious one. Some acknowledge that it is a form of public protest that was traditionally acted out by women and that was culturally accepted. Others argue that such practices could lead to a reaffirmation of the 'essentialist' nature of women as nurturers and as lacking in social power except with the help of the occult. There were also concerns raised regarding the potential manipulation of these women through such appeals to their emotions, played out at the cost of neglect of more focused political actions.

The large-scale displacement that has taken place as a consequence of the conflict has also had a specific impact on the lives of women. Thousands of women have fled as refugees to southern India, and to Europe, North America and Australia. Tens of thousands of others have been 'temporarily relocated' in state-run welfare centres and makeshift villages set up by NGOs; the 'temporary' nature of their stay sometimes exceeds ten years. The circumstances of displacement and dislocation destroy the familiar survival networks and strategies adopted by women of all communities and propels them into decision-making situations to which they are unaccustomed. The experiences of women and displacement have been well-documented,[15] and all point to the ways in which the radical reversal of gender roles and undermining of gendered power relations result in what Darini Rajasingham-Senanayake calls an 'ambivalent empowerment'.[16]

The political economy of the conflict in Sri Lanka has also had tremendous impact on the status of women in the country and on gender relations. Losses due to destruction of, and lack of access to, economically productive assets, as well as the disruption of economic activities have placed grave stress on the economy. The conflict grew intense in a period during which the Government of Sri Lanka actively pursued policies of economic liberalization as a part of the overall process of globalization that can be seen in all South Asian countries. The creation of Free Trade Zones (FTZ), the transformation of rural communities from subsistence producers to cash crop producers, the lack of adequate returns from agricultural production led to large-scale rural to urban migration, a phenomenon not experienced in Sri Lanka prior to this period. Thousands of young men and women flocked to urban centres in search of employment. Many of them sought employment in unskilled sectors in West Asia; others, mostly young women, went to work in the factories producing export goods in the export promotion zones set up around the country. This process, in turn, led to social disintegration, with families disrupted Children, the elderly and other dependents were left without adequate care once the female head of the household had left.

High defence spending by the government—at 6 per cent of the GDP, one of the highest in the world—has led to several additional taxes being imposed on the people, driving up prices of all goods and services. The LTTE has its own defence expenditure, and its own system of taxation from those living in areas under their control, from those travelling to those areas as well as from Tamils and well-wishers living outside Sri Lanka.

The expenditure on purchase of weapons and ammunition and on salaries and benefits for servicemen and women are balanced by cuts in spending on health and education and cutbacks in subsidies on food, transport, and communication. Provision of care for internally displaced persons, the payment of pensions and compensation, provision of specialized health care for those disabled by the conflict and for those affected by the psychological impact of conflict, are all grossly inadequate in a country ravaged by war.

Causes and Consequences of Conflict in Sri Lanka: A Historical Background

In Sri Lanka, the first post-Independence 'insurgency' was started by a militant youth group, the Janatha Vimukthi Peramuna (JVP, People's Liberation Front). In April 1971, in a serious challenges to state power they launched a series of attacks against police stations in several provincial towns in the south of Sri Lanka. This insurgency derived its sustenance on a collective political identity forged on the basis of economic deprivation, social marginalization, and caste- and class-based discrimination. The immediate causal factors that have been identified were the high rates of youth unemployment among young men and women from poor rural families with a secondary or sometimes an university education, and the lack of any clear expectations regarding their future.[17] This insurgency was swiftly and brutally crushed by the government. While there are no accurate figures of the overall casualties, and certainly no calculation of the loss to property, official figures state that the insurgency resulted in the deaths of 41 civilians and 63 members of the police and security forces.[18] It is more difficult to state the number of 'insurgents' killed since the security forces' reports of the time are full of vague statements such as 'a fair number of insurgents were killed', but according to all records it would seem that over 1,000 were killed during the month of April 1971. Many of the bodies were cremated unidentified. About 14,000 young men and women were detained, and many of them spent up to two years in rehabilitation centres. The all-male leadership was tried for conspiracy to overthrow the government under a special court established under the Criminal Justice Commissions Act, 1971 and sentenced to long periods of imprisonment.

Concurrently, in the north and east of the island which is predominantly inhabited by the minority Tamil community,[19] Tamil youth became increasingly restless with the failure of non-violent and democratic attempts made by moderate Tamil political leaders to resolve issues of discrimination and under-development. These young Tamils began to articulate a demand for a separate state known as Tamil Eelam. This demand was accepted as the overarching political vision for the Tamil people through a Resolution submitted to the Convention of the Tamil United Liberation Front (TULF) in 1977.[20] The key issues around which the struggle grew were the lack of access to state employment and tertiary education, very similar to the demands of youth militancy in the south. The severe and brutal repression carried out by the state security forces of any form of dissent added to this fire. In addition, the Tamils raised issues of discrimination on the basis of political and language rights, pointing to the hegemonic rule of the Sinhala majority community in the south within which minority representation was structurally diminished. Among other critical issues, the encroachment of land in the north and east was of serious concern to the Tamils. This had come by under a series of colonization and settlement schemes which brought landless peasants from the Sinhala community to the north and east, thus radically altering the demographic patterns of these areas. The consistent neglect of these areas in terms of industrial and other development since the country's independence from British colonial rule in 1948 was another bone of contention.

As the conflict intensified and became increasingly violent, the process of brutalization and militarization of society commenced. The government reacted as those controlling power structures in any society in conflict do: they set in motion mechanisms of repression and silencing. The creation of the Prevention of Terrorism Act in 1979, the establishment of a Special Task Force within the police, and various other anti-subversive measures that undermined fundamental democratic principles paved the way for the gross abuse of human rights. At the same time, within the ideological and discursive spaces of Sri Lankan society, extremist forms of nationalist thought began to emerge on all sides—Sinhala, Tamil, and later Muslim—that denied the pluralistic nature of the island and the human rights and dignity of all its peoples as equals.

In 1987, the Government of Sri Lanka entered into an agreement with the Indian Government that enabled the Indian Peace-Keeping Force (IPKF) to move into the north and east of the island in order to begin a process of disarming and demobilization of the militant Tamil groups. There was, however a strong resistance to the Indo-Lanka Peace Accord from a range of southern political actors unified under the banner of the Deshapremi Janatha Vyaparaya (DJV, Patriotic People's Movement). The protests soon deteriorated into an unmitigated campaign of terror and violence against anyone associated with the state, anyone who supported the Indo-Lanka Accord, or anyone who supported a political and negotiated settlement of the ethnic conflict. The state responded with utmost brutality. In the two-year-period from November 1987 to November 1989, over 5,000 persons were killed by the DJV and over 40,000 persons 'disappeared' (abducted, murdered, and disposed of with no trace) by the security forces and by various paramilitary groups operating with the tacit approval of the security forces.[21]

The north and east of the country has been the frontline of the war, and, therefore, has been particularly affected by it. Tens of thousands of people have lost their lives, hundreds of thousands of people have been displaced, and property worth millions of rupees has been damaged. The war has also infiltrated the southern parts of the island from time to time with large-scale bombings which have led to loss of life and destruction of property. In addition, resistance to the Indo-Lanka Peace Accord in 1987 paved the way for a massive repression in the south. The conflict in all its various manifestations—military conflict, pogroms, civilian massacres, large-scale disappearances—has posed serious challenges to the structures of governance of the country and has led to erosion of democratic freedoms and human rights of all communities, but especially the rights of the Tamil minority community. Issues of unlawful arrest and detention, torture, disappearance, sexual and physical abuse and violence are among the most common human rights violations that the human rights community in Sri Lanka has to deal with. In addition, the denial of rights to internally displaced persons has created a new discourse on the meaning of citizenship in the context of conflict.

During the years of conflict, women's groups that work for the protection and promotion of women's rights have been in the forefront of agitating against the range of human rights abuses that take place in the context of a conflict: torture and disappearance, arbitrary arrest and detention, censorship and controls on the freedom of movement. In addition, they have challenged limitations placed on the freedoms of expression and association as well as the climate of impunity that permits violations of human rights to become the rule rather than the exception.

ROLE OF GENDER IDEOLOGY IN MODERN SRI LANKAN CONFLICTS

Many feminist scholars writing on the impact of the conflict in Sri Lanka on women and on women's rights have explored the ways in which the capacity of women to reproduce the community, in both a biological and social sense, ascribe a special role for them in conflict situations.[22] On the one hand, the conflict dislocates communities and generates a process of social disintegration within which women are called on to assume roles of leadership and responsibility, at the level of the community and within their families, which in 'normal' times would have remained out of bounds for them. On the other hand, the stress on the woman's role in maintaining and defining the identity of the community leads to many restrictions on their rights, including their rights to mobility, choice of marriage partner, and, in general, control over their sexual and reproductive lives.

The involvement of women in Sri Lanka in active military service, within the state Armed Forces and armed militant or insurgent groups, has had a tremendous impact on society as a whole as well as on militant organizations which are always male-dominated and male-controlled. This aspect of conflict has been the subject of much study and analysis in past years. The tensions between traditional perceptions of women as givers of life and the contemporary reality of women as fighters and suicide bombers creates a space in which conservative assumptions about women's roles can be challenged and changed. However, it also provides an ideological and sociocultural base for constraining women within the home and the community.

The specificity of women's biological and socio-cultural existence has led to women's bodies becoming contested terrain in all modern conflicts. The ways in which women are made vulnerable to horrific sexual violence and a wide range of abuse is a crucial indicator both of their positioning within the conflict and within society and community. How society responds and reacts to these violations and to the changes that are wrought in social and cultural patterns and frameworks because of the specific ways in which conflict has an impact on women's lives are critical areas of academic and activist exploration. At the same time, conflict creates a range of situations in which women are, often without any preparation, pushed into decision-making positions within their families and communities. The phenomenon of the female-headed household has changed the reality of women's role within the family and society, and presents all those concerned with processes of conflict transformation with a major challenge of how to incorporate these changes and gains into any framework for the future.

In addition, the conflict has created a glorification of war and the mythologization of the hero who goes to battle for the defence of the 'Motherland'. Patriotism, love for one's country, sacrifice—all become paramount principles in this process. Those who die in battle are publicly revered, awarded medals, commemorated; their families derive various benefits from the deaths. The links between masculinity and militarism are very visible in this arena. The media portrays the 'brave and heroic' soldier as a man, always. 'Machismo' reigns supreme. Advertisements to recruit young men into the army show them as brave, daring, attractive to women; in turn, the women in these advertisements are starry-eyed and obviously overawed by the prowess of the military might which is integral to the masculinity of the men they are with.

JVP INSURGENCY: 1971

The JVP had been organizing and mobilizing rural youth since 1969, and by 1971 it had acquired a fairly extensive following, specially in some areas of southern Lanka. The decision to carry out coordinated attacks on police stations as a means of destabilizing the state structures and moving towards capture of state power was taken in the midst of some controversy, at a time when the JVP leader Wijeweera was in custody. However, when the attacks did take place on 4 and 5 April, the Sri Lankan security forces were caught off their guard and for a few weeks, in some areas of the island, JVP cadres controlled access roads, took over village cooperative stores, distributed food on ration cards, and conducted summary trials and punishments, including executions.

Looking at the structure and form of the JVP in this period, it is clear that the role of women was not so significant in terms of, for example, their presence in decision-making bodies of the JVP. According to Kelly Senanayake,[23] there were approximately 450 women among those who were taken into custody following the abortive uprising of April 1971. Of them, only about 150 had actually attended the indoctrination lectures of the JVP, and only about 15 were working for the organization on a full-time basis. During the 1971 period, only about six women were involved in decision-making bodies at the Action Committee level.[24] The leadership of the JVP had actively encouraged its cadres to work for the recruitment of young women, but this was primarily based on a romantic notion of the participation of women garnered from reading the example set by women cadres in Maoist China. There was also the experience of the high level of active participation by women in the demonstrations and political activities organized by the traditional left parties in 1953 against the increase in the price of rice,[25] which the JVP may have tried to emulate. What is clear from what is known of the organization at the time is that issues of gender, or of the specific problems of women's subordination, were not taken into account in the political analysis of the group.

Yet, the fact that young women from poor and middle-class rural homes joined this radical militant movement speaks of the fact that it was able to attract and absorb women. The women attended the same political 'classes' as the men and received military training. Kelly Senanayake[26] cites the names of several schoolgirls from Ambalangoda, the home town of Wijeweera[27] and many other leaders of the JVP at the time, such as Sampathy, Kamani, Sepali as having joined the organization in 1970. In addition, during the trial of the JVP leadership, names of other women were revealed, for example, that of Chandra *akka*[28] of Vidyodaya University, and of Leena Irene and Nandaseeli who were both students at the University of Colombo at the time. They were among the five women taken into custody while they were in hiding in the government flats in Bambalapitiya after an aborted attack on the then Prime Minister Sirimavo Bandaranaike's residence. There were women involved in attacks on police stations; the death of one woman cadre in Deniyaya has been recorded. Lieutenant Colonel Wickremanayake, who was in-charge of Matara district during this time, mentioned the fact that a number of 'girls' were among the attackers he personally saw; he described them as 'having hand bombs in bags which were slung across their back'.[29] In the retreat to the Wilpattu jungles of the North-Central Province, over twenty women were involved, including Sujatha Handagama, Susila Wijesinghe, Pushpa, Swarna, and Padma. 'Juliet', one of seven women involved in one particular group that hid out in the Wilpattu jungles for a five-year-period, has spoken of the feelings of 'the breaking of new ground' and a 'new-found sense of freedom' that she gained through her involvement with the JVP.[30]

The JVP adopted an extremely rigorous and almost puritanical control over the emotions of its membership, demanding absolute commitment and loyalty to the organization and denying its cadres the right to have any emotional or sexual attachments among themselves. The strict ban on intimacy between the cadres can be seen as a way in which the JVP tried to mitigate its radical departure from other social norms such as sex-based segregation and the relegation of women to domesticity. Bringing young men and women together in absolutely intimate 'life and death' situations yet proscribing intimate relationships between them, the JVP de-sexed its members, with the communist form of address, 'comrade' acting as the leveller between the sexes. This is perhaps one reason why the 'love affair' between JVP leader Wijeweera and the sister of a comrade in Ambalangoda, Yasoma, led to a huge controversy within the organization. The JVP's unwillingness to deal with woman-specific issues is clearly borne out by its absolute refusal to acknowledge the rapes and sexual abuse of women cadres during their period of arrest and detention in 1971. Senanayake refers to one particular incident in which a woman cadre who was well-known to have been subjected to sexual violence during interrogation later married a leader of the JVP who then proclaimed, at a public meeting, that she was a 'pure' woman in spite of her arrest and detention and that her virginity had not been affected.[31] This reluctance on the part of the leadership to tackle the issue of sexual violence against their female cadres also succeeded in silencing the women who had been the victims of such violence. Although in the early days after their release from prison and from detention camps the women did want to talk about it and protest about it, the silent disapproval of male comrades led them to connive at sweeping it under the carpet. Thus, in spite of its commitment to revolutionary and radical politics and its lip service to women's emancipation, in fact the JVP remained trapped within extremely moralistic and bourgeois codes of conduct for men and for women which were merely a reflection of the double standards and patriarchal attitudes about women that prevail in modern society in general.

The rape and murder of 22-year-old Premawathi Manamperi during the insurgency of 1971 was a sensational story of the time. She had been taken into custody by the army on 16 April along with four other young women suspected of being supporters of the JVP. On the next day, she was stripped and paraded through the town of Kataragama chanting 'I have attended all five classes',[32] and then shot and killed in public. The public nature of the murder made it possible to bring the army personnel responsible to trial: two people were found guilty of attempted murder and given prison sentences. Following his release from prison in 1977, one of the first public meetings to be addressed by the JVP leader Wijeweera was at Kataragama, where he declared open a memorial to Premawathi Manamperi; her murder was soundly condemned on this occasion and she became a symbol of the brutality of the security forces. Perhaps it was the fact of her death that made it possible for the JVP leadership to take up this case of sexual violence over all others.

In 1971, there were few women's organizations in Sri Lanka; those that did exist were more focused on social welfare and 'upliftment' of rural women within a traditional model. Thus, there was no mobilization of women to protest against the treatment of women during the insurgency. In fact, during this period, there were also no human rights organizations. The Civil Rights Movement of Sri Lanka emerged as a civil society response to the situation in April 1971 and was the only organization that consistently campaigned for justice for the young women and men arrested and detained as a consequence of their involvement, and often alleged involvement, in the insurgency. However, the involvement of women in the insurgency did pose a challenge to the stereotype of the docile rural woman, whose only roles in life could be those of wife, housewife, and mother. The media did pick on some women cadres of the JVP, albeit in a sensationalist way. Far more serious was the impact of the insurgency on the attitudes towards women in the villages, towns and families from which the cadres had been drawn. The idea that women could play active roles in a radical political movement, attack police stations, carry out ambushes, be detained or imprisoned, remain hidden in the jungles for years, all this was profoundly shocking to society as a whole.

THE JVP: POST-1971–1981

In 1977, the leaders of the JVP were released from prison as the result of an amnesty. Those cadres who had been released prior to this date had already begun the work of reorganization. Given the changes in the age and levels of experience and understanding of the cadres, there were some critical changes. For example, many of the cadres got married and started families. Many of the women who had been actively involved during 1971 left prison and got married, some of them to members of the JVP, others to outsiders. Very few of them remained within the organization. Among them were Leena Irene and Nandaseeli, who had been university students at the time of their arrest in 1971, and who were key to the formation of the Socialist Women's League, the Women's Wing of the JVP, in the post-1977 period. The JVP Women's Wing functioned as an adjunct to the main organization, with representation at every stage within the decision-making structures at the local level, and absolute absence of representation with the Polit Bureau and Central Committee, which were the highest bodies within the organization. It published its own newspaper, *Samajawadi Kanthawa*,[33] organized activities around International Women's Day and recruited women into its ranks. However, there were constant tensions within the organization regarding the autonomy of the Women's Wing, specially in terms of it's capacity to relate to women's movements that were emerging outside the organization. In addition, as female cadres married, they encountered problems with balancing their political commitments with their lives as mothers of babies and young children. In 1979, for example, when Nandaseeli, who was then a district secretary, requested permission to take time off shortly after the birth of her second child, she was told that if she did so she would be demoted within the ranks of the organization.[34]

In spite of all these contradictions, the JVP continued to attract young women from the educated rural poor into its ranks. However, the division between the women's wing and the main organization continued, with all male decision-making bodies at the national level.

THE SECOND INSURRECTION: JVP, 1987–1989

Following the signing of the Indo-Lanka Peace Accord and the arrival of the Indian Peace-Keeping Force on the north and east of the island in July 1987, a strong opposition emerged which was composed of Sinhala nationalist extremist forces from across the political spectrum led by the JVP and acting under the name Deshapremi Janatha Vyaaparaya (DJV, Patriotic People's Movement). Formulating its opposition to the accord in terms of 'Indian occupation' and 'no devolution', the DJV adopted a tactic of 'annihilation' of all persons who were seen to be supporting the accord. Ex-members of the JVP who had left the organization due to its increasingly Sinhala nationalist focus were among the prime targets. Also on their list were members of the other political parties, including left parties and trade unions, government servants of all levels, parents and family members of servicemen, and anyone who defied their calls to strike. Among those who were annihilated by the DJV during its two years of 'terror' were leading politicians, news broadcasters and journalists, trade unionists, social activists, and ordinary civilians. In turn, the state unleashed massive repression against the DJV using paramilitary groups not directly linked to the security forces. The state was responsible for the deaths or disappearances of over 40,000 persons during this time.

The DJV was an extremely male-centric underground organization, in which women played a role as clandestine operatives, primarily restricted to carrying messages. No women were in the leadership, or engaged in assassinations. Some women were targets of assassination; among the better known were Dr Gladys Jayawardena who was the chairperson of the State Pharmaceuticals Corporation at the time, and Sagarika Gomes, a popular singer and broadcaster. Some women members of the DJV were among those arrested, tortured, and killed. However, since the bodies have never been identified, there is no real figure available as to the number of disappeared, let alone a sex-based disaggregation of the figures. The DJV ground to a halt when, in November 1989, its leadership was assassinated by members of the security forces. There has never been an inquiry held into these assassinations.

The JVP temporarily 'disappeared' from the mainstream political scenario in the years following the deaths of its leaders. It re-emerged in the early 1990s as a political party seeking to enter the formal political arena, contesting parliamentary elections in 1994 and securing six seats. A Muslim woman member of the JVP, Anjun Umma, became an MP from the Gampaha district. She was re-elected in the elections of 2004. The JVP women's wing, the 'Samajawadi Kantha Sangamaya' (SKS, Socialist Women's League) remains within the fold, with some degree of autonomy in terms of organizing activities and recruiting new members. However, there are no women in any of the decision-making bodies, and even in 2004, on International Women's Day, the male General Secretary of the JVP was the keynote speaker at their Women's Day meeting. The group is also actively resistant to forming any links with women's groups that have been involved in any advocacy for peace, since the JVP adopts a position that rejects any formal negotiations with the LTTE.

Women in Civil Society in the South of Sri Lanka and their Responses to Militancy and War

The impact of the conflict on women has played a key role in affirming the commitment of already existing women's groups throughout the island to work for a just and sustainable peace, and also led to the emergence of new women's groups within the conflict-affected areas. At the national level, the Women's Action Committee (WAC) and Women for Peace were formed in the south in the mid-1980s, and carried out public agitations against the war and against the violence and abuse faced by women living in the conflict areas. In addition, they built concrete links with women's groups working in the north and east. Pathmini Sithamparanathan was a member of the Women's Study Circle of Jaffna who spoke at a meeting organized by the WAC to celebrate International Women's Day in March 1983. In 1990, a broad network of women from all ethnic and religious communities came forward to call for an end to the repression and disappearances, under the banner Mothers and Daughters of Lanka. Subsequently, we saw the emergence of a southern Mother's Front, which, together with the Organization of Parents and Family Members of the Disappeared (OPFMD), rallied to call for accountability for the widespread disappearances that took place in the south in the late 1980s. In the late 1990s up to the present, we have seen a number of ad hoc coalitions emerging around issues of women and conflict, calling for greater involvement of women in the peace process, and more consideration for women and women's participation in processes of reconstruction and rehabilitation.

The impact of the conflict on women family members of men in the army, and on women in the army are new arenas of engagement for women's movements in Sri Lanka. There are several organizations that have emerged out of this community, including some that focus on the rights of family members of those who have died in the conflict, and others that focus on the servicemen missing in action. One, which is called the Association of War Affected Women (AWAW) has a mixed sex membership but gives prominence to women and to women's issues within the organization. The state has made provision for the families of servicemen/women killed and wounded in action to receive the full pay of their son/brother/husband or daughter/sister/wife up to her/his normal age of retirement, and his/her pension thereafter. Servicemen and women are awarded medals and their families are called *Rana Viru*[35] families. Just as in the LTTE, there is a glorification of battle and sacrifice. Yet, the process of becoming beneficiaries from the death of a loved one also plays itself out in macabre ways. AWAW members have spoken of the problems they have faced in obtaining their dues, and of the tensions created within families as different members try to control the benefits, including the conflicts that arise between wives and in-laws, for example. In most of the cases, as much as the causes of conflict are gendered—for example, the parents of a soldier trying to control the wife/widow of their son using social justifications—so are the ways in which women respond to these conflicts—for example, by engaging in religious and animist rituals that are among the culturally prescribed emotional and psychological 'outlets' for distress. An outdated pension regulation that stipulates that a widow is entitled to receive a pension from her husband only as long as she remains unmarried is another factor that creates many difficulties for young widows. Many of them are young, and, therefore, do get involved in romantic and sexual alliances following the death of the husband: in such cases they are compelled to remain legally unmarried, and, therefore, outside the protection of the law if they wish to continue drawing the pension.

The membership of the Mothers' Front and the OPFMD were also mostly female. They reported facing problems when it came to going through the formal process of seeking acknowledgement of the death or disappearance of their son/daughter/husband/brother/sister. At every stage in the formal and legal procedures to establish the death of a missing person, for example, filing affidavits in court, making a police complaint, obtaining certification from the village headman or *grama sevaka*, they experienced hardships, including sexual harassment, violence and coercion into providing sexual 'favours' in return for processing the required documentation. In response to international and national pressure, successive governments in the 1990s set up a number of Presidential Commissions of Inquiry to investigate the tens of thousands of allegations of disappearance at the hands of the security forces. While reports from Amnesty International and the UN Working Group on Disappearances provided adequate evidence as to the situation,[36] the process of the commissions led to another round of testimonies and led to very few prosecutions. There were awards of compensation, however, but payment of these sums were delayed due to lack of funds in the state coffers. In addition, as happened with the wives and widows of servicemen, these wives and widows too were compelled to seek the support of intermediaries in order to travel and obtain the required documentation to apply for a pension, compensation, and other benefits. They reported spending substantial amounts of the money received from the state on commissions and other payments which were often forced out of them.

During this period, individual women and women's groups were involved in a very active manner in the work of broad networks such as the Movement for Inter-Racial Justice and Equality and the Movement for the Defence of Democratic Rights, and various other semi-clandestine networks such as the Movement for Socialism and Democracy, that tried to confront all forms of repression and terror, from state and non-state actors. Women's groups have also been actively involved in campaigns and activities organized by the Peoples' Peace Front, the National Peace Council and the National Anti-War Front. In 2002, following the signing of a Ceasefire Agreement between the government and the LTTE and the commencement of peace negotiations, a group of women's organizations led by the Women and Media Collective brought together an international team of women activists to visit the north and east and make recommendations regarding the deeper engagement of women with the peace process. As a consequence of this initiative and other lobbying and advocacy efforts at many different levels, in

December 2002 the government and the LTTE announced the creation of a Sub-Committee on Gender Issues to advise the peace process on matters relating to women and gender concerns.

The Eelam Struggle: Late 1970s to the Present

In the early 1970s, when militant youth in Jaffna in the north of Sri Lanka first began to agitate for a separate state, it was a largely male-dominated movement. As state repression increased, as anti-Tamil pogroms in the south led to more and more Tamils seeking refuge in the north, as the general social and political situation deteriorated, Tamil militancy splintered into several groups with ideological understandings of self-determination that differed slightly from one to the other: the People's Liberation Organization of Tamil Eelam (PLOTE), Eelam People's Revolutionary Liberation Front (EPRLF), Tamil Eelam Liberation Organization (TELO), and the Liberation Tigers of Tamil Eelam (LTTE) were among the most significant in terms of political influence. In all these groups, women cadres were a minority. The EPRLF was the first organization to recruit women, and within the organization there was an inclusion of women's issues in the general political discussion. The EPRLF women also took a lead role in organizing protests against the LTTE massacre of the TELO leadership in April/May 1986, at a time when the other mainstream militant groups remained silent. However, there were also some key incidents that pointed to the tensions regarding the inclusion of women within the Tamil militant movements. Within PLOTE, the murder of five women cadres in one of their camps in Maniamthoddam in Jaffna in 1985 created an uproar and had a very negative impact on the reputation of the group. In general, as with the JVP, there was an ideological and rhetorical commitment to the emancipation of women that was not easily translated into reality. Given the extremely conservative and caste-bound nature of Jaffna society, this was only to be expected.

As the LTTE gained ascendance in the Tamil struggle in the mid-1980s through the physical elimination of all rivals and potential rivals, the role of women within the organization began to be theorized by Adele Balasingham, the Australian-born wife of LTTE ideologue Anton Balasingham. In 1983, she published a pamphlet titled 'Women and Revolution: The Role of Women in Tamil Eelam National Struggle'[37] in which she states that among her objectives are 'to inform the women in Tamil Eelam that their participation in the national liberation struggle is crucial for the victory of the nation'.[38] According to her, this participation would be a 'springboard from which women can organize, identify and articulate their grievances and fight against the modes of oppression and exploitation perpetrated on them'.[39] Describing a 'revolutionary situation', Balasingham says 'it creates the conditions which allow for a radical rupture with traditional roles and images of women.... Women's participation in all dimensions of the struggle, including armed combat, effects a qualitative change in the sexual division of labour for women and the relationship between the sexes'.[40] The book is full of examples and photographs of women in struggle from Palestine, Eritrea, and Cuba. Balasingham followed this up with the publication of *Women Fighters of Liberation Tigers* in 1993, and *The Will to Freedom* in 2001, the first being completely focused on the military activities of women LTTE cadres, and the second being a more general narrative of the LTTE struggle, with some sections focusing on women.

In the late 1980s, the LTTE began recruiting large numbers of women and inducted them into actual battle. Radhika Coomaraswamy quotes Peter Schalk, citing figures that 8 per cent of LTTE cadres killed in combat from 1982 to 1991 were women, and that by 1986, there were 3,000 women cadres in the LTTE.[41] Observers point to the correlation between the militarization of women and the LTTE's need for a larger base for the recruitment of personnel, especially after the Vadamarachchi operation which was followed by widespread arrests of male cadres. Qadri Ismail comments that 'Until the loss of enough male cadres made it absolutely necessary to use woman, she was assumed (by the male leadership of course) to be incapable of secrecy, commitment, courage and other "manly" virtues, and, therefore, wasn't mobilized.'[42] Rajini Thiranagama explains this reality further:

> ... the nationalist fervour and the romantic vision of women in arms defending the nation ... our social set up, its restrictions on creative

expression for women and the evils of the dowry system are some of the social factors that led to their initial recruitment. Moreover, the political climate created by the struggle in the past decade and the increasing loss of men to state terrorism and the world at large as refugees and emigrants are some of the contributing factors necessitating women's recruitment.[43]

By 1984, the first women cadres of the LTTE received formal training in weaponry and warfare, in Madurai, India. They were inducted into battle in Mannar in October 1986. By 1987, the LTTE had an official Women's Wing known as the Suthanthirai Paravaihal,[44] and moved into a phase of what Schalk has called 'martial feminism'. It was during the time that the IPKF was in the north that Malathy from Mannar, now acknowledged as the first female martyr of the LTTE, died in battle. By 1990, Balasingham writes proudly of 'the rifle-carrying woman guerrillas of the LTTE in camouflage uniforms who marched into Jaffna after the withdrawal of the Indians'.[45] In 1991 came the attack on the Elephant Pass camps of the Sri Lankan Army in which waves of women fighters were reported to have led the advance; 123 women LTTE cadres are said to have died on the battlefield. Among them was Captain Vanathi, whose poem entitled 'She, the Woman of Tamililam'[46] refers to the woman's forehead adorned not with *kumkumam*[47] but with blood, and a cyanide capsule rather than a *thali*[48] around her neck.

Tensions around issues of sex, sexuality and intimate relationships between male and female cadres were inevitable within an organization such as the LTTE. As with the JVP, the fact that society looked with a certain amount of disapproval on women joining the ranks of the militant groups led to an assertion of conservative attitudes towards women within the movements. Women had to be 'protected' so that the society would not reject them. As S.J. Tambiah writes, 'After the Indo-Lanka Peace Accord was signed, parents had no problem welcoming home their (briefly) returning sons but the return to the family of the young women who have joined the movement was more difficult and fraught because of the stigma of their flouting domestic surveillance and strict control of interaction with males and suspicions of their possible sexual transgressions.'[49] In addition was the attitude that men lose their sense of purpose in the company of women. However, in 1984, LTTE leader Prabhakaran flaunted these prohibitions and declared his intention to marry Mathivathani, a young woman university student who had been 'abducted' along with three other female colleagues while in the process of a fast unto death in Jaffna and taken to Chennai. This led to an uproar within the ranks of the LTTE. Eventually, Prabhakaran did marry Mathivathani and forced the organization to open up to the prospect of marriage of its cadres.

Throughout the 1990s, the LTTE controlled large tracts of land in both the north and the east and set up a parallel administrative structure, including a criminal justice system with its own police, judiciary, and law enforcement machinery, including prisons. Women cadres played a critical role in each of these institutions. By 1993, the Women's Wing of the LTTE had expanded into a somewhat autonomous agency, having its own Political, Military and Intelligence Sections. Jeya, who had been a student at Jaffna University, was the first leader of the Political Section of the LTTE Women's Wing in 1993. Following the Ceasefire Agreement signed between the Government of Sri Lanka and the LTTE in February 2002, and official acknowledgement of the areas controlled by the LTTE and by government troops, the LTTE was granted permission to engage in political activity in the north and east. The struggle moved into a new phase, in which young men and women cadres of the LTTE established political offices in small towns up and down the coast of the Eastern Province and began to carry out awareness-raising work as well as engage in minor dispute resolution within the community.

During this period of lull, there was a relaxation of the rigid disciplinary codes that allowed men and women cadres to marry and leave the organization if they so wished. However, there were some restraints placed on them, such as their commitment not to engage in any other political activity. Some women cadres chose to move out of active involvement in the LTTE to engage in welfare work with widows, orphans, persons suffering from physical and psychological disabilities as a consequence of the conflict and so on, for example, the women in-charge of Sencholai, an LTTE-sponsored Home for Orphaned Girls. The

LTTE also began running a number of institutions within which cadres received training in vocational skills. The large bakery-restaurant complex in Kilinochchi, in which many women cadres are given training and employment, is one of these initiatives. In 2004, the LTTE had several women as a part of their overall decision-making structures. Thamilini, the head of the Political Section of the Women's Wing, is almost always present at press conferences and all other important meetings and leads the team of LTTE nominees to the Gender Sub-Committee to advise the peace process. Through the Tamil National Alliance (TNA), the LTTE also supported candidates for the parliamentary elections of 2004, nominating one woman for four of the districts for which the elections were being held. This was the first time in Sri Lanka's post-independence history that a Tamil political party had nominated women to run for Parliament. Two of the candidates, Pathmini Siddambaranathan from Jaffna and K. Thangeswari from Batticaloa won the elections, and were sworn in as MPs of the thirteenth Parliament of Sri Lanka. All these may be seen as indicators of the fact that women are playing a critical political role within the LTTE as it makes its transition from armed militant group to democratic political party.

Women in Civil Society in North and East Sri Lanka and their Responses to Militancy and War

The impact of the conflict on the women of all ethnic and religious groups living in the north and east of Sri Lanka has been tremendous. The conflict has led to a serious dislocation of 'normalcy'; large-scale displacement and the exaggerated processes of social disintegration that occur as a consequence of conflict have exposed women in the war-affected areas to violence and abuse at the hands of the military of both sides, as well as of the community and their families. While the high prevalence of domestic violence in camps set up for internally displaced persons has been remarked upon by many researchers,[50] there has also been a high rate of abandonment and desertion of women by husbands and boyfriends, many of whom have migrated or fled the country. The civilian massacres that took place, committed by the Sri Lankan and Indian security forces, as well as by armed militant groups and civilian groups, affected all ethnic and religious communities. The trauma of the exposure to senseless violence and brutality of this nature has marked many Sri Lankans for life. These processes led to the emergence of a large number of female-headed households, which challenged many traditional assumptions about power and decision-making within the family. Many more women than would have been possible in a non-conflict situation entered the public sphere as a consequence.

It was during this period, from the mid-1980s onwards, that many different women's groups and organizations emerged within the north and east. Some focused on provision of support to women from a 'welfarist' understanding of women's needs, while others adopted a feminist analysis and shaped their interventions relating to the conflict from the perspective of women's rights and women's autonomy, linking peace issues with broader social, economic, and political issues, and demanding equality at all levels including in processes of conflict transformation and peace-building. The Women's Study Circle in Jaffna was one of the most outstanding; during a very critical moment in terms of the external and internal politics of Tamil society in Sri Lanka, its members saw the need to link their struggles as women with the national struggle, yet understood that their participation in the broader struggle for self-determination 'opened new horizons' and at the same time placed many obstacles on the path of their struggle as women.[51]

In 1984, following a number of arbitrary arrests and detention of over 200 young men by the army, women in Jaffna united under the banner of the Mothers' Front and engaged in a series of public demonstrations, demanding that the army inform them of the whereabouts of their children. The Mothers' Front also campaigned against the harassment of women by the Armed Forces, highlighting concerns about rape and sexual violence by the security forces. While the activism of the northern Mothers' Front gradually receded due to a number of social and political tensions, there were other instances in which women spontaneously resisted the actions of the military and of armed groups. In November 1986, for example, women took the lead in the agitation surrounding the death of Edward from Pasaiyoor in the LTTE camp at Ariyalai.[52] Rajini Thiranagama describes the activism of women in Jaffna during this period as follows:

> The natural defiance of the women from the lower classes remained a remarkable feature as opposed to the pliability of upper class women. Village women in the East went out with rice pounders to stop the internecine fighting during the LTTE-TELO clash. When the LTTE took on the EPRLF on 14 December 1986, women from some low class villages in Jaffna near Keerimalai and Mallakam defied the LTTE by sitting on the roads armed with kitchen knives and chilly powder.[53]

The Mothers' Front, which had been reduced to a welfare organization by the increasing controls imposed on any civil society activism by the LTTE, re-emerged as a strong force in the Eastern Province in the late 1980s. In March 1988, three mothers began a fast unto death calling for an immediate and unconditional ceasefire between the IPKF and the LTTE, and for negotiations between the LTTE and the Indian government. One of the mothers, Mrs Kanapathipillai Poopathy, now revered in LTTE annals as the '*Annai* Poopathy',[54] died on 19 April 1988, and this day is now commemorated by the LTTE each year.

The situation for women in the war-affected areas in general throughout the north and east worsened during the period in which the Indian Peace-Keeping Force was based in those areas. There is some documentation of cases of rape and sexual abuse of Tamil women by the Indian Army. Among the cases reported on by the University Teachers for Human Rights were several relating to different cases of rape in Urumpirai and other parts of Jaffna, in November/December 1987 and in January 1988.[55] Molestation was very common during the process of 'checking' houses and at roadside checkpoints. Many middle-class women fled the area and even went abroad in order to hide their 'shame'. Women belonging to lower economic strata were left behind. Rajini Tiranagama and other women began Poorani Women's Centre in Jaffna in 1988 in order to support women who had been victims of rape and sexual violence, including a few who had conceived as a result of rape.

In the mid-1990s, there was a sudden influx of internally displaced persons into Colombo and its surrounding areas due to the intensification of the conflict, specially in the Eastern Province. Tens of thousands of men, women and children sought refuge in public buildings and subsisted for months on an issue of minimum dry rations of the state and the goodwill of volunteers and social workers. In December 1990, the UNHCR reported over a million displaced persons in Sri Lanka. Several women's groups in Colombo were involved in providing relief to the Internally Displaced Persons (IDP) and promoted the self-organization of women in the welfare centres. A number of women activists from the north and east who were IDPs themselves formed the Suriya Women's Development Centre in collaboration with Colombo-based women's groups. This organization later relocated to Batticaloa in the Eastern Province as the IDPs were resettled and returned to their homes, and continues to work from there in the present. There are now many women's groups throughout the north and east that work with women victims and survivors of violence (including domestic violence) and that focus on strengthening the position of female-headed households in the context of resettlement and reconstruction programmes. Demolishing the social stigma attached to widowhood, orphanhood and single motherhood, creating an environment that respects the independence of women and challenging men to reshape their attitudes and opinions regarding the role of women in society, women's groups from the Tamil, Muslim and Sinhala communities are battling entrenched patriarchal norms about women. What one sees as missing in the analysis that emerges from within the LTTE and from its supporters is, in particular, adequate focus on the role and situation of women civilians who have been affected by war as well as of women of other ethnic and religious communities who have been also victimized by the conflict.

TENSIONS BETWEEN TRADITION AND CHANGE: IN THE NORTH AND EAST

Scholars have been very divided over the issue of what participation in armed struggles in the Sri Lankan context can mean for Tamil women within the LTTE, and in society in general. Within the LTTE, the roles assigned to women have been clearly militaristic, the stereotypes of the 'martyr' and the 'hero' being somewhat feminized, of course. Malathy remains the epitome of the heroic woman on the battlefield, while Annai Poopathy remains the symbol of sacrificial motherhood. These are the two women whose deaths are commemorated each year by the LTTE. Some have linked the ideology of the LTTE with regard to women to the images of women in the *Sangam* literary tradition of Tamil Nadu, in which there is glorification of the *veera thaie* (the heroic/militant mother). The characterizing of Mrs Poopathy who died while on a fast unto death as *annai* may be an indication of the ways in which the LTTE politicized maternity. In a BBC interview in 1991, the mother of Miller, the first LTTE cadre who successfully undertook a suicide mission in Nelliady, Jaffna on 5 July 1987 articulated her sense of satisfaction at her son's sacrifice, and spoke of the fact that her own status in the community had gone up since her son's death, as the 'mother of Miller'.

There is no doubt that young women cadres of the LTTE posed a challenge to notions of womanhood in traditional Tamil society as a whole, wearing trousers, cutting their hair, shunning jewellery, and stepping beyond the boundaries defined for them by predominantly Hindu and Tamil social and cultural hierarchies. They participate actively in military operations and die in battle, they run medical bases, are members of the Eelam Police force, act as judges and lawyers in the LTTE Courts, and are among the human bombs who carry out targeted assassinations. Schalk, Balasingham and others have argued in favour of the 'heroic militarism' of the LTTE women cadres as representing an advance in the positioning of women in Tamil society. However, they have generally interpreted the role of these women as being a significant part of the national liberation struggle; the issue of whether the changes wrought in the role of women during wartime could be maintained during a transitional phase, for example, and whether the 'new' Tamil society would be willing to accept independent and autonomous women on terms of equality has, however, been relegated to the background. Other scholars, like Radhika Coomaraswamy and Neloufer de Mel,[56] have argued that the 'military' role given to women within the LTTE does not necessarily mean that any lasting transformative process is under way within the organization or in Tamil society in general, pointing, for example, to the absence of substantial numbers of women in any key decision-making structures within the LTTE in the present.

Despite the LTTE's verbal commitments to the participation and inclusion of women in the struggle, from the very inception of the organization there has been an undercurrent of resistance to demands for autonomy and for a focus on the specific problems faced by women within the struggle and within the ranks of the LTTE. The manner in which Balasingham describes the rejection of Nirmala Nityanandan, the first woman to be arrested and detained under the Prevention of Terrorism Act (PTA) in 1983, by the leadership of the LTTE as a 'contradiction in feminist perceptions' points to this.[57] These tensions are articulated by Balasingham as signifying the divide between 'Western women's liberation' and 'an emancipation that the mass of Tamil women could identify with'. Declaring Nityanandan to be 'a world apart' from the 'village girls who had come to join the struggle and fight for their homeland and had no real idea of women's liberation nor necessarily aspired for it', Balasingham affirms the patriarchal structure within which the LTTE locates its work with women by stating that the LTTE leader, Prabhakaran, has 'assumed the role of leader and mentor' of the women's wing. While it is true that differences in class and capacity may have separated Nityanandan from the rank and file of the LTTE, the framing of her rejection by Balasingham reveals a reluctance to take on some of the 'feminist' issues raised by Nityanandan regarding the role of women in national liberation struggles and the attitudes of the LTTE towards women.

Laws and social regulations that affected the lives of ordinary women in the north and east, such as dowry, caste, seclusion of unmarried women and other social and cultural forms of marginalization and exclusion of women from the public world were challenged by the inclusion of large numbers of women within the ranks of the LTTE, including the LTTE military as well as by women's groups that emerged in the region. Social disintegration and the absence of male family members because of death, arrest, flight, disappearance or conflict-related displacement also contributed to this transformative process, making it possible for women to engage with public life and take on decision-making responsibilities. As Coomaraswamy points out, 'inequitable social practices that kept unmarried women at home and menstruating women in the back garden have given way to virile forms of mobilization'.[58] Their new circumstances thrust women into the public arena. A Tamils Relief and Rehabilitation Organization (TRRO) report for the 1983–6 period in Jaffna showed 477 widows in the Jaffna district; 70 per cent of them were between the ages of eighteen and forty, and 70 per cent had no means of support.[59] The new technical, commercial, and professional skills that women gained as they were increasingly thrust into the public arena led to the unprecedented visibility of women in the north and east—in shops, in offices, on the roads. As Tambiah points out, '. . . in an unexpected way the civil war and the deaths of men may actually help to "emancipate" women and empower them while at the same time increasing their burdens'.[60]

In the areas of the north and east of Sri Lanka that have been dominated by the LTTE since the late 1980s, there is no doubt that the social changes wrought by the conflict have led to some process of transformation within the LTTE itself. This is no doubt largely due to the high visibility of women within the movement as well as within society in general due to the war and to the prominence gained by female-headed families. Although research in the LTTE-controlled areas of the north and east over the past ten years has been sporadic and ad hoc, what emerges from the investigations that have been carried out is that the LTTE has taken a strong position against violence against women, and against the consumption of liquor, since most women who are victims of domestic violence cite alcoholism as one of the main causes for the violence against them. In 1994–5, Balasingham speaks of doing research into the cases of domestic violence that were being reported to the LTTE Police with the full cooperation of the police. Among the issues that she highlights, other than daily beatings and abuse, was the 'reality of marital rape in the lives of Tamil women'.[61] In Trincomalee in 1999, Rajasingham-Senanayake recorded an interview with a young woman activist who said that women brought complaints of domestic violence to the LTTE, which 'took appropriate action'. The male offenders were given a first warning: if the violence persisted, they were fined. If this still did nothing to prevent the violence from taking place, the men were sentenced to periods of imprisonment in an LTTE jail. In the Vanni in 2002/3, Sophic Elek was told that the LTTE cadres take a proactive stance against incidents of violence and abuse of alcohol within the home. Each village reportedly has a 'good conduct unit' which reports on illegal and criminal activities within the village to the LTTE. 'Once identified, perpetrators are taken into LTTE custody, given "moral education" and, subject to the nature of their crime, sentenced to time in prison or community service. They are then encouraged to rejoin their family.'[62] However, conversations with women in the Eastern Province tell a different story, of lethargy and unwillingness by the LTTE Police and Courts to pursue cases of domestic violence.[63] Thus, it may well be that, just as in the government-controlled areas, the burden of pursuing justice for women through the formal legal system leaves much to be desired and places too much responsibility on well-intentioned individuals rather than focus on creating a systematic and systemic anti-patriarchal and woman-friendly framework for the dispensation of justice.

There has also been focus on the issue of dowry, which is an institution that is extremely oppressive of women in the Tamil community. In 1992, the LTTE women's wing put forward a call for the abolition of the dowry system as one of their demands for International Women's Day. Balasingham refers to a process of research and investigation into the willingness of people to accept such a change.[64] She refers to a publication authored by her, *Broken Chains*, in which there is a focus on *thesavalamai*, the traditional matrilineal property laws of the Jaffna Tamil community, which give women some degree of control over property, as well as an analysis of the contemporary practice of dowry within the Tamil community. Balasingham reports that in 1994, the LTTE Justice Department formulated new laws pertaining to the practice of dowry that upheld the property rights of women, including the right of married women to dispose of property without having to obtain the consent of her husband, and abolished the practice of cash donations to relatives of the bridegroom. The *thesavalamai* law which restricted a married woman's right to dispose off property was also revised.

However, in spite of these changes, the changes in the position of women in Tamil society that were wrought by the conflict may not become lasting and sustained transformations unless specific attention is paid to the processes whereby this may be achieved. Already, in 2004, as young girls were demobilized under a UNICEF–LTTE programme against child recruitment by the LTTE, observers reported unwillingness on the part of parents to accept these girls back into their homes and families. The resistance on the part of communities, schools, and other social and public institutions to welcome these girls back into their original communities was also a factor that led to the rejection on the part of the families. As a consequence, for example, there were reports of marriages being arranged for girls below the age of sixteen, with no consideration of their wishes.[65]

Some observers have commented on the allocation of care-taking and service-rendering roles to LTTE women cadres during the ceasefire period, for example, placing them in charge of service-oriented vocational training for girls and young women, and in charge of the homes for women and children who had been affected by the conflict, as an indication of there being no lasting changes in the position of women in Tamil society in spite of the experiences of the conflict period. Thus, concrete focus on retaining some of the gains made in terms of women's increased mobility and independence during the conflict period, remains a challenge in the post-conflict and transitional phases. Commitments to bring back 'normalcy' ring hollow in the ears of women for whom normalcy means subordination, economic dependence, vulnerability to violence, and lack of autonomy.

In terms of resettlement and rehabilitation programmes for internally displaced persons, too, there is a huge gap in terms of the understanding of the specific needs and concerns of women. Official programmes do not 'naturally' take women into account as independent beings capable of making decisions regarding their own lives and futures, nor are officials in charge of designing policy and programmes for the resettlement, reconstruction and rehabilitation process 'automatically' gender-sensitive. Much needs to be done in these areas. For example, the 'Needs Assessment' for the total reconstruction and rehabilitation programme for the north and east which was carried out in 2003 was found to lack a gender perspective.[66] Once the gender perspective had been 'inserted', there continued to be huge gaps in the area, for example, of health care, with reproductive and sexual health needs of women being confined to provision of contraceptives and maternity-related care. Despite the grave concerns regarding the spread of HIV in conflict areas due to a number of factors, there was no specific focus on clinics and health care to deal with sexually transmitted infections. Thus, maintaining an overview of all projects and programmes designed for reconstruction in a post-conflict situation is imperative if the specific needs of women affected by the conflict are to be addressed.

In the South

The conflict in Sri Lanka has led to severe processes of social disintegration in the south as well. In both insurgencies, young men and women were killed and disappeared, altering the lives of their families and communities as well as of society as a whole. The involvement of women in militancy has challenged some of the traditional assumptions about women in society. Yet, the changes that are visible in terms of women's daily lives are not reflected in legal, policy, or institutional frameworks. The participation of women in policy-making and decision-making structures remains extremely low, and there is widespread social resistance to any attempts to reconstitute institutional and legal approaches in a gender-sensitive manner and in a way that enhances women's full enjoyment of their rights. The impunity with which men continue to act violently against women remains a major issue.

As in the north and east, in the south too, the conflict led to fairly substantial numbers of women being recruited into the army and into the Civilian Defence Forces.[67] As the conflict intensified, women were inducted into the fighting forces as well. The entry of women into areas of the security forces that were hitherto totally male domains has led to the breaking down of some barriers, but at a cost to the women themselves. Some complaints have been made regarding sexual harassment within the Armed Forces. Within the police there have been several cases reported in which women have complained of sexual violence and abuse; in addition, there have been some cases of murder/suicide in which there has been speculation that there was some romantic/sexual encounter between male and female officers that led to the deaths. Rates of domestic violence within the families of servicemen are also quite high according to some reports. Thus, the conflict which drives both women and men into 'abnormal' situations leads to disharmony, violence, and abuse which are not mitigated through any legal or institutional framework.

There are large numbers of widows and female-headed families created by the conflict, both on the side of members of the security forces and on the side of political activists and others who were caught up in the conflict through random bombings, for example. There are thousands of 'ordinary' women who challenge traditional perceptions of a woman's role and position in society on a daily basis. Yet, they are not visible as a 'critical mass', except in a few exceptional circumstances such as through the Association of War Affected Women. There are also many disparities in terms of the benefits received by these women; while families of servicemen killed or missing in action are entitled to full salary up to retirement age, and then a pension, many of the families of those who disappeared due to paramilitary killings have never received any compensation. Even compensation that was awarded by the various Presidential Commissions that investigated these killings have sometimes been deferred on the ground that there were no funds available. These disparities create barriers and obstacles to solidarity among these categories of women who face many of the same social and cultural difficulties.

Sexual and economic exploitation of women who have been affected by the conflict often takes place without their having any recourse to justice. In families where compensation has been granted by the state for the death or disappearance of a male family member, the grant has improved the economic conditions of the family, but has also increased the vulnerability of women to abuse and exploitation. For example, young widows who live in their husband's homes often complain about their in-laws appropriating the full compensation and leaving her at their mercy. In addition, single women who have access to reasonably large sums of money on a regular basis, as is the case with those with a monthly salary or pension from a serviceman, are often the targets of 'scam' operations by men who want to get their hands on the money and have no commitment to the women or her children, if there are any. Most of these women come from traditional and conservative rural backgrounds, and are conditioned to feel 'insecure' without the presence of a male; this environment makes them play into the hands of these persons. Lack of legal rights regarding land has been another major issue, with grants of state land issued under the Land Development Ordinance not 'automatically' passing into the hands of a wife on a husband's death.

The conflict has also led to an increase in women in sex work in and around areas where large army encampments are located, such as in Anuradhapura in the North-Central Province. There has been reluctance to identify this as a social phenomenon that is a consequence of conflict. There is continued discrimination and criminalization of sex workers and neglect of their health status, in spite of knowledge that this is a high-risk area for both the men and the women concerned, in terms of sexually transmitted infections, including HIV.

During the years of the conflict, women's groups in the south have been engaged in a series of activities aimed at bringing about legal reforms in terms of divorce, abortion, and domestic violence throughout the 1990s. However, there have been few gains made in the arena of legal reform since the reforms to the Penal Code in 1995 which criminalized incest and sexual harassment and imposed a mandatory minimum sentence for rape. Proposals to liberalize the existing abortion laws in order to permit women who have conceived as a result of rape or incest have been shelved following protests from MPs and members of the public from all ethnic and religious communities. The conflict has provided an excuse for politicians and decision-makers to continually defer critical decisions with regard to women and has created an environment in which raising certain issues may be perceived as being 'anti-national'. For example, the thrust to provide contraceptives to women of minority communities is often perceived as an attempt by the majority community to control the numbers of minority communities. Although women's groups have not had great successes in terms of bringing about sustained change in legal and policy matters, their achievements in terms of social mobilization around women's issues and in terms of drawing public attention to discrimination against women have been considerable. Their role in working for an end to the conflict and for greater participation of women in the peace process has been remarkable.

CONCLUSION

The key question that continues to be asked regarding the role of women in insurgencies and militant movements, as well as in periods of demobilization and reintegration is whether they have acquired agency as the creators and visionaries of the political project which has affected their lives. Or have they been mere participants and observers of strategies designed by others, most often male, which do not radically alter their subordinate social status and their vulnerability to violence and exploitation?

The extended period of the conflict in Sri Lanka has led to a major erosion of democratic structures and institutions as well as to serious destruction of life and property. The political and economic crisis that was created by decades of turmoil has extended to the entire island, although manifest in different ways. Those who were victims of state repression in 1971 because of their association with the JVP never received any compensation or justice for the brutality and injustice they faced. The state repression and counter-terror launched by the JVP/DJV in the late 1980s saw the creation of several Presidential Commissions of Inquiry, which, to a large extent, have been futile exercises in terms of bringing the culpable to justice. However, in some cases, monetary compensation was paid to survivors. The violence in the north and east has also seen the creation of several mechanisms including Presidential Commissions. However, once again, justice has not been done. The various civil society groups that emerged in defence of human rights, democracy and peace during this period continue to function, albeit at a minimal level.

In the late 1990s, the intensification of the military conflict in the north and east culminated in the signing of a Ceasefire Agreement in 2002. A series of programmes have been designed with reconstruction, rehabilitation, and resettlement in mind. In this context, a serious reconsideration of development programmes and policies from a gendered perspective is called for; so is the development of policies that could strengthen women directly involved in conflict and women in conflict-affected zones through processes of education and training for new economic activities. Among the gendered aspects of development that need to be focused on in any process of conflict transformation, other critical issues are the feminization of poverty; the 'invisibility' of the female head of a household; and lack of women's participation in decision making. The fact is that legal and policy frameworks have hardly shifted in order to accommodate the needs and concerns of women affected by the conflict. The legal recognition of the female head of a household as a specific and special category of citizen that perhaps calls for some forms of affirmative action or special attention is something that has come to the forefront of contemporary discussions. The heavy militarization of society had led to an increase in criminality and contributes to the prevalence of high levels of violence against women. In spite of the fact that there are constitutional guarantees of equality and that the country earns large sums from women workers, there is continuing discrimination against women in general, and against some groups of women such as sex workers, lesbians, and women with HIV/AIDS in particular.

Sri Lankan women, through the years of the conflict, have confronted the challenges posed to them through changing circumstances in very powerful and empowering ways. Using the symbolic and cultural 'values' ascribed to motherhood, in both the south and the north-east of the island, Sri Lankan women organized as mothers to initiate the first public agitations against impunity and the cult of 'disappearance' in Sri Lanka.[68] At first they did it separately within ethnic categories; later, they acted together, across ethnic and religious divides. Dr Manorani Saravanamuttu, speaking at the New Town Hall in Colombo on 23 June 1992 at the Second Annual Meeting of the Mothers' Front of the south of Sri Lanka described their goal as being 'to change the social framework of our land so that there will not and never will be another holocaust as has occurred in certain parts of the country in the recent past and which still goes on in other parts of the country'.

During periods of intense conflict or in times of gross and widespread human rights abuse, when male-dominated political parties, trade unions and other social organizations remained on the margins of public discourse, and when protest against these atrocities was muted to the point of silence, it was Sri Lankan women who organized, mobilized and brought women on to the streets and into public spaces to raise their voices against injustice and abuse. Tears, which are accepted means of expression of women/mothers in a patriarchal society, were transformed into a source of strength, where the mothers and fathers wailed, shouted, ranted and raved, cursing those who had taken away their sons.[69] These public expressions of their grief and sorrow over the killing and disappearances of their children through the medium of tears and other forms of mourning specific to women has a sizeable impact on society. In addition, these actions were among those that brought the issue to the attention of the media and of the international community, and eventually led to the state establishing institutions such as the Commissions of Inquiry into the Involuntary Removal of Persons.

In the 1980s and 1990s, these initiatives were somewhat disparate, reflecting the political and geographic divides of the time which were heightened by imposition of restrictions of travel and communication between the north-east and the south of the island by the military for 'security' reasons. Despite these restrictions, Sri Lankan women worked together across the ethnic, religious and geographic separations, to stand together against the violations and abuses of women's rights that occur as a consequence of the conflict. For example, in 1989, a group of women from the south travelled to Jaffna to join a demonstration and meeting to protest against the assassination of Rajini Thiranagama, founder member of University Teachers for Human Rights (Jaffna) in September that year. In July 2003, the AWAW representing mothers and wives of soldiers 'missing in action' and the Guardian Association of Jaffna, representing wives and mothers of young men who 'disappeared' while in the custody of the security forces came together in a demonstration in Colombo at which they were united by a common demand from President Kumaratunga, Prime Minister Wickremasinghe, and LTTE leader Prabhakaran: 'Tell us, where are our children?'

At the same time, the differences in the experience of the

conflict by Sinhala, Tamil or Muslim women, and the differences in impact according to region, ethnicity, and religion have led to major realignments of women's groups and women's activism. For example, throughout the 1980s, we have seen the emergence of women's groups which mention ethnicity/religion in the name of the organization; the best-known are the Muslim Women's Research and Action Front (MWRAF), the Sinhala Women's Advancement Society, and the Sinhala-Tamil Rural Women's Organization.

The interaction between traditional notions of womanhood and femininity and the transformations of these notions in the context of conflict have evoked great academic interest. While some inquiries have been directed at the changing roles of women in the context of conflict-related displacement, widowhood, assumption of head of household status and 'imposed' independence, others have looked at the impact of the process of transformation of women's roles from mother and wife to armed militant. Women who belong to communities within which the collective identity of the community has become the defining factor in self-identification find themselves torn between different loyalties—to their community, and to the community of women. Despite the 'freedom' that women gained through the conflict period, despite their equal participation in extremely risk-laden political and military activity, despite the rhetorical commitments of radical movements to gender equality, the radical transformation of the self-image of woman that we see during a conflict period seldom lasts in a post-conflict or transitional scenario.

The framework of identity-based politics within which most women become involved in, or affected by conflict also create conditions within which women cannot raise issues that are significant for women. The fact that women are perceived as the bearers of the community honour makes them vulnerable to all forms of violence and abuse at the hands of the 'other' community in times of conflict, riot and flight. Thus, a call for equality by women within a community in a conflict situation can be often perceived as being contrary to the interests of that community. Maintaining links with women outside the community becomes complicated, because these women may more often than not belong to the 'other' community and are, therefore, perceived by men to be 'hostile'. This places restraints on the ability of women from one community to become a part of collective actions as 'women', and places them at times in opposition to 'other' women. In such a moment, unless there is critical understanding of the complexities of the situation, the divisions that are created can destroy a collectivity that has been nurtured over years of activism.

Women's activism for peace during these years in Sri Lanka has also been extraordinarily productive. Based on years of experience, women's groups have worked on developing training programmes and seminars on methods and processes of peace-building and conflict transformation from feminist and gender-sensitive perspectives, at both the conceptual and methodological levels. In doing so, they have explored non-violent forms of dispute resolution as well as traditional and customary forms of dialogue, negotiation and dispute resolution at the community level. As this process moves forward, women are moving towards concepts of transitional justice, with emphasis on processes of rebuilding communities, collective healing, and reconciliation. Their work in this area focuses on non-punitive forms of justice, including symbolic acknowledgements of injustice and violence that address broader issues of accountability and impunity within a democratic system. The new millennium is one in which Sri Lankan women will endeavour to change themselves from victims to agents of their own destiny, through the creation of institutions and structures that challenge patriarchal traditions and the subordination of women, at the same time as they strengthen democratic principles and practices. Their bitter experiences of violence and conflict as well as the courage and commitment they have shown in defying all odds to raise their voices against conflict and for peaceful resolution of conflict will no doubt empower them to shoulder these monumental tasks with the tolerance and dedication that is required.

NOTES

1. See Benedict Anderson, 'Long Distance Nationalism: World Capitalism and the Rise of Identity Politics', The Wertheim Lecture, CASA, University of Amsterdam, The Netherlands, 1992.

2. For example, in the Sri Lankan Parliament there have never been more than 5 per cent of women MPs since the country gained independence from British colonial rule in 1948.
3. For example, one may cite the role played by Medha Patkar in the Narmada Movement.
4. See Anuradha Chenoy, *Militarism and Women in South Asia*, New Delhi: Kali for Women, 2002.
5. See, for example, the work of Partha Chatterjee and Nivedita Menon.
6. Neloufer de Mel, 'Introduction', *Women and the Nation's Narrative*, New Delhi: Kali for Women, 2001, p. 2.
7. Chenoy, op. cit., n. 4, p. 4.
8. Cynthia Cockburn, 'Why (and Which) Feminist Anti-Militarism?', Discussion Paper, Women's International League for Peace and Freedom, March 2003, at: <www.wilpf.int.ch>
9. Diana Francis, 'Gender and Conflict Transformation', Discussion Paper, February 2004.
10. See, for example, the work of Sunila Abeysekera, Urvashi Butalia, Neloufer de Mel, Shobha Gautam, Rita Manchanda, Darini Rajasingham-Senanayake, and Kumudini Samuel.
11. Nira Yuval Davis, *Gender and Nation*, London and New Delhi: Sage, 1997.
12. Cynthia Enloe, *Bananas, Beaches, Bases: Making Feminist Sense of International Politics*, London: Pandora, 1989.
13. Urvashi Butalia, 'Introduction', *Speaking Peace: Women's Voices from Kashmir*, ed. Urvashi Butalia, New Delhi: Kali for Women, 2002.
14. See the submission by Amnesty International to the CEDAW Committee on the occasion of the consideration of the Third and Fourth periodic reports of the Government of Sri Lanka in 2002 for details.
15. See Sophie Elek, *Rice against Risk: Peace and Resettlement—Challenges faced by Displaced Women*, Colombo: Centre for the Study of Human Rights, 2003; and *Land and Property Rights of Internally Displaced Persons*: Colombo: Centre for Policy Alternatives, 2003.
16. For example, see Darini Rajasingham-Senanayake, 'Ambivalent Empowerment: The Tragedy of Tamil Women in Conflict', in *Women, War and Peace in South Asia*, ed. Rita Manchanda, New Delhi: Sage, 2001.
17. See, for example, G.B. Keerawella, 'The Janatha Vimukthi Peramuna and the 1971 Uprising', *Social Science Review*, no. 2, Social Scientists' Association of Sri Lanka, Colombo; also, 'Matching Employment Opportunities and Expectations: A Programme of Action for Ceylon', Report of an Inter-Agency Team, International Labour Organization, 1970 (known as the Seers Mission Report).
18. *Judgement of the Criminal Justice Commission Inquiry*, No. 1, Colombo: Government Press, 1976, p. 435.

19. The Tamils constitute almost 18 per cent of the island's population.
20. Often referred to as the Vadukoddai Resolution.
21. See the reports on visits to Sri Lanka by the UN Working Group on Enforced and Involuntary Disappearances in 1991 and 1992.
22. See, for example, the work of Malathi de Alwis, Neloufer de Mel, Darini Rajasingham-Senanayake, and Kumudini Samuel.
23. A member of the Core Group of the JVP in 1971 and the 26th accused in the main case against the JVP leadership, writing in *Eya*, the Sinhala journal of the Women and Media Collective, Colombo, March/April 1996, p. 18.
24. The very lowest level of organization within the JVP.
25. Known as the 'Hartal' of 1953.
26. Ibid., p. 21.
27. Rohana Wijeweera, leader of the JVP, was assassinated in 1989 by state security forces;
28. 'Elder sister'.
29. See the Appendices to the Report of the Criminal Justice Commission.
30. de Mel, op. cit., n. 6, p. 211.
31. Senanayake, op. cit., n. 16, p. 20.
32. Referring to the five lectures on social/political analysis which were the JVP's recruitment strategy.
33. 'The Socialist Woman'.
34. Personal communication with Leena Irene in 1979.
35. 'War Heroes'.
36. See the report of Amnesty International on their visit to Sri Lanka in 1991 and the reports of the UN Working Group on Enforced and Involuntary Disappearances for 1991 and 1992.
37. Released by the LTTE Political Committee, first edn., November 1983.
38. Ibid., p. 6.
39. Ibid
40. Ibid., p. 18.
41. Radhika Coomaraswamy, 'Tiger Women and the Question of Women's Emancipation', Rajini Thiranagama Memorial Lecture, *Pravada*, vol. 4, no. 9, 1996, p. 8.
42. Qadri Ismail, 'Boys will be Boys: Gender and National Agency in Fanon and the LTTE', *Pravada*, Social Scientists' Association, Colombo, 1992.
43. Thiranagama et al., *The Broken Palmyrah*, Colombo: Sri Lanka Studies Institute, 1990, p. 326.
44. 'Birds of Freedom'.
45. Adele Balasingham, *The Will to Freedom: An Inside View of Tamil Resistance*, London: Fairmax Publishing, 2001.
46. Peter Schalk, 'Birds of Independence: On the Participation of Tamil Women in Armed Struggle' in *Studies in Lankan Culture*, December 1992.

47. The red powder with which Tamil women place a dot on their forehead.
48. A gold chain traditionally placed by a husband around his wife's neck at the time of marriage.
49. Stanley J. Tambiah, 'Civil War and Women of Jaffna: Tales of Many Widows', *Pravada*, September 1992, p. 11.
50. There are over 800,000 people displaced within Sri Lanka as a result of the conflict, with around 175,000 still resident in state-run Welfare Centres; for further information, see Elek, op. cit., n. 15.
51. Quoted by Ismail, op. cit., n. 42, from a leaflet published in *Women's Studies International Forum*, vol. 25, Summer 1984, pp. 1–38.
52. Thiranagama et al., p. 90.
53. Ibid., p. 92.
54. 'Mother'.
55. Ibid., pp. 309–20.
56. See *Women and the Nation's Narrative: Gender and Nationalism in Twentieth Century Sri Lanka*, Colombo; Social Scientists' Association, 2001, and other writings.
57. Balasingham, op. cit., n. 45, p. 86.
58. Coomaraswamy, op. cit., n. 41, p. 8.
59. *Widows of Ethnic Violence in the Jaffna District: A Review of the Available Data: 1983–86*, Jaffna: TRRO.
60. Tambiah, op. cit., n. 49, p. 9.
61. Balasingham, op. cit., n. 45, p. 306.
62. Elek, op. cit., n. 15, p. 44.
63. Based on private communications.
64. Balasingham, op. cit., n. 45, p. 301.
65. Information gathered on visits to Batticaloa in June 2004.
66. Study carried out by the UNDP in Colombo in 2003.
67. Formerly known as the Home Guards.
68. Sunila Abeysekera, 'Organizing for Peace in the Midst of War: Experiences of Women in Sri Lanka' in *From Basic Needs to Basic Rights*, ed. Margaret Schuler, 1995.
69. See, for example, 'Notes and Comments: Tears and Curses', in *Pravada*, Social Scientists' Association, Colombo, June 1992. In traditional rituals, women are permitted to dance and shout in public in the belief that they are possessed by an 'evil spirit' needing to be exorcised; this is common to women in the north and east as well as the south.

4. On the Edge: The Impact of the Insurgency on Nepali Women

Chandra Bhadra, Ava Darshan Shrestha and Rita Thapa

This research paper is an attempt to rediscover the state, insurgency, counter-insurgency and militarization from a feminist perspective. This stance provides evidence of the extent of exclusion and the marginalization of women from the above processes. The gendered nature of the whole nexus results in profound negative implications for women.

INTRODUCTION

The Maoist insurgency that started out in three or four remote districts of far-western Nepal in February 1996 has now severely affected almost the whole country as it gathers momentum in its ninth year. The entire country in all its geopolitical reality (surrounded on three sides by open borders with India and on one side by China) and socio-economic diversity is now affected in one way or another. Two attempts at peace negotiations have failed in the recent past, during which women were never really represented in the negotiating parties on either side. The Maoists explicitly stated that gender concerns would be addressed once the class struggle was overcome, while the Nepali state, as usual, made feeble efforts at tokenism. Heavy dependence on foreign aid (estimated to be over 60 per cent) has resulted in an increase of militarization and strengthening of national security, which went hand-in-hand with a reduction of up to 20 per cent (as stated by a foreign ministry source in 2003) of the budget on social spending, mostly on health and education. Nepal's safety net lies in the institutions of family and community, and now these are being surely and swiftly eroded by the impact of the conflict, leaving the people with little else to fall back on.

A study on conflict widows conducted by Nagarik Aawaz in 2003 set the precedent for this research. Though this was a small pilot study, it gave a glimpse of the disturbing picture not only of conflict widows, but of all women caught in the crossfire. Generally, considering women's positions of social subordination, gender disparities in education, access to health, and their structured economic dependency, their risk has been aggravated by the conflict. This research paper attempts to look at the impact of this conflict on women across the board, reaching beyond their traditional roles. It has to be understood, to begin with, that not only are women not a homogeneous group along the lines of class, caste, ethnicity, age, and religion, as everywhere else, but in Nepal, the geographical and cultural diversity is outstanding and unique compared to other parts of the world. Therefore, general statements will require greater scrutiny.

METHODOLOGY OF THE STUDY

The research has been based on desktop review, newspaper cuttings, in-depth interviews, structured interviews, and site observations. In order to get the regional representation of the country, the primary research was carried out in three regions of Nepal: Sindhupal chowk and Kathmandu districts in the Central Region; Sunsari and Jhapa districts in the Eastern Region; and Doti and Darchula districts in the Far-Western Region. At the time this research was carried out, each of these regions were high security risk areas because it was immediately after the breakdown of the second attempt at peace talks. The risk to the researchers were all the more serious since a conscious decision was made to ensure that women in the armed militia were also represented in this study. The unusual timing, the situation, and the sensitivity of the subject compelled the researchers to rely on unconventional methods and procedures. Needless to say then, the costs to the researchers in the process were both related to personal safety and emotional.

The study was structured not only with the above-stated heterogeneity, but women's positions in the family, and/or their relationships to the concerned men as well. Accordingly, women were categorized as mothers, widows, adolescent girls, women at large, and women within the insurgency. Additionally, primary data was also collected from women who were/are in key positions of power to assess their agency in the whole nexus of conflict and the peace process.

The writers would like to acknowledge the efforts of Bhakta Bahadur Singh, Tara Aryal, and Nirmala Thapa for collecting primary data from the districts in very difficult situations. Acknowledgement also goes to Neeta Thapa for transcribing the interviews, and to Geeta Shrestha for collecting secondary information. Nagarik Aawaz is also acknowledged for assisting and supporting the entire fieldwork.

THE SITUATION OF WOMEN IN NEPAL

The 2001 Census revealed that women comprise 50.05 per cent of the total population of Nepal (23,151,423); 87 per cent of these women live in rural areas. In comparison to men, more women live in rural areas. Nonetheless, rural women in Nepal are not homogeneous. Because of ecological, socio-economic and cultural diversities, the constraints and opportunities for rural women vary in terms of the ecology (mountain, hill, and Terai), class, caste/ethnicity, religion, and the developmental region. Notwithstanding this diversity, the treatment of 'women as a category of gender' plays a pivotal role in the present situation of underdeveloped human capacity and lack of economic opportunities for rural women. 'Feminization of agriculture' and 'feminization of poverty' are markers of the economic status of women in Nepal. These markers are the result of historical and existing social subordination and legal discrimination against women.

According to the 2001 Census, the literacy rate of adult women (15 years and above) is 34.9 per cent as against 62.7 per cent of adult men. District-wise analysis of the percentage share of females in literacy shows that the situation is better in the Eastern and Western Development Regions (as high as 48 per cent in Syangja district, situated in the western mid-hills), but worsening in the Mid-Western and Far-Western Development Regions (being as low as 13 per cent in Mugu district, situated in the far-western high hills and mountains).[1] Among literate women, 45.9 per cent were found to have primary-level education, 30.3 per cent secondary-level education, 8.1 per cent have graduated from high schools, and 5.3 per cent have college/universities degrees. The remaining 9.2 per cent of women are literate, with no schooling. The district-wise analysis of the percentage of girls enrolled at the primary level shows a good record in districts like Mustang, Manang, and Syangja, with as high as 52 per cent in Manang (situated in the mountains) of the Western Development Region. In contrast, some districts in the Mid-Western and Far-Western Development Regions and some districts in the Terai (southern plain) belt have very low enrolment rates, with Mugu district having the lowest, at 31 per cent.[2]

As mentioned above, the 'feminization of agriculture' is one of the key indicators of the situation of women in Nepal. The district-wise analysis of the percentage share of females in non-agricultural occupations shows that women in the Eastern and Western Development Regions have better opportunities in occupations other than agriculture, with as high as 33 per cent in Syangja district. The situation is the worst in the Mid-Western and Far-Western Regions and some districts in the Terai, with as low as 8 per cent in Baitadi district in the Far-Western Region.[3]

The 'feminization of poverty' is shown by the rank of two indicators: the poverty deprivation index, and the gender discrimination index. Nepal ranks 142 out of 173 countries in the human development index (HDI), and in income-poverty Nepal ranks 76 out of 88 developing countries.[4] Similarly, in the gender-related development index (GDI) Nepal ranks 119 out of 146 countries.[5] The gender empowerment measure (GEM) is not available since the parliament was dissolved in 2001. These indicators show that poverty is pervasive in Nepal, and that due to gender discrimination there is feminization of poverty.

Within Nepal, the indices show the Mid- and Far-Western Development Regions along with a few districts in the Central Region having the least developed poverty ranks, and the same regions and districts in the Central Terai having the lowest ranks in the GDI.[6] It implies that although feminization of poverty is pervasive in the country, women from the Mid- and Far-Western

Regions face the major brunt of poverty due to the existing gender discrimination.

Interestingly, the Maoist movement ignited mainly from three mid-hill districts in the Mid-Western Development Region—Rukum, Rolpa, and Jajarkot, which are found to be the least developed in terms of the poverty deprivation index, the socio-economic and infrastructural development indices, and the women's empowerment index.[7] This situation is indicative of how the thirty years of the partyless panchayat regime and the ensuing fourteen years of multiparty democracy did not result in elimination of poverty: rather, these political regimes have continued to perpetuate the exclusion of the poor and the marginalized, especially women. Hence, after five decades of development efforts, the present conflict/insurgency is linked with the persistent state of poverty and social exclusion.[8]

Historical Analysis of the Present Context and Women's Perceptions

Nepal as a nation state emerged through the unification of several small principalities in the foothills of the Himalayas, governed by local/tribal kings or chieftains. The process of unification started around 1761 and continued until Nepal went through fourteen years of war against the British, until there was finally a peace treaty with them in 1816. King Prithivi Narayan Shah, the king of Gorkha principality, first carried out the unification, and the process of expansion was continued by his brothers and sons after his death. During the mid-1800s, Junga Bahadur Rana took hold of the premiership in a violent bloodbath, establishing a hereditary premiership thereafter. This autocratic regime provoked rebellion among the people when, in 1950, King Tribhuvan himself became the main actor in liberating Nepal as a democratic state from the clutches of the hereditary premierships of the Ranas. Although the people's movement for democracy had the full support of the king, it did not last longer than a decade, when King Mahendra revoked multiparty democracy and promulgated the partyless panchayat system in 1960. For thirty years thereafter (although it was termed as a decentralized partyless democracy), governance manifested as an absolute monarchy.

The people's movement of the 1980s and the subsequent re-establishment of multiparty democracy resulted in reformulation of the Constitution in 1991.

The role of women in building Nepal has neither been documented nor adequately highlighted. Nepal was a frontier state throughout the time of unification, expansion, and the subsequent war against the British. Generally, during such phases, women are in charge and control of the families and the communities while the men are out fighting. There is scattered documentation of the bravery of Nepali women during the war against the British. Even during the people's movement in the 1940s, many women were directly and openly active in party politics and the movement. Similarly, during the 1980s, for the first time women in large numbers openly took active roles in the people's movement to restore democracy. This reveals that during times of political instability and turmoil women have direct or indirect participation in the polity. However, history also shows that the notions of nation and State are defined within the sphere of masculinity, where women have been completely excluded from state affairs. As a result, political conflicts, wars, insurgencies and armed conflicts perpetuate within the definition of masculinity, where women appear to be 'non-doers' and just remain silent sufferers and victims.

The gendered nature of democracy, specially the experience of the 1950s, left women without many achievements in the political sphere. In his book *Women and Social Change in Nepal (1951–60)* dedicated to 'All Women of Nepal who are Striving for Equality', Thapa remarks that, in spite of the democracy of 1951, in reality, the great majority of women remained like puppets in the hands of men.[9] The partyless panchayat system (1960–89) remained systematically gendered with women secluded in the ghettoos of partyless 'women's organizations', where women could do very little for asserting their human rights. Although women's contribution to the re-establishment of democracy in 1990 was tremendous, they were once again left out of the political process as soon as democracy was re-established. The experience of the two democratic movements of the 1940s and 1980s demonstrated the treatment of women only as 'reserve forces'. Once the political goals were achieved, they were sent back home.

This negation of women in the political process was amply clear during the drafting of the Constitution, soon after democracy was reinstated in 1990. Although the Preamble of the Constitution claims that the process of writing the Constitution was made with the widest possible participation of the Nepali people, the nine-member commission was comprised solely of men, including representatives of all parties. The exclusion of women from the commission to draft the Constitution led to the treatment of women in a 'welfarist approach', rather than as equal citizens.[10]

The symbolic exclusion of women from the formulation of the Constitution resulted in the systemic exclusion of women from the legislative, judicial, and executive bodies. The minimum of 5 per cent candidature of women for general elections as mandated by the Constitution remained at the minimum level, with the actual representation remaining less than even 5 per cent both in the 1991 and 1994 general elections (3.41 per cent in each). This compelled the continuity of the women's movement for democratic rights even beyond the state transforming into a multiparty democracy. In the 1999 general election, due to women having raised their voices and demanded the raising of the minimum percentage of candidature, the major parties announced 10 per cent candidature for women. The actual candidature though, remained 6.39 per cent, with 5.85 per cent women being elected. Women's representation in the upper house, the National Assembly, was slightly better, with women occupying 15 per cent (9 out of 60) of the seats when the full house was functional. Women parliamentarians also remained marginalized when it came to sharing positions of power.

The legislative exclusion of women also extended to the judicial and executive arms of the state. To date, women in judicial decision-making positions comprise 2.5 per cent of the total, with a single woman judge in the Supreme Court among fifteen judges. Similarly, women's representation in the civil services remains 5.12 per cent of the total gazetted-level positions, with women's representation remaining about 4 per cent in the highest strata of bureaucratic decision-making positions of the special and first class civil services.[11]

From the primary data collected from women in key positions of power who are highly educated and experienced, it was revealed that even though they were either the equal or sole decision makers within their homes and families and commanded respect within their communities, they remained powerless within the structures of the state, of organizations, and of political power. All these women were intellectually aware of the grave national situation and were deeply concerned about national security and identity. However, they felt helpless in bringing about a transformation of the situation in the context of their being marginalized and excluded from the whole political economy of the insurgency, counter-insurgency, militarization, and the peace process.

The respondents of the field survey also echoed the feelings and experience of women in positions of power about their state of helplessness, exclusion, and powerlessness. The findings of the survey reveal that women in general were found to identify themselves with their immediate/personal and concrete experience of family, home, and the community at the micro-level rather than the macro-level abstractions of nationhood, national security, responsibility for the country, or the political economy of militarization. Nevertheless, it was not so with women who were directly involved as insurgents. Although, based on personal experience, these young women related their perception with the ideology of class conflict.

Women as primary respondents expressed their notion of family as immediate blood relations eating and sleeping under the same roof, fulfilling the basic needs of each other. Similarly, they saw their homes as peaceful, sacred/holy, and as permanent places of shelter. They perceived the community as consisting of different caste/ethnic and class groups living harmoniously and helping each other during times of need. Although these views were ideals that these women envisaged, the harsh realities of insurgency have resulted in separation, displacement, and dislocation of the family, shattering the sanctuary of their homes and communities. Contrary to these perceptions, women participants in the insurgency expressed that for them 'family' meant those who were members living in the same group and fighting for class liberation. Similarly, 'home' was where they could spend the night safely, which could even be an open field or the jungle. Further, for them 'community' was like-minded groups of people who shared the same ideology.

Similar to the above findings, for women-at-large, the concept of nationhood and national security was not clear, specially for mothers who belong to the older age group. They did not know what nationhood or nationality was. However, younger women who are widows or adolescent girls have some notion of nationality and emphasized that nationality was essential and should be protected by stopping the current violence. They asserted that national security had been gravely endangered due to dishonest, myopic, and selfish leaders. This was especially emphasized by women cadres of the people's army, who were very vocal against capitalism and supported the rights of the minorities manifested in diverse cultures, religions, and languages in Nepal.

Women in general did not know what their responsibility towards the nation would be, specially older women like mothers and older widows. Older women seemed to feel helpless in fulfilling their responsibilities towards the nation; for example, they said that they could do nothing but 'pray to God' for obtaining peace in the country, whereas some widows and adolescents (of both the warring factions) who are the daughters and sisters of the victims stated that they would work and serve the nation like their husbands, fathers, and brothers. Hence, the perception of responsibility seems to be instigated by women's personal and familial circumstances created by the situation of insurgency. Not surprisingly, women in the insurgency articulated that their responsibilities towards the nation were to be involved in the liberation of the people and the nation from injustice, and from class discrimination by the selfish, capitalist, and dictatorial leaders.

Women in general were also unaware about the political economy of militarization. The definition of militarization was very personalized. They defined militarization from their perspective of which warring faction they were related to. For example, women related to security personnel stated that militarization was necessary for the peace and security of the community/country, while women relations of those who had been arrested or killed by the security personnel stated that militarization was meant to harass and kill civilians. Specifically, women from the insurgents' families asserted that what the 'people's army' (militarization) the Maoists termed their army as was necessary for protecting women from the state's military atrocities. Endorsing militarization through the people's army, women militants stated that it was necessary for the political success of the 'people's movement'.

Women have differential experience of militarization. In fact, there seem to be three distinct patterns of how women have been experiencing militarization. First, those who lost their near and dear ones denounced militarization of the 'other side' of the warring faction. Second, although women face militarization of some form or the other in their daily lives, they were apprehensive of opposing it for the sake of the security and welfare of their children and other members of the family. Third, women who were active in insurgency were found to participate in military type of activities aiming to defeat and destroy old regimes/ structures and for ushering in a new social order.

It was very touching that women of one faction seemed to sympathize and identify with women from the 'other side', saying that 'they must be feeling the same sadness and desperation as I do'. They also blamed the men for creating the consequences. On the one hand, women in insurgency were perceived by other women as having been misguided and led to sacrifice their homes, families, and happiness, and hoped that some day, soon they would return to mainstream society and lead normal lives. On the other hand, women insurgents also sympathized with the other women as being poor, discriminated against and disadvantaged within the family and the larger state. Although women insurgents saw no immediate meeting point with upper-class women in the existing structure, they called upon all women to unite to establish peace and pressurize the government.

Roles of Women in Insurgency

The role of women in insurgency was examined in terms of being indirect supporters and as combatants. While the mothers were not found to have any roles in the insurgency directly or indirectly, some young widows did indirectly support the insurgency, expressing their interest in Maoist ideology. The majority of the women insurgents reported that they were involved actively in the insurgency, a few reported that they were involved, but passively, but none reported on participating forcibly. Those who were actively involved reported that they were participants in order to fight gender, class and caste discrimination in response to the demands of changing times. They said that they were active in mass gatherings, ideological dissemination, going underground and taking up arms. Those who reported of passive participation spoke of supporting the ideology, becoming a member, providing food to the cadres/ insurgents, being messengers and carrying letters.

Those who were active as fighters asserted that their involvement was to do away with women's oppression and to work towards emancipation of women. They specifically articulated the existing gender discrimination in education, property rights and citizenship rights, which needed to change radically. Some of them said that their involvement as fighters gave them a feeling of equality with men. For instance, wearing the combat uniform instead of traditional women's apparel and carrying weapons gave them a sense of equality with men. However, many argued that the Maoist leaders were playing on women's psyche of exclusion and gender discrimination. Gautam, Banskota and Manchanda (2001) argue that:

> . . . it is surprising, given the flood of women getting involved in the Peoples War, that the ideological patron of the Maoist movement, Dr Baburam Bhattarai does not engage with the women's question in his political writing on the New Democratic Revolution (NDR).[12]

The trio further support their argument by stating:

> As for the Peoples War in Nepal, four years after it was launched, women co-leaders of the movement like Pampa Bushal, are no longer prominent. Presumably she is one of the 'bourgeois intellectual women' denounced by Prachanda. There are no women at the regional and central committee level.[13]

It is further reported that young women with leadership qualities joined the rebels' party but had failed to attain the positions of power they had aspired to, and most often had ended up losing their lives.[14]

More than half of the respondents were not aware of the exact number or proportion of women in the insurgency, although one of the women leaders claimed 30 per cent representation.[15] Those who claimed to know either withheld the information as confidential, or just guessed the proportion to be ranging from 20 to 50 per cent. Although they claimed to have equal roles and responsibilities as those of men, specification of roles and responsibilities revealed a gendered division of roles such as procuring and cooking food, sewing clothes, dancing and singing, collecting donations, acting as informers, making bombs, motivating others to join the organization, and carrying guns. Similarly, women in decision-making positions were also reported to be much fewer than men; reportedly, women were evaluated for positions of power based on their ability, knowledge, and physical fitness.

The majority of the respondents reported of joining the insurgency on their own accord, but there were some who stated that they were forced to do so. There were others who outlined the atrocities of the security forces, such as village raids, terrorizing and mistreatment of women and killings of the innocent, and the sympathy extended to them by the Maoists during these situations, that motivated them to join the insurgency. Then there were some who said that the Maoist insurgency provided them with an opportunity to fulfil their desire for fighting against injustice. There were also respondents who spoke of joining the insurgency because of their husbands' involvement, while there were still others who simply desired to take up arms and learn the skills of war.

Although the majority reported no sexual abuse of women within the insurgency, there were a few instances where either women cadres themselves experienced sexual abuse or were aware of their friends having been sexually abused. Instances of sexual abuse of lower-level female cadres by the upper-level commanders were also reported.[16] Respondents also reported that there was no perverse sexual activity within the insurgent groups, as assumed by the general public of there being free sex within the insurgency. They said that this was a rumour spread by the enemy to discredit their movement. Rather, they reported that young men and women could get married and get transferred together to fulfil their sexual needs. A similar statement was made by Hisila Yami (a woman leader), who stated that a strict sexual code of conduct had been formulated so that sexual acts led to marriage.[17]

Regarding the unusual gender roles they were currently engaged in, women rebels said that they saw no difference between the roles of men and women, and envisaged continuing their present roles even after the 'rebellion' (insurgency) was over, because they perceived that class struggles would continue even after the end of armed conflict and that they had to assume leadership roles until socio-political transformation was accomplished.

Women insurgents saw a lot of difference in their roles and responsibilities after joining the movement. They saw their roles and responsibilities before joining the movement as limited to the four walls of their homes, confined to their 'selfish vested interests', and lacking self-confidence. They reported of their changed roles and responsibilities as being equal to those of men, broadened to encompass larger national concerns and having immense responsibility of liberating the country. As one respondent put it, 'Before, I was a daughter of the family, now I am a daughter of the entire nation.' This way, women in the insurgency interpreted their roles as having expanded from the micro-sphere of household and family to the macro-sphere of national liberation. However, the majority felt that even after the rebellion was over, they saw the challenges to women's liberation as remaining.

Impact of Insurgency on Women

It is evident that the whole process of armed conflict evolved from the standpoint of 'machismo' actions and reactions in which those who lose their lives or get killed are mostly men. In the process, women and children are usually the worst-hit people in conflict situations, and Nepal is no exception. Since women are not a homogeneous category, in this section, the diverse impacts of insurgency on women are discussed differentially—as mothers, widows, adolescents, and women at large. Furthermore, there was a need to further subdivide some of these categories such as mothers, widows, and adolescents, as the impact varied in terms of their relations to their men, who belong to the security forces, the Maoists, or civilians (teachers, journalists, politicians, etc.).

IMPACT ON MOTHERS

Mothers are experiencing psychological disorder and trauma have become deranged, paranoid and were hysterical, not really comprehending why their young sons and daughters are killed so young. They report 'foetal bereavement', which they explain as a sharp pain experienced in the uterus when they think of their deceased children. They ask how they would feel when somebody killed the babies they had carried inside their wombs for nine months and whom they had protected by letting them suck their souls. Mothers are found to have become deranged, crying all night, waiting day in and day out with cooked food for their (deceased) sons to come back home.[18] However, they do not shed tears, as they live out the masculine ideal of the 'brave mothers' who can sacrifice sons/daughters for national or ideological causes.

During the survey, the majority of mothers could not express how they had been affected by the deaths of their sons since they were still overwhelmed with grief. Those who responded reported of constant grief, sleeplessness, nightmares, and loss of appetite. One mother who had lost her son but was not ready to accept it, was found to be living on false hopes and waiting for her son's return. They also reported of physical symptoms of weakness and dizziness, breathing problems and trembling of the body, weakening eyesight due to continuous weeping, and throat ailments due to screaming and wailing.

The majority of the mothers lost their familial wherewithal due to the deaths of their sons, some mothers being dependent solely on their sons' incomes. All mothers (of both factions) believed that their sons had committed no crime to be killed so ruthlessly.

IMPACT ON WIDOWS

In a predominantly Hindu society, religious and cultural practices have maintained implicit and explicit rules whereby the woman has restricted mobility, virtually no hand in decision-making, and no control and power over resources and their bodies. Thus, widowhood has tremendous implications for Nepali women, specially those who are from Hindu families. The stringent and dehumanizing practices of mourning that she has to observe affect her existing condition negatively, bringing it down to the lowest levels. This makes her doubly vulnerable and at risk—emotionally and physically.[19]

In line with the findings of Thapa and Shrestha (2003), the insurgency widows are found to be generally very young (the majority being 20–35 years of age); having at least 2–5 children; mostly uneducated or having rudimentary education, no marketable skills; and no ownership of property. In the sociocultural context of Nepal, as the power and position of women is acquired through men, they are immediately slotted in positions of powerlessness and are at the mercy of relatives (primarily of their husband's side) once they become widows. Furthermore, widows have little social standing because widowhood is looked down upon as something 'inauspicious'.

After the death of husbands the responsibility of the family, specially of children, falls on the widows. So the hardship of single parenting, difficulty in continuing agricultural activities as a means of livelihood, and loss of creditworthiness were some of the problems widows have had to encounter in addition to their grief and pain. Some have even expressed suicidal tendencies in their in capacity to cope. Some, especially widows of insurgents, said that they wished to continue their husbands' missions and commit themselves to fulfil their cause.

Commenting on the health of the widows Thapa and Shrestha (2003) report that all the widows had aged prematurely. They had reduced weight and were anaemic. Gastric problems due to stress, worry, and lack of adequate food consumption were also reported. Widows also complained of kidney damage and bleeding in the uterus. Apart from these, psychological symptoms were also reported such as: difficulty in completing tasks; difficulty in making decisions on their own; lack of confidence in facing outsiders; lack of sleep; headaches; restlessness; mood swings; anger and irritation; a sense of hopelessness and sadness alternating with laziness and inertia. Lack of appetite and physical symptom of munching without being aware of the action, alcohol consumption, smoking, and severe mental problems were also found.

Almost all widows reported economic problems after the deaths of husbands. The impact of the death of the husband was felt immediately since most of the families did not even have the funds to perform the funeral rites. This was followed by children dropping out of school and less access to basic needs, such as food, clothes, shelter and health care. However, they seemed to be coping with the help of natal homes, friends, relatives and other family members, undertaking income generating activities such as livestock and poultry rearing, tailoring, selling milk, working as wage labourers, and by taking loans. Some widows were operating tea shops and local grocery shops. Some others had opened lodging houses and eateries. Some also reported receiving support from political parties. Contrarily, a Maoist widow stated that she felt no economic hardship as she was living in a commune and also that she was not interested in 'wealth'. Interestingly, there was further marginalization and a lower profile of the civilian widows and ostracism of the Maoist widows, which made this category even more vulnerable. Those who got compensation as widows of security personnel also reported that they felt threatened by their own family members who were aiming to control the compensation money.

Widows seemed to be very sensitive to cultural exclusion because of their widowhood and other psychological trauma tagged with widowhood. It was found that the media also highlighted an image of 'colourless non-entity' of young widows to get public sympathy against insurgents and their violence.[20] In spite of the psychological trauma that widows faced due to their widowhood, very few of them were found to have received psychological and medical help from hospitals. The majority did not know how to seek help or had no hope of anyone coming forward to help them. However, a few widows experienced no psychological problems in their husbands' deaths. These were all Maoist widows, and they stated that class problems were more important than personal problems. These statements of Maoist widows were indicative that within the insurgency widowhood did not have the same connotation and implication as in the general situation, which had been demonstrated by the transmogrifying action of a symbolic ritual of widows being smeared with *sindhoor* (red vermilion) on their foreheads (the Hindu symbol of married status) in Sindhuli district by the Maoists, in rebellion against the symbol of Hindu 'widowhood' which forbade Hindu widows the *sindhoor* and the red colour.

Though most of the widows were still in their period of early trauma, most widows reported no sexual desires after their husbands' deaths. Some were of the opinion that to have sexual desire after the husband's death was wrong and was against religion. Others stated that it was taken as a social crime. Although Maoist widows opined that sexual desires were normal, they should not be suppressed and that women could remarry, they also highlighted their view that their sexual desire was secondary in the face of their struggle for class liberation. Widows also spoke of verbal and physical sexual advances or sexual abuse. These were from neighbours, relatives, or strangers. They elaborated that neighbours and relatives came visiting after dark with bad intentions. These widows stated that they were fearful of even going to the toilet at night, which are generally built outside the main house.

Some widows did not know what lay in store for them in the future. They revealed fatalistic and defeatist attitudes and said that they depended on God's will and would face eventualities as they came. Other widows, specially those of security personnel, planned on sustaining themselves with the compensation money, going back to farming, and also undertaking income-generating activities. Maoist widows, on the other hand, were of the opinion that when people were at war they did not think of the future, and that they coped with the situation through group solidarity.

IMPACT ON ADOLESCENT GIRLS

Generally, for girls starting as early as 12 to 13 years, it is a period of more intense initiation into roles of domestic and sexual subordination, leading to their seclusion and restriction in mobility. For many girls, adolescence is more a preparation for marriage and domesticity. Quite often, she is a mother at 15 or 16 years. Her ability to look after her young children is severely compromised by her enormous work burden, lack of education (even illiteracy), lack of access to contraceptives, and lack of control of the family income and decision making.

Adolescent girls have been affected by the insurgency in diverse ways. Many girls are now barred from pursuing their education. Some had to flee and leave school in fear of being abducted or forced to attend mass gatherings by the Maoists. Others simply lost interest in schooling due to fear of the school becoming the battleground between warring factions. Some were simply unable to meet school expenses due to the death (in insurgency) of their fathers.

Although both adolescent boys and girls have become targets of recruitment or abduction by insurgents and arrest or detention by the security personnel, when it comes to girls, their sexual vulnerability emerges as a matter of great concern. Adolescent girls are found to be verbally or physically abused with sexual implications. Those who fled were actually the ones who felt they were lucky. They related stories of how their close friends had been raped and impregnated by members of the state or non-state militaries or even third parties who pretended to be either Maoists or security personnel.

The cultural value of a girl's virginity being synonymous with family honour is considered to be violated when girls are raped or even physically molested. When young girls are forced to join the rebellion, parents and other guardians fear the young girls' loss of virginity, resulting in the loss of family honour. This has resulted in a new trend of adolescent girls being married off at very early ages/underage.[21] Accentuating this problem, in many villages security personnel are marrying young girls by giving false identities in terms of their names, addresses, and marital status. In these uniformed men, parents also see good nuptial matches for their young daughters, an opportunity of enhancing the family reputation and maintaining the family honour. However, in many instances girls are deserted when these men are posted out, without any trace. In these cases, girls are devastated, specially when they are left behind pregnant without any support. In many instances, these girls have taken up arms for revenge.

Interestingly enough, although the purity of a girl's body is valued, in recent times when forced to send children to join

Maoist training programmes, parents are found to be sending the daughters instead of their sons.[22] This is because girls have a low value for their parents as providers/supporters in their old age as compared to boys.

Adolescent girls also revealed health problems that were related to stress. It was understandable that young girls were in a constant state of worry and stress because of their being the targets of abduction by the Maoists and arrest by the security personnel. For example, stories abound of Maoists abducting girls from Accham district,[23] and security personnel arresting girls on the way to temples, their whereabouts still being unknown even after a year of arrest.[24] It could be true of other members of the family, but adolescent girls reported that even a small ailment would turn into a serious health risk since they could not travel to the health posts/centres for medical treatment due to security hazards.

Adolescent girls were also found to be away from home and separated from their families. In many cases, male members (fathers/brothers) had either migrated to cities in Nepal or in India, or the security personnel had arrested them without their knowledge or giving their whereabouts. Some girls were sent away from home and family for their own safety and security. All these girls missed their homes and families one way or the other.

The majority of the girls had not received assistance of any kind. Those who had were from the government or from NGOs. The types of assistance received were financial, skill training, accommodation, inputs/materials for income generation, and also counselling and moral support. Those who had not received assistance from the government or NGOs reported that they would rely on their relatives for helping them. Family members of insurgents were receiving support from the Maoist party in the form of moral support and assurance of security.

IMPACT ON WOMEN AT LARGE

The insurgency has not only impacted women as mothers and widows, women at large are also affected in many ways. Because of the conflict, male members of the family, specially the able-bodied and the young, are migrating out from villages to cities in

Nepal or across the border to India or to other countries. They have fled villages either fearing for their safety from the Maoists, or seeking livelihood options as traditional sources of livelihood opportunities have been disrupted or destroyed due to the insurgency. Women are left behind with the elderly and very young children when men migrate, or join the insurgency, the security forces, or just leave the villages in search of work. The absence of male members in the family or the village has resulted in women being forced to undertake additional activities, which were traditionally performed by men.[25] This has further burdened the already overworked women. So women are left not only with the responsibility of taking care of the elderly and the young children, but also with the sole responsibility of undertaking agriculture and farm activities, resulting in the increase of female-headed households. In the absence of adult males in the family, women are in a constant state of anxiety, stress and fear. This finding is also supported by the Thapa and Shrestha (2003) study.

Many families had been displaced from their homes. Many mothers reported that they could not bear to continue staying in the place where their sons had been killed brutally. Widows migrated for their children's safety and education, while adolescent girls got displaced due to fear of being abducted by the Maoists or being harassed by the security forces. Many even moved out of the country to India to save their lives or in search of work. The displacement poses other problems to girls and women, such as becoming easy prey to human traffickers and subsequently being forced into prostitution.

Women's Agencies

Mothers were rarely found organized in self-help groups to deal with their grief or for economic activities. All the widows reported that they had not received any support from organizations to deal with social problems. The Royal Nepal Army Wives' Association has supported widows of army personnel based on women's traditional roles, by conducting training like sewing and providing sewing machines after the completion of training. There were other widows who had organized themselves into self-help groups conducting activities such as building collective strength and organizational power, coping with grief, and discussing and developing future livelihood strategies. These examples clearly reveal that the relief provided by the state is purely based on a 'welfare approach', while self-help groups initiated by women's organizations show a trend towards a 'rights-based approach'.

None of the mothers had taken any initiatives in the peace process. They said that they were too old and dejected to be able to participate in a peace process. Some widows had participated in the peace process by attending peace rallies and peace-related meetings organized by NGOs.

Workshops held in Doti (far-western Nepal, Illam, and Biratnagar), eastern Nepal, and Janakpur in central Nepal during the period of survey reveal that the few women's groups active in these districts had not yet come together to do collaborative work in conflict management and peace-building work. This may be a small sampler for the relatively fewer number of women's NGOs in Nepal. Generally, most of the organizations were doing issue-based work and were heavily dependent on donor funding for running their programmes. Therefore, clearly, not enough women's groups were working in this area either within the donor's 'partner networks' or independently. The observation was that conflict was a fairly new issue for Nepal and civil society had not sufficiently mobilized around it. Also, the security restrictions and the increasingly shrinking space for civil society due to militarization of both warring factions meant that women's mobility and voices were further stifled and security threats heightened.

The above findings of the primary data are not surprising considering the fact that those women who are/were in positions of power (including a woman minister who was a member in the peace talks), had been excluded from the whole process of insurgency, counter-insurgency, militarization and the peace negotiations. Interviews with women in key positions of power revealed that although they were in total control of their lives within their families and had good social standing and leadership in the community, they felt marginalized within their own organizational/power structure. All these women in positions of power felt that women at large were treated as second-class citizens, and that women had been totally excluded from the state processes.

While all of the above is true, it is also noteworthy that in this relatively short period of time and very difficult times for Nepal and the Nepali people, women have done some groundbreaking work. They have led some critical research, done advocacy and lobbying work on both sides for peace, and have also done some relief and response work for conflict widows, children, and the displaced population. The following cases provide examples of how some women's organizations are providing safety nets.

Case Study 1: Shakti

When violence escalated after the palace massacre of 1 June 2001, Shakti, a feminist activist with over two decades of experience in the field of development, began to mobilize civil society to work for conflict transformation and peace-building. In recognition of the fact that this was going to be Nepal's precondition for any development gains in the future, an organization was founded soon after.

The organization has focused on the following:

- advocacy to understand the conflict situation and work for peace in civil society;
- support to displaced youths as a way of 'saving seeds' in times of famine;
- relief support to victims of the conflict including widows and children; and
- a nationwide initiative for peace through collaborative action with other local-level organizations.

In less than three years, the organization has expanded its learning and experience, initiated strategic programmes for peace-building work, and gained recognition for its cutting edge quality of work. There are probably very few other organizations in Nepal that have grounded themselves in such a well-thought-out approach in response to present needs despite explicit threats to leadership, and the obvious climate of instability and insecurity when fear rather than action prevails on the ground.

Despite looking for support locally and approaching some aid agencies in Kathmandu, the organization has not received funding other than from one source. It is lucky that owing to the network and credibility of its leadership at the international level, this organization has been able to meet its very frugal overheads and programme costs.

According to Shakti, the pressure for programme response is coming from all sides, they have a proven capacity for programme delivery and expansion, yet they continue to have to spend a great deal of time and energy looking for funds. In an overtly aid-dependent Nepal, when many key donors have set up a basket fund for peace and development, Shakti could find no logical answer. However, she could foretell that this would not forebode well for Nepal, or those who have committed to supporting it.

Case Study 2: Women for Human Rights, Single-Women's Groups

The Women for Human Rights (WHR) single-women groups was established in 1994. There are now twenty-six single-women's groups in Nepal's 75 districts covering all five development regions and involving 1,374 registered young single women. WHR targets and works with widows who are in isolation and are dependent on their families. WHR connects widows with each other in the single-women's groups.

WHR conducts awareness orientation workshops on various issues, such as the role of society, culture, religion and law concerning single women. WHR also provides legal counselling and trains them in leadership building, thus creating a platform for women interested in political participation at the district level, where women's participation is minimal.

Economic independence remains the most crucial step for single women to have a say in the decision-making process at home. Thus, WHR has started various programmes with the aim of promoting entrepreneurship among women as a means to achieve economic independence. WHR established a micro-credit programme called 'Aadhar' (Support) to assist the needy single women to obtain micro-credit at a minimal rate of interest with only their membership fees of WHR as collateral. The Single Women's Entrepreneurs' Group has also been formed with the objective of promoting the products of single women and making them self-sustainable. WHR coordinates exhibitions where the products of single women have been promoted. WHR has established an 'Opportunity Fund' to provide scholarship to the children of needy single women, and to provide financial support to single women to pursue training and education.

WHR's work has spread to different communities and segments of the population, for example, specific groups for the Dalits (the occupational groups who are treated as Untouchables), and for the victims of Maoist insurgency have been formed in Dang, Surkhet, and Bardiya districts.

Beginning with the family, WHR invites single women to emerge and join the company of their peers. The groups give the widows the term 'single women', which has been passed as a declaration in a national workshop agreeing to replace the heavily negatively symbolic 'widow' to help build a new future. Thus, WHR moves isolated women who have been considered unlucky and unwanted, into a possible force for self-transformation and for changing their communities positively. The urgency of the problem increases daily because of the Maoist insurgency. Hence, WHR gives priority attention to the single-women victims of conflict.

The impact of WHR's work is also evident in the increased attention to single-women's issues on the government agenda. The National Planning Commission of the Government of Nepal incorporated the issue of the empowerment of single women in the 10th Five Year Plan. Presently, the CEDAW (Convention on the Elimination of all forms of Discrimination Against Women) Committee has also emphasized the single-women's question as an emerging issue.

Despite the limitations owing to a non-conducive environment and the restrictions and constraints owing to the escalating conflict and violence, the women's agencies observed are doing remarkable work. This must also be looked at in the context that the area of work is 'new' to Nepal. Often, this work has required personal risk taking, and has been in a constant state of precarious balance. On a broader note, Nepali women in general and the involved women's agencies in particular seem to account for whatever remaining strength and hope the country can claim. Yet, the state's inability and capability to support and sustain these agencies is tragic.

VIOLENCE AGAINST WOMEN

In the game of man-made war and armed conflict, women's bodies and sexuality become the battlefields. Both warring factions have stories to report of 'their women' having been raped and sexually assaulted by the enemies (men). Gautam, Banskota and Manchanda (2001) report of the police brutality against women Maoist cadres:

> . . . women's defiance of traditional roles and empowering themselves by taking up arms in the jungle, may have provoked a double punishment for what is seen as a double challenge to the social-political order. In this context, the rape and killing of women 'Maoists', is not an aberration but a systematic instrument of terror and repression. Rape is routine and the 12 women interviewed in Lalitpur jail from Gorkha district, spoke of rape and torture when in police custody.[26]

Equally brutal are stories of armed Maoists gang-raping a mother of a 3-month-old baby, a woman who was still in her confinement, of girls and women being hounded and raped in front of their helpless fathers, brothers and husbands.[27] Adolescent girls related stories of how their close friends had been raped and impregnated by perpetrators of state or non-state militaries or third parties who pretended to be either Maoists or security personnel. Instances were also reported where women cadres either themselves experienced sexual abuse or were aware of their friends having been sexually abused within the insurgency.

Many have been raped and killed.[28] For women, death is easier to endure than the violation of their bodies. Many have committed suicide and gone unreported as that brings 'shame' to the family. Those who cannot commit suicide, and are pregnant as a result of rape, are ostracized within the family and the community. There are reports that women are even banished during childbirth and they go to jungles or caves for delivery.[29] Reports of physical brutality such as beating of women and girls from both parties on the pretext of being informers are also not uncommon.

During the period of research, it was found in western Nepal that alcohol consumption by men was found to be very high. In these districts, in the early 1990s, anti-alcohol movements had been very successful and had become exemplary for nationwide initiatives. Now, it is a common scene that hard drinks are served throughout the day along the roadside and that frustrated, jobless and desperate men are seen consuming alcohol. From this it can be logically deduced that domestic violence and crime have increased in severely affected areas. Informal discussions affirmed this presumption.

Abduction of schoolchildren, youth (both men and women) and their use as human shields by the Maoists speak of another level of violence. Additionally, abduction and forceful recruitment of women and girls has also become a matter of daily news. The abduction of women and girls is suspected to serve the purpose of sexual slavery.

FURTHER IMPACTS

Since the state offers so little, the only safety net for the Nepali people generally lie in the institution of the family and the community. When this is upset owing to political divisions,[30] displacement or migration due to the conflict, or disruption in traditional and cultural ways of life, there is very little else to fall back on. In this situation, the question of responsibility towards the conflict-affected elderly, the disabled/maimed, children, orphans and women becomes crucial.

Owing to security restrictions or reasons, women's mobility is further restricted, impacting on legal, cultural, economic and political mobility. A general shrinking of civil and political spaces has inevitably had larger implications for women than for men, specially to the women's movement.

The conflict has had a very negative impact on children. The widows interviewed were finding it very difficult to support the education of their children. This necessitates contemplating on the future of these children who have lost their educational opportunities.

The incidence of women delivering babies without fathers due to rape, lack of fathers' identities, false marriages and desertion raises the issues of the identity of the children and their citizenship. The Nepali civil code mandates only the father's lineage for citizenship and children cannot get citizenship rights through their mothers. So the national identity and the citizenship of children become crucial issues of concern.

The death and disappearance of men, and desertion by men are worsening phenomena resulting in increase of 'singlehood of women' as widows, half-widows, and single mothers. This category of women is found to be shunned by the families and by society. The question of assimilation of these women into society as dignified citizens becomes a challenge due to the existing sociocultural norms of Nepali society.

Displacement of families and individuals could be in the millions by now. The question of these people having to be in-country refugees is a reality. However, they cannot access international support extended to refugees due to the legitimacy of their status as refugees. On the other hand, the government has done nothing for this category of displaced people.

Political Economy of the Armed Conflict and Militarization

Although women at large are oblivious to the whole political economy of armed conflict and militarization, all women in key positions of power stressed that there was interplay of national and international power games both in terms of polity of warfare and the economy of warfare and that all the players were men. These women saw that the game of divide and rule had been played by international forces, and that the leadership of all the players involved was dancing to the tunes of those outside forces. Further, they felt that there were those who made economic gain from the militarization of conflict. These agents were both national and international. It was especially so for Nepal, which does not manufacture arms and ammunition.

After the experiment with multi-party democracy in 1990, Nepal announced a state of emergency for the first time in 2001. Historically, the Royal Nepal Army looked after national security and the Nepal Police civilian law and order. The emergence of armed insurgency necessitated the creation of a third military order named the Nepal Armed Police Force to counter the armed insurgency in civilian guise. However, the subsequent result of the armed insurgency becoming more bloody forced the government to use the Nepalese military in countering insurgency. All these induced expansion in the militarization and diversion of resources in the name of strengthening the peace and security of the country, which called for a manifold increase in military expenses. Furthermore, financial demands for reconstruction of the destroyed social and economic infrastructure such as schools, health posts, bridges, communications, and electricity, among other things added to the strain on the already-overburdened state coffers. The review of the national budget allocation from a gender perspective reveals reduction in development expenditure in general, and that on women-focused programmes in particular. This way, women have been impacted indirectly due to reduction of the budget or elimination of women-targeted/pro-women development programmes.

Conclusion

It is clear that whatever little gains were made for women post-1990 have been washed away as an effect of the protracted conflict. Owing to the feminization of poverty and the existing gender discrimination, women in general bear profound negative impacts of the armed conflict. As the identity and the very existence of women are generally tied to their menfolk, the varying nature of their relationships impact different categories of women differently as mothers, widows, and adolescent girls. Further, variations in impact are also found to depend on which warring faction the man is aligned or not aligned with. This calls for identification of differential treatment or intervention to women of different categories.

It is evident that in the whole process of insurgency, counter-insurgency, militarization, and the peace initiative, women have been treated only as 'victims of armed conflict' and women's agencies in the whole nexus have been completely negated. Women are either 'invisible', or they have been completely excluded from the whole process. The only time when women have been highlighted or made visible is as 'women insurgents', specially for daring to break the stereotype. However, the present study, based primarily on the response of women who are currently within the insurgency, discloses that the roles, responsibilities, and rights seem to follow the conventional gender line. Further demystification of the gender relations within insurgency seems to be necessary.

Although women as victims in the different categories are intimately related to men of different warring factions, surprisingly, all of them (including women insurgents) have empathy for the 'women from the other side'. This seems to arise from the fact that all these women are conscious of the existing gender discrimination and women's exclusion horizontally and vertically. Embracing this empathy towards the 'other women', all women have strong feelings that 'to correct the present wrong' women should come together and take active roles in the peace-building process. This finding is very close to the feminist theory of masculinity equating with violence, and femininity equating with peace.[31] It calls for the imperative of bringing women from the periphery to the centre, and transforming them from 'non-doers' to 'active agents' to give peace a chance.

A number of women's agencies which were observed are doing remarkable work which requires personal risk taking. However, the efforts of these agencies towards relief, reconstruction/rehabilitation and their tireless actions towards peace-building do not seem to be valued by the parties concerned.

RECOMMENDATIONS

Based on the above findings, short-term and long-term recommendations are proposed as follows.

SHORT-TERM RECOMMENDATIONS

On an immediate basis, the Nepali state must provide necessary relief outreach pertaining to food, health, and education to all the displaced population, and others caught in the crossfire. The compensation policy must be revised to encompass all categories of widows of the conflict and families impacted, rather than only the families related to the security forces. The state must also ensure the facilitation of easy access to necessary legal documents like citizenship hapens, passports, and other state identification documents prioritizing women.

Additionally, the Nepali civil society must come together, organize, advocate, and demonstrate for peace and against all forms of violence from all sides, and also organize creation of alternative safety nets for the displaced and needy people.

All parties concerned should develop the culture of observing the ground realities and trying to interpret them through women's perspectives. For this, the state, civil society, and the insurgents should work together to bring affected women from the periphery to the centre of the peace-building process, because they are the ones who, at the personal level, undergo the pain of violence and conflict while for others it is only a distant reality. Hence, the Maoist party should come forward for peace initiatives and end this plight and pain of women and children.

It is high time that the state becomes ready to confer women's legal rights to citizenship on their children, lest in the very near future Nepal have a significant number of its population without citizenship. These are children born to single mothers who have been raped, deserted, and lured into false marriages.

The slow but steadily increasing number of women's agencies from the local to the national levels should be strengthened with all necessary support. These women's agencies should increasingly adopt a rights-based approach of empowerment. Women from all walks of life should take the initiative and get organized to play active roles in the whole process of peace management.

The military and other security forces must be humanized through gender sensitization (not merely as a token as in the past), to truly serve their people, which is to ensure the safety and the security of the public.

LONG-TERM RECOMMENDATIONS

In the longer term, the state must revise or redraft all discriminatory laws, including the Constitution, and enforce the implementation of all the UN conventions and treaties it has signed. Social justice and a rights-based approach must be enshrined at all levels of application and implementation, ensuring 'inclusive' and 'self-representative' nation building. The state is also responsible for putting in place a social safety net designed to suit the demands of armed conflicts benefiting all citizens not allowing anyone to fall through the loopholes of governments existing policies—most of whom will undoubtedly be women.

Additionally, all players with a state in Nepal's future will have to build consciously and at large a culture of peace (for which Nepal used to be world-renowned till the recent past). It is necessary to strengthen overall communication through education, and build skills in conducting peace negotiations, mediation and conflict resolution, counselling and healing.

NOTES

1. International Centre for Integrated Mountain Development (ICIMOD), Central Bureau of Statistics (CBS)/His Majestys Government of Nepal (HMGN) and SNV, Districts of Nepal: Indicators of Development, Kathmandu: ICIMOD, update 2003.
2. ICIMOD, CBS/HMGN and SNV, *Mapping Nepal Census Indicators 2001 & Trends*, Kathmandu: ICIMOD, 2003.
3. Ibid.
4. United Nations Development Programme, *Human Development Report 2002: Deepening Democracy in a Fragmented World*, New Delhi: Oxford University Press, 2002.
5. Ibid.
6. ICIMOD et al., op. cit., n. 2.
7. ICIMOD et al., op. cit., n. 1.
8. D. Thapa, *Understanding the Maoist Movement of Nepal*, Kathmandu: Martin Chautari, 2003.
9. K.B. Thapa, *Women and Social Change in Nepal (1951–60)*, Kathmandu, 1985.
10. C. Bhadra, 'Gendered Culture and Gendered Democracy: Maoist Insurgency and Implications on Women (A Feminist Critique)', Keynote Paper presented at the International Workshop on Cultural Exchange Between Nepal and Denmark on 'Gender and Social Change in Nepal—Political and Cultural Implications', Alborg University, Denmark, 30 September–1 October 2003.
11. Ibid.
12. Ibid.
13. Ibid.

14. Jagaran Nepal, *Fact Findings on Violation of Human Rights of Women on Conflict Areas: Case Studies from Dolakha District*, report submitted to DANIDA HOGOU, 2003.
15. S. Gautam, A. Banskota and R. Manchanda, 'Where there are No Men: Women in the Maoist Insurgency in Nepal', in *Understanding the Maoist Movement of Nepal*, ed. D. Thapa, Kathmandu: Martin Chautari, 2003, pp. 93–124.
16. Ibid.
17. Ibid.
18. Sharmila Karki, 'Conflict Affected Women', presentation during the national consultation on preparation of the CEDAW Shadow Report, Kathmandu, 24–25 September 2003.
19. R. Thapa and A. Shrestha, *Fact Finding Study on Conflict Widows*, Kathmandu: Nagarik Aawaz, 2003.
20. Bhadra, op. cit., n. 10.
21. 'Increasing Under Age Marriage of Girls Because of the Fear of Maoists', *Rajdhani*, 30 January 2003.
22. Ibid.
23. 'Six Adolescents Abducted From Cowshed', *Kantipur Daily*, 25 February 2004.
24. 'Even After Truce Daughter and Sisters Did Not Reach Home', *Rajdhani*, 29 March 2003.
25. 'Women's Pain in 30 VDCs Sans Men', *Rajdhani*, 30 January 2003.
26. S. Gautam, A. Banskota and R. Manchanda, 'Where there are No Men: Women in the Maoist Insurgency in Nepal', in Manchanda, R., ed., *Women, War and Peace in South Asia: Beyond Victimhood to Agency*, New Delhi: Sage, 2001.
27. Bhadra, op. cit., n. 10.
28. 'Revolutionary *Muna* Killed After Rape', *Saptahik Disti*, 31 March 2003.
29. 'Main Target Women in Government–Maoist Conflict', *Rajdhani*, 19 July 2002.
30. Ibid.
31. J. Galtung, 'Woman: Man = Peace: Violence?', *Peace by Peaceful Means: Peace and Conflict, Development and Civilization*, Oslo: Sage, 1996, Ch. 3.

5. Post-9/11: Terror, Terrorists and Women

Saba Gul Khattak

For us, the sky and earth are both spitting fire,' said Dilawar Khan, sitting next to his four injured children at a local hospital. 'From the sky, helicopters are targeting us, and from the ground the mujahideen are firing. We poor tribesmen are sandwiched between the Al-Qaeda and Pakistani forces.

OWAIS TOWHID, 'The New Frontier', *Newsline*, April 2004

INTRODUCTION

Systems of governance and their linkage with the legitimate or illegitimate use of violence by states, armed groups or other organizations impact peace options and the future roadmap for a peaceful world. To understand security in its multiple meanings, the intersections between structural (often institutionalized) forms of violence and direct violence need to be understood. Often, women's concerns are overlooked both in the context of the effects of violence and their requirements for peace.

Specifically, this paper examines post-9/11 impacts of the US-led global war on terror in what is designated as Pakistan's 'tribal areas' that border Afghanistan. This paper provides the historical and political background within which we need to develop our understanding of the present violence and conflict generated by

*I am most grateful to Saleem Shah at Sustainable Development Policy Institute (SDPI) for his help with collecting the information for this paper and for continuously discussing different dimensions of the issues involved. I am equally grateful to Aimal Khan Khattak for providing me material for this paper (acknowledged specifically within the paper) and for his insights. Thanks are also due to the students of Gomal University who helped fill a survey questionnaire for SDPI with displaced women from Wana.

the global war on terror between the Pakistan Army and local inhabitants of the tribal areas. This writer asserts that the present-day violence in the tribal territories is an intermesh of past and present-day 'terrorisms' spawned not only indigenously, but with the critical interventions and support of US funding and strategies.[1]

After providing the background of the area and its relationship with the centre, this paper specifically analyses the impacts of the global war of terror in two contexts: the first attempts to connect the discursive representations of these tribal areas with the past and highlights the continuity in their representation in British colonial and Pakistani discourse. Further, it asserts that colonial-style renderings that kept emerging in the discourse on the Wana Operations in the tribal areas during 2004 perpetuate the justification for the exercise of violence in these areas without confronting the thorny issues of human rights and structural violence. Second, and equally importantly, this paper places women from the tribal areas in the overall context of the recent conflict in the area by attempting to highlight the unaccounted impact on ordinary women's lives there. This paper, thus, analyses the recent military operations in the tribal areas, and argues that the archaic colonial laws that still apply to these areas (together with local customs) reinforce women's invisibility.

Political considerations, ranging from local micro-level concerns to grand mega-strategies, are formed in response to various events. This complexifies every phenomenon forcing us to seek the historical, social, cultural, political, and economic developments of the region. Does the post-9/11 time signify a greater degree of violence than that which we have encountered in our past? We have intimate histories of violence that form part of our collective memory, because the defining moments in the formation of our identities are ridden with metaphors of violence, whether 1857, 1947, 1971, 1974 in Balochistan, and post-1985 in Sindh. We need to take a closer look at our history and our relationship with that past, both in the context of politics and of development. The Wana Operations, in this regard, appear to be a continuation of the historical manner of dealing with political problems, and simultaneously outlines new contours in international politics.

When the global war against terror was initiated in response to 9/11, America's first strike, the indiscriminate bombing of Afghanistan, was understood by few Afghans to be about making the world safe from terror. For many, it was a continuation of the 22-year conflict that they had been subjected to, but with a difference: the intensity had been unknown before. This was followed by the invasion of Iraq. In both cases, the world—or at least the US—was to be made safe from terrorism. The global war against terror follows in the footsteps of the Cold War in that it is a replacement. The Afghanistan context provides the continuity between the two political eras in that the US fought a proxy war in Afghanistan to finally oust and dismantle the Soviet empire, and then came back to bomb Afghanistan to punish it for the terrorist attacks upon the US. While the first 'war' (the Cold War) was against the Soviet Union and its satellite states, the second is aimed against the Muslim world.[2] The Afghan case constitutes a convenient link. It was here that the Soviet Union met with its Armageddon fighting the US-backed Afghan resistance. It was also here that the US created and later destroyed the conservative Islamic government constituted by the Taliban that became a symbol of the values that need to be destroyed if the US and the Western world are to be made secure.

What is the connection of the war against terror with the tribal areas? Briefly, this area borders Afghanistan and served as a 'launching pad' to initiate military resistance to the different Soviet-backed governments (1980–92), and later the internecine fighting within the mujahideen (1992–6). After ousting the Taliban from power in 2001/2, the US installed the Karzai government in Kabul (2002–present), whose writ does not extend much beyond the capital, resistance and internal strife having continued within Afghanistan. The Taliban and their various sympathizers, who crumbled under US firepower, took refuge in the tribal areas of Pakistan. They knew the terrain well, having received their training there earlier during the Afghan imbroglio. With pressure from the US, the Pakistan government, that till recently had supported these 'jihadis', changed its stance and took on the responsibility of 'flushing out' Al-Qaeda men and their supporters. The process involved violent military interventions in the areas at the behest of the US FBI since June 2002 leading to a heavy casualty rate and the death of over a hundred people on both sides. Aside from the violence, a large number of houses were damaged by the bombing, or occupied by the soldiers and those were broken into or looted for personal gain. These incidents raise fundamental questions of state-society relations in post-colonial contexts and questions regarding women's status and rights as well as their security in conflict situations within the backdrop of masculinist politics in their extreme forms.

Below, we discuss the larger context of the Frontier Province politics followed by a section on literature review. A chronology of the events that took place in Wana during 2004 and where sporadic fighting continued to be reported throughout that year and into 2005 is provided. Finally, we discuss the implications for women and children, whose voices have been next to impossible to record, but who are, nevertheless, silent witnesses to violent change in their own lives. Women's views are derived from a survey conducted by Sustainable Development Policy Institute (SDPI) and the issues reported in the press.

HISTORICAL BACKGROUND OF THE AREA (OR, THE LARGER MASCULINIST FRAMEWORK)

The tribal areas were divided into two: the Federally Administered Tribal Areas (FATA); and the Provincially Administered Tribal Areas (PATA). Pakistan's tribal belt has been traditionally considered to be the buffer between Afghanistan and Pakistan. The Durand Line, established by the British with Amir Abdur Rehman Khan, the first ruler of the modern Afghan state, signed in 1893, was an arbitrary border drawn to demarcate Afghanistan and what today are Pakistan's North-West Frontier Province and Balochistan. While Afghanistan was maintained as the buffer between tsarist areas of influence and British areas of influence in the 'Great Game', the British further created another arbitrary line between what came to be called the 'settled districts' and the 'tribal areas'. The 'tribal areas' in a sense constituted a buffer between Afghanistan and the British Indian empire. In so doing, the British ensured that Afghan incursions into British India would be limited through the maintenance of the 'tribal system', thereby absolving the British India government of the necessity to maintain armies along the frontiers. The differentiation was cemented through administrative arrangements and resulted in the direct control of the British over the 'settled areas' and indirect control exercised through the appointment of a political agent to the territory. The tribal areas, in their role as a buffer, were spared (colonial) state interference and continued to practice traditional ways of governance. The structures for justice, governance, and legislation depended upon centuries-old traditions and codes of conduct known as *Pukhtunwali*, exercised through the *jirgas* (a council of village and tribal elders) that existed at different levels. The British formalized this system by setting up a system whereby Maliks and *lungi*-holders (wrap around cloth wear by men) were paid a stipend by the government when they were granted recognition as chiefs or influential men by the British India government and made responsible for the maintenance of their respective areas. The institution of *khassadars* (local police), who bore responsibility for maintaining law and order, was established; in addition, each tribe was also awarded a specific number of jobs in the local militia. If a tribesman violated the Frontier Crimes Regulation (FCR), his fellow tribesmen would not be paid their monthly salaries, and in extreme cases, could be dismissed. Similarly, the practice of demolishing houses was cemented through the FCR. Thus, policing, defence, and political governance were conveniently ensured.

Pakistan chose to continue with this arrangement when Jinnah signed the Instrument of Accession with the Bannu Tribal *Jirga* in January 1948. The settled areas, on the other hand, experienced a different form of political development under British colonialism, whereby they were under the direct rule of the centre. As such, they were the beneficiaries of the political rights that were slowly and grudgingly granted to the subject peoples. In addition, the British laid down the canal irrigation system around the River Indus that created new prosperity for many districts and won the British the loyalty of the local elite. Thus, the economic and political histories of the two parts became very divergent even before the creation of Pakistan in 1947. As the Pakistan government chose to continue with the status quo regarding the tribal areas, and continues to implement the FCR of 1901 to date, little has changed by way of economic and political development for the ordinary people. Few schools and health facilities exist. 'The literacy rate in FATA for men is 18.09 and a miserable 0.79 per cent for women.' (ibid.) The development figures for the area are even worse than those of the Frontier Province, which is among the worst-off provinces of Pakistan.

The concept of 'settled areas' and 'tribal areas' was a construct, which created and reproduced the ways in which the British looked at this area and these representations spilled over into post-colonial Pakistan. For example, though the people of these areas had their centuries-old laws and codes of conduct, due to the inapplicability of all colonial British laws there, the area was referred to as *Ilaqa Ghair* (Outsiders' Area, implying Outlaw Territory) and the people as lawless, underscoring British perceptions, rather than local ones, of the times. Recent reports have also repeatedly referred to the tribal areas as the 'wild West', thereby reproducing British perceptions. It is true that not all British and later Pakistani law and systems governance applied here, but that is a different issue coming out of different political arrangements.

The different rules and regulations for the tribal areas under the FCR ensured that security and order was maintained through the elaborate systems put in place, which, in some instances, only extended to the roads in the areas. The writ of the government did not extend beyond the roads. Hence, anyone committing a crime (vendetta has always been common) could escape to the tribal belt, request refuge, and live in the hard terrain as an outlaw. Hired assassins would often gun down the escapee/criminal involved in vendettas. The political agent, through his network of spies, would usually know who was in hiding and the protection money that was involved. It is this tradition that many people allude to when they discuss tribal traditions and their critique. Afrasiyab Khattak maintains that harbouring terrorists or giving them refuge in the tribal areas could not be possible without the tacit permission or knowledge of the political agent. Thus, the presence of hundreds of foreign terrorists in the area could not continue had the Pakistan government disapproved of it. He maintains that the Pakistan government's intelligence agencies were supporting and maintaining the Taliban and their sympathizers as 'strategic assets' for Pakistan in the negotiations with the Kabul government. Ironically, it appears that Islamabad and Kabul have reversed their roles with regard to the treatment of the tribal areas. Sana Haroon asserts that the absence of modern state structures created a vacuum and given the appeal of religion, the mullahs (clergy) gained a far greater foothold than would have been their due had other institutions been present in the area.

Pakistan's uneasy relations with Kabul also played a significant role in the lives of local people living in the tribal areas. Afghanistan was the last UN member to grant Pakistan recognition in 1947 when Pakistan was created, because Afghanistan had claims over territory that belonged to Pakistan. The different tribes in the tribal areas were granted special favours by the governments in Afghanistan; they had representation in the Afghan civil bureaucracy and had seats reserved for them in the Afghan parliament. The implication was that this territory belonged to Afghanistan. In the late 1950s till the early 1970s, Afghanistan and the USSR also funded a movement for an independent Pukhtunistan (land/country of the Pukhtuns) comprising areas belonging to Pakistan. This had its basis in the different resistance movements launched in the tribal areas against the British from time to time. Kabul-based Radio Pukhtunistan used to air a national anthem for Pukhtunistan as well as programmes in Pushtu even in the 1970s. The lure of Pukhtun identity and rebellion against the Punjabi-dominated centre created ambivalence among the Pukhtuns and Punjabis that continues to play a role, albeit a dormant one, at present. It made many Pakistanis suspect and stereotype the Pukhtuns as traitors who wanted to break away. It divided the Pukhtuns over which side they wanted to be. All this changed once the Soviet Army physically entered Afghanistan in December 1979. Afghan Pukhtuns were now used as the main resistance to the Soviet occupation of Afghanistan. They received refugee status, with material aid ranging from food, shelter, health and education facilities, weapons, money and other supplies to indoctrination and training to fight modern warfare in the name of jihad in Afghanistan. Women and children suffered specially through this terrible period, because their conditions and agency were often unrecognized. It comes as no surprise then that there were a number of 'foreigners' who had received indirect patronage from different countries:

> There are many other foreign mujahideen, particularly from Uzbekistan and Chechniya, who settled down in the tribal belt after the first Afghan War. Since the region was used as a 'launching pad' into Afghanistan for thousands of anti-Soviet mujahideen, trained and funded by Pakistani and American intelligence agencies, fighters, who over the years became familiar with the terrain, never left. And two decades later, these foreign fighters were no longer seen as aliens by local residents. But it was only after September 11 and the ouster of the Taliban by US forces that the ideological bonding between the locals and the Al-Qaeda fighters turned into a real relationship. '*They look like Waziristanis now. The foreign mujahids residing here wear the traditional dress, speak fluent Pashto, and follow our traditions*,'[emphasis mine] said a tribesman, Saeed Wazir, himself a former mujahid. 'Some of them do farming, others do jihad, but all of them are pure Islamists. They have never harmed Pakistan.' (Towhid 2004, p. 35)

As mentioned earlier, given this state of affairs, and the installation of the Karzai government in Kabul by the US, for the first time tribes from the border find Kabul to be hostile towards them. Thus, escaping into Afghanistan, receiving any material or moral support are not options for these mujahideen. Until recently, they enjoyed the tacit support of the Pakistan government, but amid reports of Pakistan's support for the ousted Taliban and their connections with the Al-Qaeda, and, therefore, 9/11, Pakistan has been under pressure from the US to purge the tribal belt of 'terrorists'. The ISPR (Inter-Services Public Relations) has used terminology akin to the US when talking about the tribal areas by claiming to have 'flushed out' the terrorists who were 'holed up' in the harsh terrain. Meanwhile, this policy and the accompanying attitude created rifts within Pakistan and the people of the tribal areas of Pakistan. Mehbat Khan expresses his sense of alienation regarding the Wana Operations:

> It is an attack against Pakistan-loving tribesmen and our motherland; it is the same thing the *goras* [fair-skinned people; Westerners] did during British times . . . we never expected it from our own forces. Look at the misery the operation is causing among civilians. Not every

tribesman is involved with Al-Qaeda and they cannot all be punished for somebody else's sin or crime. (Mehbat Khan, reported by Towhid, p. 28).

Although Mehbat Khan asserts that not every tribesman is Al-Qaeda, some people from the area have joined the Al-Qaeda. Therefore, Al-Qaeda not only consists of foreigners but also of Pakistanis. This is in contradistinction to the Pakistani media and official descriptions that consistently repeat that local people have given the 'terrorists' refuge, but that the local people are not part of the Al-Qaeda; the myth/stereotype that only Arabs (with a few Chechen and other foreign fundamentalist militant groups) are its members is constantly reproduced. The politics of 'othering' through the creation of the category terrorists = non-Pakistanis is effected, thus distancing Pakistanis from Al-Qaeda. But gaps or aporia in this discourse of othering and distancing keep appearing that present a different interpretation of events which challenges the categories of terrorist and non-terrorist, Pakistani and foreigner, Pukhtun and Muslim identities vis-à-vis a Pakistani identity, us and them. For example, the above quote indicates that many of the foreigners had integrated into the local culture and were accepted as such. There were intermarriages not only among the foreigners and Pakistanis but also their children. It also appears that for many local people, the unifying element were Islamic and Pakhtun nationhoods (though the foreigners were Chechen or Arabs, they were all Muslim, and adopted local dress and spoke the local language) rather than Pakistani nationhood. The primacy of Pakhtun and Muslim identities over a Pakistani identity creates the image of 'us' and 'them' in both official and local discourses.

The process of othering created by the official political discourse is contested and assimilated in a complex manner. The presence of local (Pakistani) recruits to Al-Qaeda, intermarriages, the physical presence through settling down of the foreigners' foreign/Arab widows, and the acceptance of the foreigners by the locals as being part of the local landscape indicate the existence of contested realities. The resultant clashes, not only at the discursive level but also in real-life violent politics, have, thus, not only resulted in death and destruction, but also cemented the ideological walls that have been created following 9/11.

The different representations of the Wana Operations on either side have one overwhelming point in common: the absence of any discourse on or from women of the areas. There is little space within the complex political identity issues, largely dictated by male-centred 'high' politics that does not provide any weight to aspects concerned with women, both in their concrete physical reality as well as at the ideational level. Most reports and representations have concentrated on providing details about the weapons used, the strategies and tactics executed by the opposing sides, the deadliness of intent and threat emanating from either side, the level of death and destruction as indications of the relative power at the disposal of each side. Simultaneously, the two sides are depicted as equally threatening: one backed by state power and the unmatched military power of the US and the other by the covert but 'high-tech' tactics employed by a secretive, well-organized, petrodollar-backed web-like organization with tentacles all over the world and manned by professional and ideologically driven minds. Such depictions leave little space and importance for everyday issues facing ordinary women and fade into nothingness in the face of the immediacy and intensity of conflict situations and their reportage.

THEORETICAL LITERATURE REVIEW

The well-known political philosopher Hannah Arendt (1969) wrote about the relationship between violence, power, and authority, asserting that the first two are mutually destructive, that is, that violence destroys power and indicates its loss. Why is it important to understand the underpinnings of violence in our society? What is our history of engagement with different types of violence? We enter difficult terrain when we begin to debate the legitimate right of a state or government to exercise violence against its own people (whether in civil wars, secessionist struggles, or supposed terrorism) or those of another state (as in situations of war and armed conflict). Violence in its so-called legitimate context is exercised by the state and may or may not be questioned. It has limits on it and is circumscribed by law, making it possible for citizens to challenge an act of violence. Violence that may be currently acceptable might not be so with the wisdom of hindsight.

To analyse the Wana Operations within the immediate 9/11 context, we need to understand the relationship between state and society in Pakistan. This relationship needs to be problematized not only in its colonial and post-colonial contexts, but also before Western colonialism. After all, the latter relied upon an existing blueprint and then executed changes in it. If the state, in Pakistan's context, has acquired unbridled power vis-à-vis its people, the roots can be traced to the pre-colonial 'Western' period when governance arrangements were localized. Conquests from neighbouring areas and regions took place without too many changes in the local structures of governance. The onset of the Mughal conquest of India saw some changes in governance arrangements as systems of taxation and land tenure—which was maintained through the construction of roads for purposes of communication and control. These systems coalesced under British colonialism, whereby increasingly the centre connected with the remotest parts of the country through the construction of railroads and roads. The codification and formalization of legal structures, some adapted from British laws, ensured the existence of competing governance structures at the grassroot and higher levels. These arrangements varied, but one can assert that while local patterns of governance were selectively allowed to operate in some areas, other areas were completely absorbed under the centre and empire. The patterns of centralized state structures, deeply inscribed with ambivalence towards local people in general came to be formalized. The colonized Indian population was seen at once to be immature, unenlightened, crafty, untrustworthy, and unreliable.

How was colonial discourse enacted in the Frontier Province? The answer provides a critical insight into the continuity of the past with the present as one sees the specific employment of language to provide justification for a particular way of seeing and acting. These connections between present-day discourse and the past underscores the continuous othering of the Frontier to justify the treatment meted out to its people, which would otherwise have been considered unacceptable in Britain in the past and in Pakistan today. For example, in many instances, colonial discourse about the Frontier Province resonates with metaphors of a hunt, underscoring a relationship of the conqueror/hunter with its prey that has to be civilized and changed. This spilled over into post-colonial arrangements. Such imagining resonates in interviews with high officials. For example, Lt. Gen. Safdar Hussain, in charge of the Wana Operations, said, 'They are professional fighters who exercise great patience as they lie in wait for their prey' (Towhid, 2004, p. 28). Similar statements have also been issued by various state functionaries at different points, while the political agent in the different tribal territories has behaved like his predecessor in British times. Additionally, just like terrorism on the one hand and predefined rules of violence by the state on the other hand are predictable in their symbiotic relationship with one another, a different set of criteria apply to 'tribal' and 'pre-modern' societies (Mamdani 2004). When a particular set of people are equated with being pre-modern, it gives the state the authority to treat them as subhuman because they are assumed to be without any standards of modern conceptions of justice. In a sense then, it is all right to apply different rules of justice and violence to such societies. Such an institutionalization of violence is not endemic to the Waziristan issue. We find varying echoes coming from other parts of South Asia.

Neloufer de Mel, writing about the Sri Lankan state, explains how violence was institutionalized in Sri Lanka:

> The UNP government was able to act with such impunity because violence had been a systematic tool of socio-political control by the state in both colonial and post-colonial Sri Lanka. As marked in the introduction to this book, it had operated under several states of Emergency. But from 1977 onwards, under the leadership of President J.R. Jayawardena, the systemic use of violence for political gains became heightened. The landslide electoral victory of J.R. Jayawardena and the UNP in 1977, as well as the new Constitution of 1978 which ushered in a Presidential system to Sri Lanka with wide executive powers for the President gave the party a sense of untrammeled power. It institutionalized violence as a defining aspect of the state apparatus as never before.

In a more or less similar manner, we see a strengthening of the state and its coercive apparatuses in Pakistan, whereby, increasingly, violence has been used to settle political and economic differences. Such practices impact in multiple ways, ranging from economics and development to formal arrangements between the people and the state—the social contract. The increasing use of violence as an instrument of policy indicates a breakdown of the social contract. Thus, the question raised at the beginning of this section becomes critical: the relationship between violence and power. Furthermore, when the state is variously depicted as the protector (e.g. the patriarch, the home/place of security), its relationship becomes even more problematic vis-à-vis the people whose bodies and homes and environments are inscribed with violence, e.g. violent deaths, torture, rape, and the element of a public/open spectacle when conflict sanctions destruction and violence to take place. In these encounters, retaliation from the other side often involves the same tactics also (de Silva, 1997: 23–4).

Feminists have analysed the state extensively, pointing to its limitations not only from the angle of political economy, but from a feminist women-centred context. They point out to the collusion between patriarchy and capitalism and assert that the former is the pillar through which the edifice of the state and exploitation are maintained. Many feminist writers have likened the state to the patriarch at home and assert that the role that it plays is similar, i.e. the family is a microcosm of the state, and both structures are important for the maintenance of a particular 'order' that works to the systematic disadvantage of women. This 'order' ensures that the dichotomy between the public and private spheres and gendered hierarchies are maintained, and that women's unpaid labour in the home continues. Further, it ensures women's subordinate role in almost all contexts, ranging from unequal wages to unequal rights. The edifice of the state and inequality are maintained not only through mystification of the power structures, but also through elaborate mechanisms that persuade people to treat the state as home with all its connotations of protection and shelter. Thus, for example, citizenship with its related paraphernalia of identity cards and passports that provide the means to leave or enter a country, the existence of the police force (for internal order) and the militaries (for maintaining the boundaries and identity of the state) all help to reinforce that the state is the ultimate patriarch and home:

Home entails a sense of belonging, a sense of identity, a sense of security, a sense of grounding and a sense of rootedness. All these associations, with home are experienced in both a narrow and broad sense; narrow in the sense of being restricted to the structure of a house and an individual, and broad in the sense of a community, a place or country, and a broader or deeper sense of being—of collective identity immersed in a culture, a time, a history and a civilization. (Khattak, 2002, p. 2)

I believe that one of the central themes in the context of any kind of conflict is the centrality of home and its connections with security. When one is forced to abandon one's home or when it is destroyed as a result of conflict, a fundamental human need is being targeted. This destruction and threat to the home is a central theme of all conflicts, and has the deepest impact on women and children because it is a clear invasion of the private sphere and poses a direct threat to individual security. In the context of the Wana Operations, people's houses were razed under the provisions of the FCR, as if this was business as usual. It was justified on the basis of past practice; no one was expected to question or object to the practice, since it had the sacrosanct consent of time and codification. Taking war from the public into the private sphere has its repercussions:

The construction of gender renders women's and men's experience of violence and, therefore, lives very different from one another. While men are usually engaged with the public sphere, in the present context with political activity or its suppression, women are often the ones who suffer the consequences of these moves or counter moves. A larger politics, whereby the state as well as political parties negotiate at the community level and upwards, controls the parameters for action among and between men. (Khattak, 2002, p. 2)

Women's invisibility in matters of violent conflict, thus, acts to their disadvantage because they do not have a voice in the initiation, negotiation or settlement process, while this violence affects and impacts their lives deeply. This combination of being passive recipients of a fate that is not for them to inscribe, where their voices do not receive any space, makes it imperative to underscore the need for changing the way we view and understand politically motivated conflict.

What I wish to underscore here in the context of Wana is that, first, the Pakistani state has treated this area in the colonial manner in which the British treated it; second, the present-day violence witnessed in the area is perceived to be carried out by the Pakistan Army at the behest of the US for the sake of regime continuation rather than any other motive; third, women are worse off than the men of the area due to the structural and customary forms of discrimination that together push them further back than the women belonging to the rest of Pakistan.

CHRONOLOGY OF THE WANA OPERATIONS

The Pakistan Army launched four major operations in the tribal areas from 11 September 2001. The first began on 27 June 2002, the second on 2 October 2003, the third on 8 January 2004, and the fourth on 16 March (Nuri, 2005, p. 131). The first three operations involved the death of at least 30 soldiers, although it is said that the military has not released the exact figures of those killed and injured to avoid demoralization in the Armed Forces. Further, this does not indicate the loss of civilian lives and injuries as well as damage to property and the environment, and the social impact on people's lives such as the closure of schools, water supply and health facilities.

This section provides a chronology of the Wana Operations conducted in March 2004 to capture the dramatic manner in which the situation changed for ordinary people living in the area, and to convey the intensity of violence and resultant insecurity.[3]

- Started on 16 March 2004, stopped on 28 March 2004.
- Began in a limited area of Kalo Shah, 12 km. from Wana, south Waziristan, later spread to an area of 60 sq. km. and most of the area remained under curfew-like situation. The area was cordoned off and house-to-house search was conducted.
- The Wana Operations have been described as the biggest hunt ever launched against 'foreign terrorists' in . . . south Waziristan (Towhid, 2004, p. 23).
- Officials said that some 400–500 'foreign terrorists' [Uzbeks, Chechens, Arabs] were engaged in the fighting. Local tribal sources estimate their number at 600 and state that in

addition to these fighters there were some 2,000–2,500 Al-Qaeda local tribesmen, trained and recruited by the foreign militants (ibid., pp. 24, 28).

- Schools and hospitals were closed and were used by the Forces.
- According to the AFP report of 17 March (also published in many newspapers on 18 March), due to the tension, a large number of tribesmen started shifting their families from Azam Warsak, Sarkai Khel, Karmzai station, Ghawai Khwa, and Zhera Ghunday areas to safer places. On 17 March itself, more than 500 persons left the area either by vehicle or on foot. Ali Shah, a local resident, told the media that they were leaving the area, fearing aerial bombing.
- Naseemullah, a local class nine student, told the BBC Urdu Service on 18 March that fighters and gunship helicopters were continuously patrolling the area by air. Schools were closed down. People were tense. They were facing problems in shifting women and children from the conflict-hit areas to safe places.
- Surat Khan, a local resident, said that the Pakistan Army had desecrated the sanctity of *chadar* [the outer garment of a woman] and *chardeewari* [the household].
- According to a report published on 19 March in *Ummat* (Karachi), the mosque's loudspeaker was used at 7 a.m. on 18 March to warn the local people to vacate the areas by 8:30 a.m., later extended to 10:00 a.m. The announcement caused panic among the locals. Hundreds of men, women and children and the aged came out from their houses in search of safe places. They used trucks, tractor trolleys, jeeps and even donkeys as modes of transportation, while some left the area on foot. Some people preferred to stay. Then, at 9:30 a.m., without warning and without waiting for the deadline to pass, the army started shelling the area, and at 10 a.m. a full-fledged attack was launched. Some houses were attacked, around 12 civilians killed, and some women and children also injured. Due to a bombshell hitting a house in Kazha Panga, Azam Warsak area, three persons were killed and six injured. According to a report on 20 March in *Ummat*, migration from the area was still going

on and the number reached 60,000. There was a curfew-like situation in the area and the communication systems were disrupted. Due to the shelling, the Gomal Public School, the only high-standard educational institution in the area, with 800 students on its rolls, was completely destroyed. To reach safer places, people were using unfrequented and tough routes due to the security problems on ordinary routes.

- '46 military and paramilitary personnel lost their lives in a fortnight of combat, in which the government claimed to have killed 63 militants and captured 166, among them 73 foreigners. And that's not all. Several innocent civilians were killed in the crossfire, around 100 houses of "errant" tribesmen were demolished and 100,000 of a population of 160,000 tribesmen were displaced . . .' (Rehana Hakim).
- The UNHCR refused to undertake relief measures for the Wazir tribesmen displaced by the operation against Al-Qaeda, stating that their help to the IDPs in Afghanistan was a totally different matter as 'there was no functional central government in Afghanistan. In Pakistan's case, there is a functional central authority', said Jack Redden, the UNHCR spokesperson.
- On the day the Frontier Corps *jawans* (men) were ambushed, some of them were killed by the rockets that hit them. They returned the fire, and bodies of slain militants could be seen on the ground (Towhid, 2004, p. 24).
- In the deadliest attack 12 [soldiers] were killed when a convoy carrying military supplies was attacked. Eight bullet-riddled bodies of soldiers were later found in a well. The authorities received yet another setback when they recovered the bodies of two kidnapped administration officials riddled with bullets from a well, despite an agreement that the militants would release them (Towhid, 2004, p. 32).
- According to a report on 22 March in *Ummat*, as the result of firing by a gunship helicopter, 13 civilians were killed in Dog, near Wara Ghunday.
- According to a report on 22 March in *Ummat*, authorities asked the residents of Shah Alam village on 22 March to vacate the area. In Wocha Wana, the authorities started demolishing 400 houses of the Yargul Khel and Ali Khel

tribes. Around 2,000 shopkeepers belonging to the Yargul Khel tribe were served notices for demolition of shops in Wana. The tribesmen were asked to surrender the wanted persons to the authorities, or face closure of their businesses and the demolition of their shops. Most of the shops in Wana, agency headquarters of south Waziristan agency, remained closed due to this, and the shopkeepers were busy transporting valuable goods from the shops.

- According to a report on 29 March in *Ummat*, Malik Anwar Ali, a local tribal elder from Wana, told the BBC Urdu Service on 28 March, that due to the end of the blockade and opening of roads, and the result of the agreement between the militants and authorities, people started returning to their homes. He added that those returning to their homes said that they saw bodies and injured lying on the ground. He said these bodies were of those who probably wanted to flee the area but became prey to firing. He said that more than two dozen civilians were killed in the operation. Due to the firing, about 150 houses were partially or completely damaged. The security chief for Federally Administered Tribal Areas (FATA), Brig. Mehmood Shah (retd.) told the media on 28 March that 60 suspects were killed, 163 arrested, and 83 houses demolished during the operation. According to independent sources, the majority of those killed and arrested were locals.
- Two students, Mansoor and Daud of Iqra Public School, Azam Warsak, arrested on 16 March had still not been released. It has to be mentioned that despite repeated appeals and contacts with the higher authorities by Mohammad Nawaz, principal of the school, the names were not included in the list of 50 persons agreed on 24 April to be released in a grand *jirga*.

Issues Emerging in the Context of Women and Children

This section highlights two aspects about women's lives. The first analyses some of the issues that women face in the light of the overarching historical discursive contexts. Here, the absence of women's voices in the public sphere and their double oppression is raised. The second aspect, depending upon a small survey questionnaire (hereon referred to as the SDPI Survey, 2004) and the few available press reports, attempts to capture women's everyday concerns as well as the effects of politically motivated direct violence in Wana. Specifically, the latter deals with the effects of loss of home (whether through deliberate destruction as a matter of policy, or bombing, or due to looting and pillaging), changes in everyday life during the conflict and subsequent displacement, the fate of women due to sudden marriages and widowhood.

We try and place women within the overall context of a racist discourse inherited from the British that Pakistanis (whether state officials or independent mediapersons or intellectuals and activists) reproduce unintentionally. The British discourse consists of the overall sensibility of trying to be just and fair by giving the enemy its due—an enemy that in the final analysis is unequal and needs to be civilized. Thus, the civilizing mission takes over. In all equations, this basic premise manifests itself in different ways, but the question of women is seldom raised because the hunt and civilizing mission is aimed first of all at subjecting the 'independent scoundrels' who give them a good fight for their bucks. The complete invisibility of women of the area in even colonial discourse on the tribal areas is probably because a first step was the subjugation of the men, which was to be followed by the granting of rights to the women. This is a deviation from the norm in India, whereby the white man's burden included emancipating the brown woman from the brown man's injustices.[4]

Since it was decided for reasons of expediency to keep the tribal areas as a buffer between British India and Afghanistan, the legal arrangements were different. Tribal men, while being held accountable to the FCR vis-à-vis the British Indian government, were given powers over decisions pertaining to civil private matters (Aziz, 2005: 121). These were not brought within the ambit of British Indian laws. Civil/private matters pertained to the implementation of *riwaj* (customs) through a *jirga*. *Riwaj* included issues of inheritance and other practices related to women's lives such as marriage, dower, *swara* (exchange of women to settle disputes), *walwar* (bride price), and women's mobility.

The FCR ensured that the question of women did not arise in public discourse during British times. Any reference to women's rights was considered an attack against the culture and traditions of the area.[5] No further justification was needed to 'civilize' the land; therefore, women were left alone, untouched by any public discourse. Since Pakistan continued with the same policies, the Pakistan government also did not raise the question of women in any context, whether political (voting rights, the right to be elected), economic or legal rights (including right to life and other rights with regard to marriage, divorce and inheritance, education, and health). The government also did not feel the need to do something about the status of women or their oppression through customary laws such, as the practices of *swara* whereby a woman is exchanged as part of a dispute settlement with the enemy as *walwar*. The issue of past prejudices and racism combined to produce a double oppression for women of the area. They have been disadvantaged for being 'tribal', and disadvantaged again for being 'tribal and being women'. For them, both their own men and the Pakistani state are sources of inequality, as both pursue masculinist politics and discourse.

During the 1990s, human rights and women's rights activists raised the question of women's rights in the tribal areas. First raised in the context of women's political rights in the face of an agreement between political parties to disallow all women from voting in the 1990s; even at present, women are informally denied the right to vote, highlighting the patriarchal nature of politics and political parties in Pakistan. Such attitudes mark the continuities between colonial times and present-day arrangements when it comes to women's issues. Governance structures and institutions do not interfere in matters concerning women of the area.

In the context of the Wana Operations, the issue of women's rights was underscored yet again. The former chairman of the Human Rights Commission of Pakistan (HRCP) and National Awami Party leader Afrasiyab Khattak stated that, 'Women and children are present in the areas which have turned into battlefields. They deserve rights, not bombs.' Hina Jillani, a lawyer and women's rights activist stated that such operations could not be condoned merely because they were anti-terrorist in nature. Referring to the ruthless manner in which the area was bombed and houses destroyed, she said, 'It is important to emphasize the manner in which the state carries out operations' (Siddiqui, 2004).

There is an assumption that the houses of the 'tribals' can be destroyed, that they have been traditionally objects of destruction due to *jirga* decisions, later systematized under the infamous FCR, and hence do not have any rights. The very use of the word 'tribal' is pejorative, with its connotations of backwardness in every context. It is racist: associated with being pre-modern, and, therefore, subhuman. It makes it easier for government representatives to order the razing of the tribals' homes under the FCR as part of official business so that the act does not represent any violation of human rights in the minds of the administrators. No one has so far looked into how women and children are affected by this custom or law because if the 'tribals' (read men of the area) disapprove of any discussion with or about their women, then surely that must be respected. Tribal women's concerns or feelings are not allowed space to exist at the level of public discourse. They are made invisible twice. Not only does no one talk about them, no one even thinks about what they have to undergo. The masculinist systems of thought and belief in the public sphere that operate on both sides make women's concerns un-voicable, as the women themselves are denied any voice.

Home as the site for security and identity is critical, especially for women. The Wana Operations resulted in both the deliberate destruction of people's houses as punishment and also the mass displacement of over 100,000 people who had to leave their homes for safety. In the section on chronology, we have recorded that according to different accounts, between 83 and 400 houses were razed by the military as punishment to 'errant' tribesmen for not handing over the wanted terrorists. Further, notices to 2,000 shopkeepers that their shops would be burned down led to their closure, disrupting people's businesses and livelihoods. On 22 March, a mass displacement of people took place when they were warned to leave their homes in view of the operation that was to be undertaken. According to eyewitness accounts:

> Hundreds of people, including women and children, were seen leaving the scene of the Tuesday's bloodiest clashes in Kaloosha, 15 km. west of the regional headquarters Wana, and adjoining areas. 'People are fleeing the area using whatever they can get, tractors and trucks, fearing a retaliatory action from the government,' a resident reached on phone in Wana said. 'The situation is very tense,' he said. (Khan)

Many people had to leave their homes in a matter of a couple of hours at the most: under the circumstances, they carried what they could but had to leave much behind only to discover their houses pillaged, looted or used by the military in their absence. Their livestock was also either killed in the bombing or stolen. Many had to go and stay with relatives, and those who had nowhere to go took up abode under the open sky. Some old men who chose to stay behind to guard their homes were rounded up and taken by the military, which accused them of being terrorists. Some people reported (see chronology) that on their way back (after a settlement was reached), they saw the dead bodies of people killed in the bombing lying on the ground. Throughout these traumatic events, the UNHCR refused to help the internally displaced people from Waziristan (see chronology), and government agencies did little to help them either. In the end, some reported that they were sent tents by one of the most wanted men on the list of terrorists, Nek Mohammad, a Taliban sympathizer (Towhid, 2004).

The loss of home and accompanying displacement has been confirmed to lead to depression and stress.[6] In the Waziristan case, people, especially women, have also experienced depression at the loss of their homes and material possessions. Some women responded to our survey questionnaire and explained that the continuous shelling in the area and the destruction of their homes were the hardest parts of leaving home. An anonymous Afghan woman said that the most difficult aspect of leaving home was '. . . the home itself. Could there be anything more than that?' she asked (SDPI Survey, 2004). An anonymous widowed Pakistani woman said, 'Our own government and Muslim brothers expelled us from our own houses'(ibid.). Another young woman, widowed during the conflict, said that when she hears any firing she thinks a woman/women would be widowed on either side (ibid., Rukhshanda Begum). Many report that they and their children were mentally disturbed and frightened by the raids, firing and shelling which felt like 'doomsday' while they were trapped within their homes like criminals (Adil Bibi, ibid.). Some women's homes were burnt while others' were demolished, and they hold the political agent responsible for what happened. Since their displacement was forced, resulting from the suspicion that they were sheltering mujahideen,[7] they feel they were unjustly victimized for a situation in which they had no hand. This makes the financial, material and mental difficulties of displacement from their 'birthplace to an alien land' more intolerable for them. Many respondents said that they could not describe the misery they experienced, while Adil Bibi said that they were living like pitiful nomads, facing hardships all the time (ibid.). Some women reported that they were working in people's houses to obtain a few rupees, while others reported being dependent upon charity since their meagre savings went into payments for the medical treatment of their injured relatives.

Being witness to violence or being exposed to its aftermath such as decomposed bullet-ridden dead bodies produces post-traumatic stress syndrome.[8] Although no one has assessed the psychological impact of the bombing and violence upon the minds of innocent civilians, we may assume that there is differentiated impact upon children, women, men and the elderly. The SDPI Survey records a variety of responses ranging from describing the bombing and firing as the day of judgement producing hysteria in some, while others coped with it by saying that life and death were in the hands of God. Some reported that their children, specially those under five, tried to hide under the beds while others ran out to witness what was going on. One woman said that her children start crying when they hear the sounds of a helicopter. Many women reported that the closure of schools and shops led to difficulties; children were confined to homes and had no recreational activities, while they found it hard to obtain items of daily use including food with a curfew-like situation.

Many women said that their life in the 'big city' had not improved at all because they were living in an alien environment. They explained that life was hard at home also, where water and food supplies had been affected by the conflict along with their livelihood systems. For example, in some places the destruction of the *karez* system (underground waterways), that the military presumed were tunnels through which terrorists escaped, made children and old men walk miles to fetch water, which they stored and used sparingly. After the destruction of their homes, they would also expend physical labour in the rebuilding of their homes with help from their men. They did not expect any help or compensation from the government.

Politically motivated violence often results in sudden marriages for young girls. While these have been reported from Wana also, they have been reported from conflict-affected sites of Karachi in Pakistan as well.[9] It appears that there are multiple reasons for such sudden and quick marriages sans formalities. In Waziristan, the need of the men on the run appears to have guided their decision to marry their daughters off overnight as they wanted to ensure that they would have the protection of another man and family at a time when they could not protect them.[10] During the Wana Operations in March 2004, young girls were married off as well, though we have no means of knowing the number of such overnight marriages. 'After the bombing started, many Al-Qaeda mujahideen married their daughters off in a rush to the sons of tribesmen, whom they had known since the jihad against the Soviets. Dozens of weddings were arranged overnight,' said a local tribesman, Nasir Khan. Describing one of these alternate 'shotgun' marriages, he recounted, 'There was no decoration, no singing of traditional songs, no celebration. After the *nikah* was read, a meal was served, everybody offered prayers for the couple, and the evening ended with the guests taking vows to wage jihad against the US forces in Afghanistan' (Towhid, 2004). While we lack details about these marriages, they have been confirmed by the SDPI Survey as well, where some respondents report that the young girls were unhappy, some protested, while others were resigned to their fate. One respondent said that some of the young girls had been married (and widowed) twice or thrice and did not know if their husbands would return alive or not. While we do not know what their fates have been, it is clearly not unusual for young girls trapped in conflict situations to undergo marriages for which they are not mentally prepared and where they do not know how they will fare. Given that their fathers and/or brothers are on the run, the husband's family may be unkind and harsh in their attitude due to her complete dependence upon their mercy. This is an area where further investigation is required.

While some marriages took place overnight, there were others that are anomalies for the Pakistan government as they problematize women's citizenship rights. Given that the 'foreign jihadis' have lived in the area for over a decade and in some cases two decades, many settled down and the area became home. They married locally and raised their families. Now that they have become *persona non grata* and either been captured or imprisoned without the family knowing where they are or what the case against them is, some women have come forward and filed for their husband's disappearance in the local courts in Peshawar. They feel that their husbands should be produced in the courts and tried according to the law of the country. Citizenship issues further compound this situation. There are, thus, many examples of foreigners who have been more than accepted into the community, having settled down in the land. Their children cannot be denied citizenship rights even if they, the 'foreigners', are denied this right. And with the local women who are married to them exercising their right of habeas corpus [production of a person in court], the situation has become more complicated than the black and white situation that the Pakistani authorities have painted.

Equally problematic is the presence of Arab/African women in the area, many of them widows. Local people, the SDPI Survey as well as independent media affirm that there are people originally from other countries living in the area:[11]

> ... The present top-most man in Pakistan and the Pakistan Army—from former dictator, Zia-ul Haq's time—have themselves been involved in training the Taliban. In fact, they have trained not just Afghans, but also many other Muslims [involved in guerrilla warfare]. But now because Mr Bush says we are all terrorists, [we are expected to agree] our maulvi is a terrorist, our soldier is a terrorist, and our herdsman is a terrorist. These are poor people, what do they have? They have brought up to 25 helicopters in the area—for what? They claim to have arrested Al-Qaeda people. Who are they? *In fact, they*

only arrested a few Arab widows who had no spouses or sons and had taken refuge here. Where should they go?' [emphasis mine] (Rashid 2004, p. 23)

Some respondents in the SDPI Survey divulged that a few Arab/African women had married their men and become second or third wives and bore their children. They also asserted that some had independent sources of income and were better off than the local population. While a majority of the respondents were sympathetic towards the foreigners, a few said that these people should go back to their countries as their presence had caused them hardship. An anonymous Afghan woman said that they had more money and arms, and that the local people were afraid of them. Describing them as harsh and strict, she said they discouraged women from getting an education or working in the fields and orchards. They were also against the dish antennas and music, and felt that the tribal laws should be Islamized. However, a majority of the respondents said these people were mujahideen who had lived in the areas for two decades, therefore, how could they now become terrorists? (Bibi, 2004).

Umme Aiman (Bibi, 2004), originally from Sudan, said that their men abandoned them as they needed to escape. She asserted that families whose houses were razed were the ones who sent their children for jihad. She believed that their jihad against the infidels was for Allah, and therefore, their sacrifices and hardships were immaterial. She said that that though they were used to the firing and shelling, their major worry was about their children's safety. Depending upon her past savings, she said they were dependent upon friends, well-wishers and relatives to guide them, however, since most of the men were in hiding, she feared intrigues and people's greed. The latter implied that there could be spies who might tell on them.

Should these widows be forcibly sent back to their countries of origin where they can be prosecuted for marrying men who were possibly dissidents in their own country? Or, can they stay on and seek refugee status as a matter of right? Why did they make the decision to accompany their husbands into an uncertain and difficult future? How have they been able to integrate themselves into the local milieu as widowed women, without a reliable source of livelihood and social support structures? These are some of the issues that need to be explored further in order to be able to situate the lives of foreign women married to local men who are constantly on the move, fighting a war they believe is for righteous reasons in the name of Allah.

Exploring the situation of women from the tribal areas, we find out that while they share the same experience of violence in the confinement of their homes that were the targets of raids and bombing, their grief and coping mechanisms were different. While they have been displaced, their origins and roots determine the extent to which they can fall back on family for help. For the Afghan and Arab/African women, there were fewer support systems, while the Pakistani women were insecure due to their poverty. Few of them knew what had happened to their men and had to live in uncertainty, dependent upon charity while coping with their own and their children's needs and insecurities. Some were afraid of one another, while being unified in their condemnation and dislike of the Pakistan Army.

In the final analysis, their perception that they were the victims of a situation they had no hand in creating was correct. The masculinist politics whose impact they were suffering confined them to the homes that could turn into their graves. They simultaneously felt lost during the process of displacement as they were used to 'guidance' and advice from their men. The absence of the men, in their capacity as breadwinners and protectors, made them feel doubly insecure. This disruption, coupled with the mistrust within the different groups of women, was all the more hard to cope with in the absence of any financial security.

Conclusion

While the present 9/11 context would divide the world into either friends or foes, it is clear that real life situations are not so simple. This paper underscores the intricacies arising out of the mishmash of the past with the present, of the interaction between Cold War politics with present-day 9/11 considerations that have led to a reversal of who is a friend and who an enemy. There are several important implications of the Wana Operations aimed at 'flushing out' Al-Qaeda suspects from remote hideouts. These range from human rights concerns, concerns for women's and children's rights, local governance arrangements, centre-periphery relations, regional implications, and international pressures or constraints.

This paper is also concerned with the specific ways in which particular ways of representing contested realities help to justify and perpetuate violence as legitimate. The state as well as civil society in Pakistan have continued to use similar language and even words as the British used. This indicates that the processes of exacerbating violence are not only about firepower, but also about ways of seeing and of discursive representations. This paper has highlighted the continuities with racism as well as the perpetuation of inequalities within a masculinist patriarchal framework. While men from the tribal areas are treated as disposable items, their women are worse off for belonging to the areas.

Specifically for women, the dual oppression of being tribal and being women is a structural issue that urgently needs to be addressed. The destruction of homes in all the different contexts ranging from being razed under locally applicable laws that are over a century old to homes being targeted by military action and being looted afterwards, the issue of displacement and homelessness, the issue of marriages, whether quick and quiet overnight ones or of being married to the 'foreigners' and having children are all problematic aspects about the lives of women living in the area that the state will have to contend with. Issues of citizenship, specially for the children and 'foreign' husbands of local women, will need to be addressed by the state.

Most importantly, the developments emanating from the current tensions will influence the future options and arrangements of state-society relations. In this sense then, it is important to debate the Wana Operations in Pakistan in view of the larger masculinist policy background. In the final analysis, if terrorism and violence are to be rooted out, simplistic solutions such as 'smoking out' terrorists or a head-on military confrontation will not resolve anything for the state or for the so-called terrorists. To be able to understand the root causes of violence, one will need to begin with deconstructing the exercise of masculinist power in its different forms ranging from racism to the need for influence and justice. One will also have to redefine power so that it does not depend upon the hierarchies that produce and perpetuate injustices, whether among races, countries, or people. Such a task, though Herculean, will have to be undertaken, even in small ways, in order to be able to progress towards a meaningful world.

NOTES

1. I maintain that Zia-ul Haq's long rule in Pakistan was only possible with American support; his mysterious death in a plane crash is also attributed popularly to the CIA's machinations. While this belief gives too much credit to the CIA, it is not impossible to think that it might have had a role.
2. For details, see Mahmood Mamdani, *Good Muslim, Bad Muslim*, 2004.
3. I am grateful to Aimal Khan Khattak for compiling the chronology and sharing it with me.
4. For example, banning the practices of sati (widow immolation) and child marriages.
5. Such stances were used by the British to their own advantage against the kings in Afghanistan. For instance, a rebellion was incited by tribal men when King Amanullah's wife, Queen Surraya, who wore Western dress and removed the veil to come out in public in 1929. In an interesting commentary, we find that the infamous Lawrence of Arabia was instrumental in fomenting this rebellion by inciting tribal elders with stories of the king disrobing Afghan women, and, therefore, their honour (Pukhtun, 1929: 15). Thus, imperial powers (specially the men who ruled) were not averse to using the symbolic importance of women to women's disadvantage if it served their purpose. This is in contradistinction to the dominant colonial discourse that justified colonization in the name of liberating women.
6. According to Azizuddin Himmat, President of the Psychological Association of Afghanistan, 'As most of the homes of the returning Afghans have been completely demolished due to heavy fighting back home for about 25 years in some cases, now when they return to Afghanistan and find their homes in ruins, they become extremely depressed.' According to him, 98 per cent of the returning Afghan refugees suffer from psychological problems when they come to know that the houses have been reduced to rubble (staff correspondent, 'Destruction Upsetting for 98 pc Refugees', *Dawn*, 3 May 2004, p. 18).
7. Many women maintain that the mujahideen were/are not terrorists and take strong exception to the word 'terrorist'.
8. Purnaka L. de Silva, writing about political violence in Sri Lanka, asserts that Post-Traumatic Stress Syndrome (PSTT) is brought about as a result of torture and/or participation in/exposure to 'violent' actions (1997: 21).
9. See, for example, old issues of *Newsline* and *Herald* reporting about young widows of MQM activists in Karachi. Many of the young girls

were motivated by the political cause espoused by the MQM and felt they were serving their cause by marrying wanted men on the run and on government hit lists and were proud to bear the children of these men.

10. Similar marriages, but also abandonment and divorces, specially of women of Arab descent who had nowhere to go, have also been reported from the post-Taliban government phase of conflict in Afghanistan (for evidence, see interviews with Afghan refugee women in the SDPI archives on Women and Security, 2002).
11. For instance, see the chronology section for details.

REFERENCES

Aziz, Khalid, 'The Frontier Crimes Regulation (FCR) and Administration of the Tribal Areas of Pakistan', in *Tribal Areas of Pakistan: Challenges and Responses*, ed. Pervaiz Iqbal Cheema and Masudul Hasan Nuri, Islamabad: Islamabad Policy Research Institute, 2005.

de Mel, Neloufar, 'Crossing the Issues—Mother Politics and Women's Politics: Notes on the Contemporary Sri Lankan Women's Movement', in *Engaging Difference: Gender and Nationalism in 20th Century Sri Lanka*, New Delhi: Kali for Women, 2001, p. 213.

de Silva, Purnaka L., 'Hatred and Revenge Killings: Constructions of Political Violence in Sri Lanka', in *Matters of Violence*, ed. Uyongoda and Biyonwila, 1997.

Khan, Ismail, 'Reinforcements sent to Wana', *Dawn*.

Khattak, Saba Gul, 'Violence and the Centrality of Home: Women's Experience of Insecurity in the Karachi Conflict', SDPI Working Paper Series, Islamabad, 2002.

Mamdani, Mahmood, *Good Muslim, Bad Muslim: America, Cold War, and the Roots of Terror*, New York: Pantheon Press, 2004.

Nuri, Maqsudul Hasan, 'Soviet Withdrawal: Security implications for Pakistan' in *Tribal Areas of Pakistan: Challenges and Responses*, ed. Pervaiz Iqbal Cheema and Masudul Hasan Nuri, Islamabad: Islamabad Policy Research Institute, 2005.

Pukhtun 'Da Jalil Mulaa Cheetaii' (Jalil Mullah's Letter), *Pukhtun* (Pushto), April 1929, pp. 11–18.

Rashid, Haroon, 'Interview with Malik Behran Khan, Chieftain, Zalikhel tribe', *Newsline*, April 2004, p. 23.

SDPI, 'Women's Voices and Wana Operations'.

Shinwari, Sher Alam, 'So Near and Yet So Far Away' web article, accessed June 2004.

Siddiqui, Niloufer 'Human rights state dismal in Pakistan: report', *Dawn*, 19 March 2004.

Towhid, Owais, 'The Warrior Tribes', *Newsline*, April 2004, p. 35.

6. Resources or Symbols? Women and Armed Conflicts in India

*Anuradha M. Chenoy**

India has witnessed long-drawn-out armed conflicts in several regions. Of these, Kashmir and the North-East have suffered years of political violence and trauma. The structures and ideologies of this region have been militarized in this process. Women have lived through, reacted, suffered and been victimized by these conflicts. They have viewed and resisted these conflicts in different ways and developed agency and strategy within these militarized and gendered structures. This essay highlights some of the experiences of women in conflict zones to show that a parallel discourse and history is being lived and written.

In writing this, we have taken up two regions from the North-East, Nagaland and Manipur, because of the length and intensity of the conflicts, as well as Kashmir as comparative case studies. We have used available literature, reports written by human rights activists and others, conducted in-depth interviews with women, and done a survey in some of the affected regions of Nagaland and Manipur.[1]

*I am grateful to my students from Nagaland, Manipur, and Kashmir who have helped in this work. I would especially like to thank Phyobenthung Lotha (from Nagaland) and Homen Thangjam (from Manipur) for their extensive field surveys in Nagaland and Manipur. I would like to thank Khatoli Khala (Nagaland) for some interviews. Some Naga and Manipuri student organizations had banned any 'outsider' from conducting research in these regions. I am thus grateful to several women's and students groups for giving us special permission and allowing my students access to their cadres. I am grateful to Prof. Kamal Mitra Chenoy for his comments and suggestions. The faults in this paper are my own.

NATURE OF CONFLICT

The politics and nature of the conflict in the North-East and Kashmir differ as does the culture and society in these regions. A brief background brings out these differences and yet also shows the commonalities of conflict zones and their implications.

The north-eastern region of India, comprising the seven states: Arunachal Pradesh, Assam, Tripura, Manipur, Meghalaya, Mizoram, and Nagaland has witnessed armed conflicts for decades. The anti-state movements in several of these regions including Mizoram, Assam, Tripura, Nagaland, and Manipur are called 'national liberation' movements within the region. The Indian government labels them 'insurgencies' and their cadres as 'extremists' or 'militants'. Those involved in the movement call themselves 'freedom fighters' or 'national liberators'. Others in the region refer to them as 'the underground'.* In some regions of the North-East, like Mizoram after the Shillong Accord and in parts of Assam after the Bodo Accord in 2004, there were some positive results and active conflict ceased. In Assam, several movements like the United Liberation Front of Asom (ULFA) continue to be active in some regions. In the two states of Nagaland and Manipur, the long-term and intense nature of armed conflict remains unresolved, though in Nagaland a 'ceasefire agreement' has been signed between the NSCN (I-M) and the Government of India.

The Nagas have had aspirations for independence since colonial times and believe that they constitute a separate nation and did not accept their status as part of the Indian union. They have argued for the right of self-determination and this has led to a history of armed conflict between the Naga National Council (NNC) and the union of India since 1947. The Government of India (GoI) passed national security legislation with which it has fought this movement. These legislation have been used in most regions where the GoI has faced insurgent movements. These were the Assam Maintenance of Public Order (Autonomous District) Act, 1953; the Assam Disturbed Area Act of 1955, and the Armed Forces (Special Powers) Acts (AFSPA) in 1958 and 1972. In addition, the GoI used the Terrorist and Anti-Disruptive

*I use these interchangeably and without prejudice.

Activities Act (TADA) and later enacted the Prevention of Terrorism Act (POTA). All these National Security Acts have highly draconian features that give the military and paramilitary wide-ranging powers with little accountability, grossly restricting civil liberties. With these, the military and police operate independently and often without the knowledge of civil society. These Acts are some of the most obvious reasons for the militarization of these regions and the consequent deep alienation of the people.

The Indian Government and the NNC signed the Shillong Accord in 1975, which deeply divided the Nagas, who split into factions. Of these, the National Socialist Council of Nagaland (NSCN) contested the accord. This group also broke into two factions in 1988, one led by S.S. Khaplang (NSCN-K) and the other led by Isaac C. Swu and Th. Muivah (NSCN [I-M]) and both have run parallel governments in different parts of Nagaland.[2] With this, while there has been an elected government, the parallel governments of the NSCN and the Naga underground struggle also continue. The factional feud not only caused loss of life and bitterness but also was deeply gendered as women became victims of rival forces.[3] Women became subject to parallel patriarchies, those of the state, the underground, and the community. This region is heavily armed, with a proportion of one security person to every 10 civilians. Since April 1995, all of Nagaland has been under the AFSPA which virtually places the state under continuous emergency provisions and under central rule. Despite the July 1997 ceasefire between the NSCN and the GoI, the national security legislation and sense of fear remains.

The state of Manipur faces multiple conflicts. The hill districts of Manipur like Ukhrul, Senapati, and Tamenglong are inhabited by Nagas who share the aspirations of a 'Greater Nagaland' and the ideology and political commitments of Nagas from Nagaland. They are in conflict with the Indian state and face opposition from the Meitis of Manipur Valley regarding their aspirations for a greater Nagaland. The Meitis, who are primarily Hindu, see themselves as culturally distinct (and superior) to the Nagas, and want to safeguard the integrity of the state of Manipur. The Meiti underground movement though, does not identify with the Indian state. The Naga demand for a greater Nagaland that includes the hill districts with a Naga population has been vigorously rejected by the Meitis. Rifts have also been created between the Nagas and Kukis in the hill districts, and this conflict peaked between 1992 and 1996. There has been rivalry and conflict between the Kukis and Paites tribes that resulted in killings in 1997–8. A number of Manipuri extremist groups in the Manipur valley like the Peoples Liberation Army (PLA), the United National Liberation Front, the Peoples Revolutionary Party of Kangleipak (PREPAK) and others (almost 20) have been leading a resistance seeking secession from the Indian state. These groups draw their strength from popular history of the Manipuris and are hostile to the Manipur Agreement of 21 September 1949 under which the state acceded to the Indian union.

Manipur has been under the AFSPA, 1972, since 1980. Manipuri society, specially the women, are acutely aware of the historical women's movements like the First Nupi Lan 1904 and the Second Nupi Lan 1934, in which women took up arms against colonial rule. This tradition serves as a context for all women's movements in that region. The Meira Paibis (torch-bearers) lead the women's groups amongst the Meitis and see themselves as heir to this tradition. Women's involvement in historical anti-colonial movements has clearly influenced women's activism in this region.

KASHMIR

Jammu and Kashmir acceded to the Indian union under very special circumstances in 1947, with Maharaja Hari Singh's hand being forced by the Pakistani-backed invasion of tribal raiders. To fight these, the maharaja needed the services of the Indian Army. With the help of Sheikh Abdullah, the most popular leader in the state, who rallied the Kashmiri people in supporting the accession to India, Kashmir was formally incorporated as a special part of the Indian union, a fact that Pakistan has contested since then. Pakistan-organized raids into the northern part of Kashmir led to the division of Kashmir into Pakistan-Occupied Kashmir (POK) and the Indian parts of Kashmir, divided by the contentious Line of Control (LOC). This has led to unending hostilities between India and Pakistan that range from low-level conflicts to wars. It has meant that families and communities have been divided along this border for decades, with little possible communication.

The Indian government guaranteed special status and greater autonomy to Jammu & Kashmir through Article 370 in 1952. Relations with Kashmir have been complicated since Sheikh Abdullah was incarcerated on grounds of suspicion of pro-Pakistani sentiments during the 1953–75 period until the Indira Gandhi–Sheikh Abdullah Accord of 1975. In the interim period, making use of pliable governments elected in elections generally believed to have been rigged in favour of the ruling party, the greater part of the autonomy given to the state has been systematically taken away by successive union governments. This has deepened the popular alienation in the Valley and increased anti-Indian sentiments. Though Pakistan continued to support secessionist forces in Kashmir from 1947 onwards, the critical event that led to a major insurgency in the Valley from 1989 is widely believed to be the rigged elections of 1987.[4] This increased alienation in the Valley and a demand for self-determination backed by Pakistan became the basis of conflict, and terrorist methods against the state. The state responded by clamping down against the militants and others by declaring the area as 'disturbed' and using laws that gave the police and paramilitary extra-judicial powers that violate civil freedoms.[5] The civilians have always been caught in the crossfire between the extremists and the Army. Thus, there have been many recorded human rights abuses, including rape, custodial deaths, and missing people in the Valley. Women have been victims of terror from both the Army and the militants in this highly gendered conflict. The basic civil rights along with violations of international humanitarian law by all parties in Kashmir are important reasons behind the continuation of the disturbed situation that prevails there.

The conflicts in the regions of Jammu & Kashmir and the North-East thus have multiple dimensions and variations. The longest-standing conflict is between the underground/militants and the state. There are factional conflicts between the underground groups; there are ethnic clashes in Manipur between the Nagas and Meitis, and Nagas and Kukis. There are killings between factions of Kashmiri militants, encounter killings, and inter-communal violence. Each of these conflicts entails illegal killing, kidnapping, rape and sexual abuse and extortion. In addition, there is large-scale militarization and the easy availability of small arms. This deeply affects women and children and the development process gets distorted. Each of the groups involved in the conflicts is militarized and uses militarist methods and tactics to deal with essentially civil society issues. These impact every aspect of civil society, which gets gendered and structurally biased.

COUNTER-INSURGENCY METHODS

States, including India, follow military methods of counter-insurgency tactics based on ruthless militarist and gendered traditions designed to destroy the will of the people through 'psychological operations'.[6] Various means that include encounter killings, disappearances, rape, and destruction of livelihood are used. The Army regards the entire region as a conflict region, whether market, field, workplaces, homes, churches, or schools. All people in the 'disturbed area' are linked to the underground, and, thus, no one is above suspicion. Movement of all local people is restricted. Since ordinary people do not have identity cards and lack proof of identification, their mobility is limited. Body searches and house searches are common. Certain areas are delimited and 'inner line permits' are required to go to those regions: these regions are, thus, completely inaccessible to journalists or human rights activists, and others without special 'permits' issued by the Army.

In a situation of low-intensity conflict, the army uses counter-insurgency tactics designed to destroy infrastructure. Army officers argue that insurgents use women as shields to dodge security personnel.[7] In such circumstances, where the war has shifted from the borders to the homelands, civilians, including women, are seen by the Army as security risks. The security personnel conduct body searches, searches at night, in homes and at workplaces. There is, thus, no difference between the private and the war domain. Besides having no personal security, women have to work from homes and infrastructures that have been destroyed by the Armed Forces. In addition, they are sexually abused in order to humiliate the 'enemy'. Their homes become battlegrounds and life and community becomes militarized. Women feel the wrath of the Army, especially when they fail to resist an attack by militants. Their anger is turned on women and those left behind when the attackers have escaped. As stated repeatedly by the local press, it is a 'habit' of the security forces to target innocent villagers after every attack of militants to compensate for injury to the Central Reserve Police Force (CRPF). The attempt is to destroy self-esteem, specially of women.[8]

The major Act that governs military action in the North-East and in Jammu & Kashmir is the Armed Forces (Special Powers) Act, 1958 [as amended in 1972]. The Act gives no precise definition of a 'disturbed area'. Even a non-commissioned officer can order his men to shoot to kill if he thinks that it is necessary to do so for maintenance of public order. This gives very wide discretion to even very junior officers. Similarly, the Act allows such military personnel to destroy any shelter from which, in his opinion, armed attacks can be made or which has been utilized as a hideout by absconders. This latitude has permitted the destruction of large numbers of dwellings and other buildings in these states, including in collateral damage when buildings adjoining the one targeted have been damaged or destroyed.

The Act permits arrest without warrants, with whatever force necessary of any person against whom suspicion exists. This has provided the basis for indiscriminate arrests, and the use of brutal force including firing against innocent civilians. It authorizes the entry and search, without warrant, of any premises to make arrests or to recover any person or confiscate any property. For military personnel operating in a culturally alien terrain, 'beliefs' and 'reasonable suspicions' are often wholly unfounded, leading to human rights abuses, as documented by many human rights reports.[9] Acts like TADA, POTA and others further supplement this Act. The state legislature has absolutely no jurisdiction in the matter and the AFSPA thus bypasses civil authority. Thus, officers guilty of rights violations often get immunity because of this Act, instilling a deep sense of collective grievance within the community.

In the North-East, especially in Nagaland and Manipur as well as Kashmir, the insurgency and counter-insurgency operations by the Army and surrendered militants have led to a structural pattern of state-backed violence and a vicious circle of counter-violence. All these states have a history of human rights abuse and gendered violence against women as a tactic against insurgency, recorded by human rights groups.

SOCIAL AND ECONOMIC IMPLICATIONS

Years of conflict, violence, lack of economic opportunities, breakdown of the rule of law and military presence has militarized society and led to much alienation and despair. It is commonplace in Manipur to see in a weekly paper reports of murders, kidnappings and disappearances (by both the underground and the army), rape, molestation, cases of child abuse, sit-ins, strikes, bandhs (closures) by student's and women's organizations, all merge as unending and commonplace events.[10] In militarized societies, all institutions get gendered and male privilege dominates as women get confined to their homes because of the atmosphere of insecurity.

The restrictions because of the national security legislation, the common instances of crossfiring, low-intensity conflict in army areas, specially outside the state capitals of Imphal and Kohima, the imposition of curfews, have adversely affected the economy of these regions. For example, the town of Mokokchung in Nagaland, which witnessed conflict and firing by the Army in December 1984, had its commercial value destroyed for years as commercial buildings were destroyed.[11] Though the central government has poured in money in grants-in-aid, local people argue that this has rarely led to people-oriented development projects, but rather to corrupting official sections of the regional governments and bureaucracy. Locals complain that the 'official' regional government and administration have a 'nexus' with the underground groups. It is common knowledge that the 'underground' groups have penetrated the local administration in many areas in both Nagaland and Manipur. Money is made through civil contracts, and the contractors are linked to the underground. Underground groups extract taxes and non-payment can be fatal.[12] Instead of income generating projects and industry, these regions have become heavily dependent on central government funding.

Economic life and movement is disrupted due to emergency orders, curfews, and restrictions. Women, being already unequal, are unequally affected. Most women feel there is restriction on economic activities. Economic restrictions, they strongly feel, include payment of double taxes, extortion on the highways, confiscation of goods and money by state commandos and other paramilitary forces, bandhs and curfews.[13] The women believe that their struggle to eke out a livelihood is carried out under personal risks. Unemployment is very high in all regions of conflict. In Manipur, of the four hundred thousand registered unemployed in 2003, one hundred thousand are women. But there is vast underemployment and women often do not go to employment exchanges to register. The successful initiation of a ceasefire in Nagaland has removed some of the earlier restrictions, but 80 per cent of the women we interviewed in Manipur argue that they are restricted physically, and these impact negatively on trade and economic activity.[14]

The per capita income of Manipur in 1998–9 was only Rs. 7,132 and 10,287 in Nagaland, making them the lowest amongst Indian states. Both states continue to be agriculture-based with small-scale and handloom industry as big employers. The land/person ratio is very low and the tribal population is rapidly losing their land, their only asset, and to make things harder, there is a very low utilization of human resources.[15] Further, surveys confirm that while there is high literacy and enrolment in these states compared to the national average, there is low per capita income, low consumption levels, and inadequate health care systems. Women's role in the decision-making process is minimal. In fact, in the ongoing modernization, participation of women in productive work has been falling as compared to their participation in traditional productive activities.[16] The reasons are that the scope of employment of men in traditional productive activities has fallen and the burden of maintaining families through earning in traditional activities is on women. Denuding forests and receding water have increased the burden on women as they walk miles to collect water and firewood.

Social norms break down and women have to bear the burdens of traumatized and alienated youth. Alcoholism and drug abuse are very common in areas of the North-East and have been identified by women as causes of sexual abuse and violence, as also responsible for destroying family structures and impacting children negatively. Women in all these regions in both rural and urban areas have complained of intolerable situations, as the consequences of this abuse have made women's tasks more arduous. Years of conflict have resulted in human rights abuses and trauma and the region is in a state of siege. At the same time, as women take up new roles in the absence of men and find work outside the home, these new roles are not empowering. As young women have stated, 'This has only added to our responsibilities. The traditional ideal of a "good woman" has been reinforced.'[17] The question remains as to whether the larger picture is positive.

The consequences of conflict in Kashmir are enormous in terms of human and social costs, with gender implications that skew terms of relations against women. The area is obviously militarized with some 500,000 Indian soldiers, paramilitary and police, fighting an estimated 3,000 militants. Figures show over 50,000 dead, around 30–40,000 young widows, and about the same number of orphans.[18] An atmosphere of fear and despair stalks the state. Civil life is so disturbed that the minimum basic needs of the people, especially women and children, are not met and no one has time to look into these matters seriously. Children constitute about 38 per cent of the Jammu & Kashmir state's population, and of these, over 3 per cent are either orphans, destitute, or neglected, not getting the basic needs of protection, health care, food, education or love and affection, security, learning, through exploration and safe environment.[19] Rough estimates of the number of orphans due to the militancy are said to be between 10,000 and 20,000. Only the handful of private orphanages that exist are expected to deal with a calamity of this scale.[20] Intellectuals, including journalists and the faculty in Kashmir University are wary and even scared of speaking openly, particularly against the militants and the army, since any specific comment has had, on occasion, serious, even fatal, consequences.

The reports of Amnesty International and other inquiries on human rights in Kashmir reveal flagrant abuses of human rights by security forces who then get cover by the AFSPA which insulates the army personnel from action in these cases of violation.[21] Several thousand civilians have been detained under the Public Safety Act and the Terrorist and Disruptive Activities Act.[22] This has led to the phenomenon of missing persons and their 'half-widows'. The state government claims that about 3,000 are missing, but human rights groups show the figure to be 8,000.[23] There are thousands of abductions and victims are often found dead. Amnesty International has given a number of instances when the Special Operations Group (SOG) has fired on peaceful demonstrators.[24] Besides the continued use of national security legislation, there is the simultaneous decline of government institutions, specially the local judicial and criminal justice systems. Further, direct rule from Delhi have been imposed from time to time. Though the panchayat (local council) elections were held in Jammu & Kashmir in 2000, there has been a decline of secular democratic institutions that accounts for the decline of civil and political rights of individuals.[25] Women's rights are not even talked about, as they remain largely under-represented in all institutions of decision-making, even though the ruling coalition after the 2003 elections represented by the Peoples Democratic Party has a woman president, Mehbooba Mufti. The people, specially women and children, live in a situation that looks and feels like a permanent war zone. Women-headed families remain the poorest. It is for this that the region has come to be known as the Valley of fear.

The militancy has increased every year since 1990, involving about 63,387 cases in a 10-year period.[26] Property and infrastructure have also been destroyed by militants and crossfiring by the army in just one year (1990) amounts to as many as 802 public buildings, including 129 schools, 172 bridges, and 501 other buildings. This has continued every year. Other attacks by militants include the use of explosives through mines, RDX, and so on. Apart from the security forces that are targets, innocent civilians, including hapless women and children, are also killed.

The most tragic human rights violation in the Valley has been the forced exodus of the 150,000 Kashmiri Pundits (upper-caste Hindus) since 1990 who were an integral part of Kashmiri society. Despite repeated promises, no viable measures have yet been taken to bring the Pundits back. Even today, others occupy Pundit homes. Villagers from border areas of the state, specially in a radius of 5 km. of the Pakistan–India border, have had to flee their homes because of Pakistani shelling, and live in considerable hardship in makeshift refugee camps as in Devipur. Thousands of them too are suffering, and will continue to do so, until there is a political solution involving Pakistan.[27] Here too, women are the worst sufferers, as the attempts that are made rehabilitate the men first. Health care and education in the camps is very limited: shortage of materials and lack of basic amenities hamper educational development amongst children.[28] There is one tent per family which serves for cooking and sleeping space. There is one toilet for every twenty persons and sanitation is very poor. It is now recognized that the displacement of the Kashmiri Pundits out of Kashmir Valley has affected the secular traditions the Valley was historically known for (*Kashmiriyat*). With this, not only has a significant aspect of Kashmiri culture been displaced, the vacuum has been filled with a constructed culture of extremism not real to the Valley.

The literacy rate in Jammu & Kashmir in 1981 was 27 per cent, compared to the average of 48.2 per cent in the whole of India. With disruption of schools as we showed earlier and increasing security risks and poverty, literacy and schooling have been adversely affected.[29] Prostitution is on the increase as women get destitute. People have been displaced, and migration of all communities out of the Valley has crippled the economy. By 1993, almost 150,000 Kashmiri Hindus were in refugee camps where conditions have been abysmal. Women are particularly traumatized and are often at the mercy of male supervisors. Health care and education for children is very limited, putting a further strain on women.

The exact costs of the conflict and militarization in Jammu & Kashmir in economic terms has been difficult to calculate, because data is based on informed estimates and the information is based on qualitative accounts. Since the conflict is an ongoing process, the costs keep changing. As we have shown, the costs in terms of human lives, infrastructure, education, and health are tremendous. In addition, agriculture, trade, tourism, and the cottage industry on which the economy of the state was based have all been severely affected. Thousands of people within the state were employed in these branches of industry. Lack of electricity, breakdown of infrastructure, and decrease in credit facilities have all adversely affected these crafts and unemployment in the state is very high. Thousands of shops and factories have been destroyed in the crossfire and in arson and grenade attacks. Daily wage earners have been badly affected. The Kashmir Council for Human Rights reports that 15 per cent of the people have had to migrate in search of work.[30] This also provides a basis for recruitment of youth in militancy or counter-militancy operations and other such activities. The economy and environment of the area feel the structural impact of the conflict. The tourist industry has suffered greatly and the handicraft artisans and skilled craft persons languish or have taken to other occupations. Women, thus, not only face the daily overt violence of militancy and counter-militancy of the state, but also the structural violence that comes with poverty and unemployment.

The killing of Hindus has already ensured their silent exodus from the hilly tracts of Rajouri and Poonch districts of Jammu & Kashmir. Among Muslims, it is usually the Gujjars who are targeted. They are suspected of being loyal to India. In the recent past, Muslims were attacked in a number of places like Doda, Mahore, Shophian, and Rajouri.[31] When the elections approached, some militants formed a special group to disrupt the polls and coordinated their activities with jihadi (Islamic extremist) groups. This was to ensure those moderate elements in the Hurriyat Conference (a 28-party conglomerate in Kashmir Valley) and other separatist groups stayed away from elections.

Militants have attacked moderate Kashmiri politicians, and ruthlessly quashed dissent or pluralism within their ranks. Their ideology is based on a communal understanding of their proposed vision of the state of Kashmir based on the sharia, which would alienate other minority communities. Ideologically, the frequent statements by its leadership and religious bodies equate the secessionist movement in Kashmir with jihad or holy war which has only given an impetus to militancy. Fundamentalism from within the movements in Kashmir and that emanating from Pakistan have tended to merge. The Kashmiri militants do not deny the Pakistan link.[32] The Jammu and Kashmir Liberation

Front (JKLF) started a programme for Islamization in 1990 with an order to shut down all cinema halls and liquor stores. Pakistan has supported militancy in Kashmir in various ways. Thus, there has been an enforced change in the very traditions and culture of the Valley from one of a liberal syncretic Islam to one that imposes the rigours of a jihad influenced by the sects that founded the Taliban.[33] Such change impacts women severely, as we examine below. Militants, and the Pakistan government, have argued that in the Kashmir case, the special concept of jihad or holy war applies, which supersedes all international humanitarian law, not to speak of Indian law. This form of enforced Islamist tradition has had the deepest implications specifically on minorities and on women in general.

The combination of militancy, security forces, a crippled infrastructure and unproductive lives have meant a distortion and militarization of structures that women, children and men live in.

WOMEN AS CULTURAL SIGNIFIERS

A woman plays multiple roles, but her value is judged in relation to her chastity, and her role in life is linked to childbearing and care giving at home, and, thus, she is deemed to be unequal to men. A woman's identity and status is linked to that of her father/husband, and her community/society exercises control over this. She has little independent status, autonomy, or agency. Societies perceive women primarily in gender-stereotyped roles and women are brought up to carry out, accept, and conform to such roles. This perspective follows them from the private to the public domain, and in instances of conflict is further reinforced as conceptualization of masculinity sharpens and contrasts with femininity.

Manipur Valley, where Meitis comprise two-thirds of the population, are distinct from the tribals, many of whom live in the surrounding hills.[34] Social norms are based on patriarchal structures and the joint family system is common, increasing women's dependence on the larger patriarchal family. Women remain dependent on husbands, even though Manipuri women historically have had positive economic roles. There are education differentials, with female literacy at 59.70 per cent and male literacy at 77.87 per cent. Manipuri women had a historic mass movement, the *Nupi Lan*, against British colonialism and the feudal regime of the king. The site of the women's movement was the all-women market in Imphal that continues to form the basis of social interaction even today. Yet, traditional beliefs still consider women as inferior and subordinate.

Women are carriers of cultural symbols, and values and family rituals like *Mangba-Sengba* (pure-impure) are to be carried out by the daughter-in-law under strict supervision of the mother-in-law.[35] Women bear the complete responsibility for all housework and childbearing and care. By tradition, women are prohibited to eat the offerings of the ancestral God (*Apokpa*). The right side of the Manipuri household is reserved for the son. Dowry in different forms like gifts is on the increase. Women's place in the family is, thus, always secondary to those of the males. Polygamy, though illegal, is widely practiced in Manipuri society. There have been cases where a man 'caught misbehaving' with a woman has been forced to marry her, despite his already being married.[36] Here, society, the families involved, and even women's organizations have compelled the accused to marry 'the woman victim as punishment'.[37] So, clearly, the accused is punished with the right of polygamy, while the victim is made to believe that she is given justice by marriage to the perpetrator of the crime, and made to live life as a 'second' wife and count for nothing. In primordial societies where concepts of 'purity' are valourized, women's and men's roles are essentialized and predetermined. Conflict situations only exacerbate these roles.

For Naga women, discrimination begins at birth, when the birth of a male child is considered more auspicious than that of a girl, since the perception that men are the breadwinners and protectors of society and women are subordinate to their husbands is widely accepted. Analysts, however, believe that a Naga woman has more equality because 'she participates freely in singing and dancing in festivals, chooses her own partner and controls domestic affairs'.[38] But customary law permits only males to inherit property.[39] Thus, women work, can get gifts, but do not inherit. Writers have argued that modernity and Christianity have led to more participation of women in society.[40]

In some cases, when women get employed and contribute to the economy they are seen to be free, specially in the North-East. But in this sphere too, their value is not the same as men, and social controls on them continue.[41]

In Nagaland, female literacy is 62 per cent and male literacy 72 per cent. Women form the largest workforce in agriculture, sericulture, weaving, and handicrafts, but they lack infrastructure support. Due recognition is not given to their input, and there is little profit from their labour. They do not control factors of production that continue to be held by men. Women are the worst sufferers in health, poverty, and illiteracy. Naga customary laws are gender-discriminatory and the government is codifying these. Women are not represented to a large extent in their village *ho hos* (councils) of their tribes and at district level, so their concerns are not represented.[42]

The role and status of Kashmiri women combine the ideas of women under Islamic laws with those of a special Kashmiri tradition of Sufism. Kashmiri Pundit society conceptualizes women as Hindus outside the Valley do. Men are privileged from birth, while women are seen as a burden. With the birth of a boy a mother is honoured, but the birth of a daughter is identified as a problem.[43] This discrimination follows her through every aspect of life. The gender-inequality of women is evident in every aspect of state and society. Despite constitutional guarantees, women are not considered equal citizens. One instance was the attempt by the Jammu & Kashmir legislature to pass the Jammu and Kashmir Permanent Residence Status (Disqualification) Bill, 2004. This Bill bars a Kashmiri woman from inheriting, passing on the inheritance, selling or alienating property if she married an 'outsider' (non-Kashmiri). No such law is applicable to men. This Bill was supported by the popularly elected People's Democratic Party and by the main opposition, the Peoples Conference. Women's groups in the Valley have also supported the Bill and argued that it is in keeping with Article 370 of the Constitution that gives Jammu & Kashmir special status and protects its identity. The politics around this Bill show that women cannot claim identities besides those of their husbands either in the eyes of law or society. So women who symbolize a nation's honour and identity clearly do so only as long as patriarchal structures will let them.

In all three societies, the Kashmiri Muslims and Hindus, the Hindu Meitis, and the Naga Christians, men see themselves as 'protectors' of women whom they honour as long as women conform to the patriarchal patterns set for them. On the other hand, women are raped and abused by other men when they want to 'dishonour' the entire community. Women's bodies, thus, determine their values and undermine their roles. Women's roles are linked to reproduction, childcaring and rearing, and restricted to the private domain. Motherhood creates and sustains a cultural image of all women as caring and nurturing, which is necessary for the survival of all of society. Unmarried motherhood is unacceptable, so status for women is possible only within family and bound to husband. The family provides protection and the chastity of women is part of its 'honour'. Fathers and brothers have unilateral responsibility for protecting the virginity of daughters/sisters. They exercise power over her to the extent of killing her if this honours is at stake.[44]

Similarly, in all three regions/societies, the nation is viewed as 'motherland' and women's bodies are linked to this concept. Protection of women and motherland intersect as ideologies of masculinity, power, protection and virility intersect. It is, thus, an intrinsic part of a man's/community's honour to protect women/motherland, just as to dishonour/capture a nation and rape become instruments of humiliation and symbols of victory. Underlying this is the concept of protection that is part of masculine right and domain. This right to protection gives them access to force and power over others. Similarly, the state's right to protect its citizens gives it the right to use legitimate force. At the same time, however, those who are protected (mostly women and children but also men) have to give up many of their rights.

Women accept the roles accorded to them in most circumstances without questioning gender discrimination in most cases and most women (94.11 per cent of respondents in our survey in Nagaland and Manipur) felt this restriction.[45] Most of the women combatants and activists who felt equal to men while carrying arms and being part of a liberation movement, and were interviewed in Nagaland and Manipur showed respect for the given, traditional family roles, even when they were patriarchal and exploitative. For example, the chairperson of the National Socialist Women's Organization of Nagaland stated that household chores are traditionally women's tasks, and 'when one does things which do not belong to his or her normal task the balance of tradition is broken. You will always be who you are though you want to deny it.'[46] The pervasiveness and universalization of patriarchal ideologies account for this acceptance, and even when women begin to examine such ideologies, their nature and necessity for coexistence is such that they are the ones to accept and wait for incremental changes.

The fragmented nationalism and conflicts in all three regions of conflict reinforce concepts like 'brotherhood', 'martyrdom', 'manhood' and 'need to love motherland and its culture' and place emphasis on women as cultural symbols. At the same time, conditions of conflict increase women's insecurity and restrict their autonomy.[47] Laws such as the AFSPA (in use in all three regions) that give unlimited powers to the paramilitary curb women's physical mobility and threaten their lives even when they are not involved in the conflict. The body searches that are routine in such areas often lead to molestation and sexual harassment and women and the community feel violated and 'dishonoured' as ethical and cultural questions are raised about such searches. Women and girls get restricted to households. At the same time, the 'national liberators' impose restrictions, e.g. Manipur has witnessed a ban on clothes such as the salwar and sari and ordered that the traditional Manipuri dress, the *phanek* (sarong) be worn by schoolgirls and schoolteachers as part of the compulsory dress code.[48] Underground groups declared that this symbolizes their cultural identity and 'instils a sense of nationalism' and 'spirit of patriotism' necessary to 'save Manipur' from outside influence.[49] State ministers at public meetings have supported the dress code for women: 'Our noble practices of our forefathers are carried forward.'[50] There have been cases of restriction on marriages of Naga girls to 'outsiders'. There has been no call by underground groups in Nagaland regarding a ban on a certain dress/fashion or on the broadcast of Hindi channels or screening of Hindi movies.

But there have been instances of banning the writing and research of Naga history by non-Nagas.

At the same time, however, it is necessary to add that women also identify themselves with such cultural codes, as one activist had to say: 'We have a very clean and respectable discipline of dress in our culture but these days the dress code keeps changing everyday.' And 'among the Kabui women we decided to wear white clothes during death ceremonies and during functions'.[51] In fact, 71.42 per cent of the respondents in Nagaland felt that the dress restrictions were positive, 5.9 per cent were indifferent, and 28.6 per cent felt the restrictions were negative. Of the respondents, 64.7 per cent felt that the National Liberation Movement (NLM) did not reinforce traditional roles for women. One social activist argued: 'Local handloom and weavers prosper out of such a restriction on Indian clothes, and at the same time we can preserve our culture and identity by being what we are and by wearing our clothes.'[52] Most of them felt that the portrayal of women as symbols and custodians of tradition and culture is a 'fortunate blessing' and they did not take it as a burden. Clearly then, given the universal ideology of women as bearers of cultural identity, the restrictions on autonomy are an acceptable part of the unequal code for women.

In Kashmir Valley in October 1989, some militant groups opposed sterilization and abortion. Banners and leaflets to this effect were pasted all over the hospitals.[53] This order was based on the belief that the primary role of women should remain at reproduction, and that the choice for reproduction did not rest with women but with the patriarch of the family/community or militant group that appropriates this patriarchal role. Nationalism, for women, was to be centred on her body, as she was to reproduce for the nation.

In Kashmir, girl students have complained that militants came into classrooms and insisted that all the girls cover their heads and wear burkas (veils). The Hizbul Mujahideen decreed that women must not visit restaurants, hotels and parks. The Lashkar-i-Toiba decreed that Kashmiri women either 'wear burka (veils) or face bullets'.[54] They clearly do not believe in the emancipation or equality of women. Girls have been shot at by 'suspected militants' for wearing jeans. Their argument was that this 'protected women'. Militants fired on beauty salons, and banned women from public places. These kinds of orders put pressures on women to conform or face punishment, but women have both contested and supported such orders. Some militant women's organizations like the lone all-women militant outfit, Dukhtaran-e-Millat, had called upon Muslim women in the Valley to observe strict purdah.[55] They supported militants who sprayed acid on women's faces for violating the dress code, and Asiya Andrabi, leader of Dukhtaran-e-Millat, declared: 'I am happy that 80 per cent of women in Kashmir Valley have adopted [*sic*] Islamic dress code.'[56] Others have not responded to the decrees that demand change in their lifestyles. But in the winter of 2004, there was what was described as a 'purdah wave' where wearing *hijab* became so common in the Valley that there was hardly any woman seen without it.[57]

Women's dress code was enforced because it symbolizes cultural and national tradition that must be borne on the bodies of women. These norms also revealed the changing pattern of culture in Kashmiri society where the historic and distinct traditions of *Kashmiriyat* were being replaced by a more militant jihadi culture that was alien to that society and had more in common with the Talibanized kind of jihadi culture that was being imposed.

The pressure on women from militant groups to conform to dress codes is being contested by other cultural mores like globalization and the Hindi film driven culture as represented by 'Bollywood' (the Mumbai [earlier Bombay] film industry). For example, it is noticeable that girls and boys are taking to Western clothes and that bodybuilding and gyms have become very popular in the Valley, where the role models are Arnold Schwarzenegger and Hindi film actor Salman Khan, known for their 'muscle power'.[58] While muscle power is in keeping with the militarist image and has been accepted, it is the changing pattern of girls' dress that continues to irk the hard-line and conservative militant forces, who accept this image for men, but deny it to women.

Women wear the cultural symbols of society on their bodies and are signifiers of their communities' honour. In conflict situations where identity politics and ethnic nationalism are played out, women's bodies acquire greater symbolic significance, as they become markers for such politics. Simultaneously, patriarchal control at all levels increases in the name of 'honour', 'protection', or culture. In this way, fundamentalist, patriarchal, militarist policies intersect to control women. By contrast, men can shake free their cultural impositions and are not questioned when they move away from their traditional or indigenous cultural beliefs.

Location of Women

Women's involvement in armed conflict can be strategic, circumstantial, or by choice. Very often, women relatives of militants and security forces have no choice but to be part of the 'infrastructure' in conflict situations. As Kashmir Women's Commission member Girija Dhar said:

> Women have to perform the role of wife, mother and daughter, all rolled into one. . . . If her husband or son picks up a gun she has no choice but to protect them. She does not want to go against them. She has to abide by them, at times she does it willingly and at times she is forced to. . . . She has no choice.[59]

These women get classified as combatants by their sheer location. Most women activists in Nagaland and Manipur came to support the underground either because of relatives who were members or out of the sense of deep injustice prevailing in their society.[60] Women relatives supported, gave shelter to the militants and played active roles in the militancy. They suffered severe consequences if the police/army discovered their linkages to extremists.

Women relatives of state officials like police and army wives have been termed by analysts as the forgotten and invisible 'other', who have to grapple with trauma, widowhood and tragedy and have generally been ignored by human rights activists of the region and by the state.[61] State and society treat relatives of victims in different ways, depending on their status. Relatives of anti-state militants are treated callously and become victims of human rights abuse. The relatives of army and paramilitary officials are treated as dependents who get caught in the combat and become symbols of nationalism. Widows of officers are privileged over wives of ordinary soldiers. Stereotypical images of armed conflict, the 'sacrifice' of the son, the grief of the mother/widow are replayed to garner support and nationalism by both sides. Mothers of disappeared and dead sons evoke feelings of nationalism and martyrdom and have become icons of concepts like motherhood and patriotism in all these conflicts. Martyrdom is reconstructed to focus on select aspects of the victim and move the gaze from some other crucial issues like the politics behind the martyrdom.

Women victims of crossfire who are often ordinary citizens get a casual mention in the newspaper and feed into the sub-nationalism of insurgency and local movements. Little is done, however, to give relief to such victims or their families, who are left to rehabilitate themselves. Women are identified with their relatives, even long after the relatives are dead. A woman, thus, gets bracketed as a 'martyr's widow', 'bereaved mother', 'war widow', and carries this reference all her life.

VIOLENCE AND VICTIMS

Women are the greatest victims in conflict situations, targeted especially to cause humiliation to the entire community and indirectly as victims of violence in militarized societies.[62] At the same time, women have been typecast as passive victims in press reports and in the human rights discourse. While highlighting victims, it is clearly important that women's heroic roles and agency and their resistance need to be simultaneously saluted.

Women are the long-term casualties of war as widows, caretakers and wives of missing persons. Studies in Kashmir revealed that widows faced emotional stress, denial of inheritance rights, sexual harassment, and social undesirability. They have to contend with problems of economic sustenance, losing control over their children in addition to loneliness, physical insecurity, and being overburdened by domestic chores. Though their first priority was getting their children educated, 60 per cent could not get achieve this. Of the 300 children surveyed by one study, 48 per cent faced economic hardships, 66 per cent suffered from psychological setbacks, and a number of them spoke of apathy and denial of love and affection.[63] Children who could not go to school because of economic hardships became engaged in household or other forms of child labour. There also exists the problem of an increasing number of women called 'half-widows', those whose husbands are missing. These women have no status since they cannot perform the rituals associated with the dead. They cannot remarry or claim relief or hereditary rights. They become dependents and are vulnerable to societal pressures.

The state has done little for any rehabilitation for widows, and given the conservative culture, they remained dependents of their families or became completely destitute. Further, these women and children get minimal support from either the government or even NGOs. Surveys have revealed that of the thousands of widows, 20 per cent have not been able to claim their share in property and more than half are dependent on others.[64] Clearly, the emotional and material consequences of the conflict are inextricably bound together.

In situations of economic and environmental destruction, women are left to fend for themselves and traumatized children after the death and torture of husbands/sons/fathers. The widespread incidence of psychosomatic disorders caused by grief and poverty represent a serious health problem among women and recovery will take a long time. A survey carried out by Professor Dabla and his team from Kashmir University in Kashmiri villages found that one-third of the widows were in the age group of 31–45. Over half of these women, 53.67 per cent, live alone and even though remarriage is not forbidden, only 8.66 per cent remarry. In fact, 89 per cent said they did not want to remarry. The majority of the women (72 per cent) lived in villages and were insecure because of their meagre earnings and dependency on others. Long-term psychological trauma is the most likely result.

In refugee camps in Jammu, Kashmiri Pundits have been living for more than ten years since they were evicted from the state, and women have the complete responsibility for children and the elderly. They complain that the government has done little to address basic issues like education, health care, sanitation, or employment. Women have tried to resist pressures and rebuild their lives in the camps. They have formed groups like the Migrant Women's Association formed in 1991. The Mahila Mandal (Women's Association) had been formed to fight corruption in the camps. Women have reported that aid and assistance that could be used for schools has been siphoned away. The state, news agencies and most groups have forgotten these women. Some right-wing groups use their plight to mobilize political support for themselves.

Human rights violations and violence by both state and non-state armed forces are so high, and carry on for such long periods of time that tensions and trauma affect everyone and violence becomes structural and endemic. The records and newspaper files of the region are dominated by reports of such abuse: for instance, almost 81 per cent women activists in Nagaland and Manipur conflict areas feel affected psychologically, 70 per cent are economically affected, 58 per cent felt it affected them socially, and 47 per cent physically. Several women said that they were affected in multiple ways.[65] This instils a sense of grave injustice in the minds of people who carry this fear and trauma as part of a collective history.

Rape and molestation are the most common crimes committed by soldiers in these regions. For instance, based on statistics of courts martial provided by the army itself, in the last one decade, the army got 1,426 complaints, they court-martialled 50 men, dismissed 17 in the North-East, and punished 61 soldiers in Kashmir.[66] Human rights groups show through documentary evidence that this is a gross underestimation. A human rights report on Kashmir in 1996 reveals that at least 13,000 women had been molested in the past years after the Army crackdown.[67] Cases of rape are dealt with differently, as the Kunan Poshpora case in Kashmir and numerous such incidents have shown. Women victims of sexual abuse have been shunned by their families and by society, though in recent times, women's organizations have helped in their rehabilitation and rebuilding of their confidence.[68] Women tend to deny the incident when they are raped because their 'honour' has been violated and their family and community shuns them. The state, in any case, does little to address their trauma or problem.[69]

Raped women fall into two categories: either they are shunned, or they become symbols in the conflict. For instance, they are used by the state to regain legitimacy, by showing the atrocities committed by the militants in an attempt to isolate them, as one report released by the army in Srinagar states: 'The women of the state have been constantly subjected to brutalities of the militants. Rapes, thrashing, and other atrocities are common. All this over a period of time has created a dent in the psyche of the women of the state.'[70] Similarly, extremists show state terrorism and mobilize support for their cause with the example of victims. As a woman supporter of the extremists in Kashmir, Asiya stated, 'We thank the forces for their excesses. The more atrocities they commit, the more people will be prepared to take to arms for the struggle.'[71] Women lose agency as this victimization leads to their being secured or 'covered up' by veils or walls.[72] Women's bodies become the sites for collective punishment and claiming honour/dishonour. The trauma of women is then used for building nationalism and pain transformed into militarism and the politics of revenge. In these process, women become subjects of militarized politics.

Besides the violence from the armed forces and retaliation by the underground and insurgency groups, there is intergroup and factional violence, as between the NSCN groups, and between the Nagas and Kukis (where Kukis claim that Nagas have indulged in territorial exclusiveness and resorted to ethnic cleansing). There is aggression between underground groups in Manipur and between extremist groups and communities in Kashmir. For instance, an armed combatant woman from the underground told us that in 1988 she was caught between the factional fight of Naga groups. 'There was no sense of courtesy even among the old colleagues after the Burma siege.' She was summoned to serve the 'other' faction as 'bonded slave and looted'. She had to beg that she not be left naked in the forests.[73]

In conflict, men get brutalized and all levels of relationships are determined by the use of force over the 'other', and consequently all types of violence are perpetrated. Domestic violence is a frequent occurrence in these regions also. All the women interviewed in Nagaland and Manipur stated that they 'knew of someone' who suffered domestic violence.[74] Many women, however, do not complain against 'their men' in circumstances where there is a national liberation struggle. Further, they believe that men are already subject to much abuse by the armed forces, and complaints from within the family would de-legitimize and dishonour the men and the entire family.

In Manipuri society, violence against women is incredibly high, and 99 per cent of the maintenance cases filed under Section 125 of the Indian Criminal Procedure Code in the family courts of Manipur are the result of domestic violence or polygamy. Sophia Rajkumari reports, 'I have seen almost all men beating, abusing their wives in Manipur'; even when women are financially independent, matrimonial violence is pervasive. Further, women who leave their matrimonial home for any reason are not accepted by their family or by society.[75] Women from Nagaland and Manipur said during interviews that 'tradition was against physical punishment in families', but most of them knew of domestic violence. Many of the women cadres in Manipur stated that they had intervened in cases of domestic violence.[76] This revealed the allegiance that women had to insurgents or the National Liberation Movement (NLM), and their ability to take action in the absence of state institutions or the local police, which women did not trust.[77]

A large number of women interviewed (72 per cent) felt that 'the presence of national liberators' had helped reduce domestic violence against women. Local women's groups recounted instances where the 'national liberators' punished men for domestic violence; the insurgents take quicker and harsher action than the recourse to law. However, 21 per cent felt that the presence of the 'national liberators' made no difference, and 9 per cent felt that their presence had actually escalated the situation.[78] It was clear that complaints of domestic violence were being made to insurgents who had formed parallel power apparatuses and exercised local authority along with or even opposed to government authority. This local control has been used for other types of social control also, like enforcing dress codes and moral policing and young couples have been beaten up when found in restaurants.[79] Domestic violence is routine, but at times of armed conflict, it merges with the extreme violence of armed conflict, since both state and civil society actors indulge in violence as a method of resolving issues.

It is noteworthy that for women as victims, the cultural significance is given more weight than other issues. For instance, in cases of widowhood it is 'helplessness', 'burden', honour and martyrdom that are highlighted. But methods of rehabilitation, trauma counselling, property rights, citizenship rights and other such rights are barely discussed, even denied. Women's victimhood is used as a factor to garner or resurrect nationalism as her hurt is depicted as the collective hurt of the community. Women see themselves in this role also. Thus, one activist, Meira Paibi, who was threatened for opposing a kidnapping case in 2003 said: 'They call us mothers yet threaten to kill us.'[80] There is, however, a politics of collective memory where martyrdom or victimhood is remembered.

Records of these conflicts almost till the 1970s focused largely on women's victimhood. A number of the women's movements and peace movements and activism started as a consequence of these. The Meira Paibi women's movement in Manipur regards its growth and focus as having been on 'checking the excesses, random detention and harassment of men, especially youth at the hands of security personnel'. The movement first began for the release of a youth who had been detained by the Army in December 1980, and then developed further to take on other issues. A number of women combatants from the North-East told us that they had joined the underground because of the victimization that they had felt, combined with a sense of nationalism for their cause. They insisted that women were increasingly joining the insurgency because 'they were unable to bear the open injustice and harassment'.[81] The effort to transform victimization to agency, through the method of a counter-nationalist militarization was, thus, common to many women in the underground.

Women are inevitable parts of conflict, as it enters their homes even before wars actually begin, and stays with them long after wars are over. The nationalism and militarism that comes hand-in-hand with war affects their everyday life. Systems of violence merge during conflicts and women are victimized by each of them. While their status as victims is graphically described, they have been combatants, peacemakers, and providers for victims, heads of households and agitators. They have used all spaces available to them to negotiate a life for their families and for themselves.

Women as Supporters and Armed Combatants

Women have supported liberation/ethnic subnational movements in history, but their support has been valued differently than that of men and viewed as part of infrastructure rather than agency. Nationalist structures that are patriarchal in method, ideology and leadership are accepted by women. Women give up their struggles for equality until the goal of nationalism is achieved. Women's support and roles in these movements is significantly influenced by cultural factors. Increasingly, women are becoming armed combatants, but this phenomenon is common in the North-East while it remains largely absent in Kashmir.

In Nagaland and Manipur, women cadres are present in significant numbers in most of the insurgent and national liberation groups. The figures of women cadres are not recorded, but are supposedly about 1:14 as the 'nearest guess'.[82] Military training and organization follow masculinist traditions, and though war and armed conflict are seen as men's domains, women cadres interviewed by our team stated that except for 'some biological differences' they felt as capable as men.

In Manipur and Nagaland, most of the women cadres are educated, ranging from high school to graduates. This cadres joined liberation organizations for specific reasons that ranged from nationalism, ideological appeal and their concern with social and political factors of their region and their strategic location. For several of them, victimization and bad experience gave them a sense of injustice and took them to the underground. They felt that more women were joining the underground because they were 'unable to bear injustice, harassment and the destruction of their homes and people'.[83] Fighting 'for the motherland' was also a reason cited by some combatants.[84] Sustained human rights abuses led to a band of women joining the Nationalist Socialist Women's Organization of Nagaland, with its commitment to supporting the cause of Nagalim. This militant women's organization was concerned with promoting a women's army, creating a women's federation and giving awards to heroes and martyrs. Women cadres stated that 'their way of thinking changed' after joining and they became more ideological and political. Most considered their organizations gender-sensitive, but many of the cadres admitted that they faced gender discrimination.

The functional role of women cadres depended on the nature of the unit to which they belonged. Leadership hinged on their capability and length of service. Decision-making, they conceded, was restricted to the (male) leaders (executive members of the central committees), and if women were part of these, some were part of the decision-making. Some of the women cadres stated that 'women do not appear in the top structure but they did have indirect and important role[s] to play'.[85] The Peoples Liberation Army (PLA) of Manipur has several women cadres in higher positions like A. Mema Devi, who was member of the Central Committee of the PLA and was arrested in March 2003. Other women fighters killed during the armed conflict in 1998 have been reported by the PLA, like Lance Corporal N. Surkala, Bala, and Ranita.[86]

Several women had been with the underground for 17–19 years, and had felt 'overwhelming suppression' while countering the military, but felt that being 'different' (as women) did not mean inferiority in combat. All had personal difficulties but the commitment to the cause kept them going.[87] Women in the movement felt that they could move up the hierarchy depending upon their discipline and activities. Still, the domestic responsibilities remained theirs. They accepted these roles since 'it was his or her normal task', and to go against it would 'break the balance of tradition'.[88] At the same time, they felt that the physiological differences affected and 'limited' women.

Most women combatants felt 'empowered' after joining underground movements and felt that joining such movements liberated women and gave them responsibility. They believed that women joining the insurgency would decrease violence against women.[89] Several of the women combatants stated that they began 'running errands' for the insurgents and then joined the movement. Women cadres said that they had the autonomy to make personal choices like marrying and raising a family, as long as it did 'not harm the organization', and 'preferably being within the organization'.[90] The responsibility of children and domestic chores, however, 'always fell back on women's shoulders'.[91] Thus, socialization could be done with friends, but organizational matters best shared with fellow cadres. The women cadres said that while they did face problems that 'were specific to women', there were no 'grievance cells' for women-related issues. Everyone had to follow a 'code of conduct' and the organizations were against gender discrimination. Thus, the party committees looked into any problem and dispensed justice.[92]

Most of the women cadres said that more women should join the liberation movement to ensure the victory of their movement and were against the laying down of arms even if there were peace talks or a ceasefire until a political solution was reached.[93] However, most activists supported the ceasefire and wanted a just solution. Thus, for the women cadres, nationalism preceded women's issues and rights. Their commitment was to the 'motherland' and they followed the same codes and discipline as men, even though they also had to carry out roles that were confined to women. They did not challenge male hierarchy or patriarchal privilege. Their belief of empowerment was to replay masculine and militarist roles.

In Kashmir, on the other hand, some women's organizations defending extremist positions exist, but women are not represented in the existing political organizations of the militants. Organizations that are based on jihad and Islamic laws exclude women from the public sphere, and advocate that the rightful place of women is behind the veil. Some women have responded to militarism by becoming activists in the few women's organizations that have come up since 1986. The Dukhtaran-e-Millat (Daughters of Faith) and the Khawateen-e-Markaz (KEM, Council of Muslim Women) are groups based on the principles of spreading the correct message of the Koran on the role of women in Islam and the politics of jihad and revenge. Cultural politics is part of their responsibility. Their role is to spread their version of the 'true' form of Islam. They are organized essentially on Islamic lines and seek to bring reform from within Islam.[94] They dedicate their lives to the cause dictated by religious institutions and structures. Some of these organizations have moved away from the Kashmiri traditions of Sufism, and resorted to the practice of

Islam dictated by the jihadi trends that are attempting to revamp the earlier ethos.

Initiated as social service organizations in 1986, both these Kashmiri groups took up cases of rape and massacre by the security forces, like the Kunan Poshpora rapes in 1986, and the Gaunkadal massacre when security forces fired on a peaceful demonstration in 1990, killing 60 persons. Both these groups have organized peace marches and tried to negotiate on behalf of victims. They provided emotional and material support to victims and their families. But they have also played a role in indoctrinating women into accepting the rigours of militancy.[95] They have provided shelter to the militants, defied the security forces, and acted as couriers and information gatherers. But because of their own unstructured organization and the physical and ideological restrictions on women's mobility, they remained limited in their political agency.

Both organizations have specific political views, with the Khawateen-e-Markaz advocating an independent Kashmir and represented in the Hurriyat Conference (which represents 27 organizations of Kashmir). The Dukhtaran-e-Millat combines social and political activities and has spoken of a merger of Kashmir with Pakistan.[96] These organizations take up problems of dowry, marriage of poor women, and other such issues. The Dukhtaran-e-Millat carried on an aggressive campaign of enforcing burka on Kashmiri women: many students resisted this and the organization lost some amount of support. Women have increasingly come out on the streets to demonstrate against state policies and killings. But given the Islamic political culture, they have not become actual combatants. In the Kashmir conflict, there was little proof of women combatants in militant organizations. Women had their own way of resisting oppressions. In September 2003, however, in Shateng, outside Kashmir, the Army arrested a woman militant Mehbooba Akhtar.[97] This would indicate that some women militants may be part of the underground militant forces.

Women militants in the Valley have largely confined themselves to secondary roles, like nursing, care-giving and mobilizing, thus, have been politically mobilized within the confines of the cultural patterns that exist for them. They take up issues of justice and human rights simultaneously with social issues and political issues. At the same time, they do not take up leadership roles, and are not likely to have any presence or representation in the peace talks as and when they are held.

Women's roles as combatants is clearly a culture-specific phenomenon. In some armed conflicts as in the North-East, women are active participants and the phenomenon of women combatants is on the rise. In Kashmir Valley, women's roles in armed struggles are linked to their more traditional roles of socialization, caring, and being couriers and supporters of infrastructure. Women who have become combatants feel empowered, yet they have to continue to play their traditional roles simultaneously. The question whether the new militarized roles for women empowers them is one of deep concern for women's movements. The debate on this issue becomes clearer when the roles of women as peace activists is highlighted.

WOMEN AS PEACEMAKERS, ACTIVISTS AND ORGANIZERS

Women become activists and support peace processes in different ways during conflicts, from their homes, through community interaction, and as active negotiators. In Kashmir and the North-East, women have supported struggles in their daily chores, by bearing the burden of missing men, by their songs and stories that they pass on to children and by their caring roles. Women do not have to be in the public sphere to be activists, since politics enters the private domain especially during conflicts. Their very struggle to survive, fend for their families and eke out a living require tactics and strategies no less than those on the war front.

The method and agency of women is culturally driven and flexible, changing with the increased flow of information and greater politicization. Women's roles in the conflicts in Nagaland and Manipur are clear examples of how women are active in civil society as peace activists. Women from Nagaland had earlier written, 'Women here are excluded from the decision-making processes both in the traditional and modern Naga society.' They are excluded from the traditional village councils and tribal parliament, and 'they have not yet been accorded the respect due to them'.[98] Women continue to be absent from the established decision-making bodies, but they have found other ways to voice their concerns and emerge as mediators in conflicts that affect their being in such fundamental ways. We highlight some experiences from the Meira Paibis and the Naga Mothers as activists in civil conflicts.

The Meira Paibis women's movement is a unique response to the situation in Manipur brought on by conflict and militarization. The Meira Paibis began as small groups of women taking up the issue of alcoholism and initiated a *Nashabandi* (Stop Alcohol) campaign in 1975. Their role expanded rapidly, specially after December 1980 when they campaigned for the release of a youth from army detention and against insurgency-related violence. The Meira Paibis state that they work to check excesses, random detention and harassment of men, specially youth at the hands of security personnel.[99] This movement, like many other women's movements, started with social issues, turned political, and combines these issues according to the situation. There are many Meira Paibis organizations and they are also known as 'Mothers'.

The Meira Paibis have opposed the AFSPA consistently by public demonstrations, hunger fasts by individual members, and protest meetings. One of them, Sharmila Chanu, undertook a fast unto death in September 2001 against this Act. They have systematically showed the abuse of this law, brought out the plight of victims, taken up cases of rape by the armed forces, and taken up issues legally. Some human rights groups argue that this movement has not raised gender-related issues because 'probably there are more pressing and important public issues'.[100] This discourse is a very typical nationalist-patriarchal discourse, where women's problems and inequities are always considered not important enough compared to other problems of society, and, thus, left for resolution at some later stage, after 'the more pressing and important public' issues are resolved.

Women's groups have gained status in Manipuri society, and in many instances run parallel systems. They work closely with the students unions and have confronted the army on several occasions. For example, in the Namching area, the Meira Paibi fined a youth a large sum of money (Rs. 150,000) for raping a minor girl. When he failed to pay the fine, the Meira Paibis stated in a press conference that 'they would no longer act as mediator or be responsible for any consequences that may befall' the man or his family.[101] The Meira Paibis had clearly stood between the underground taking direct action against the perpetrator, but would no longer do so. Sections of the Meira Paibis were attacked by the Army in Imphal in September 1998 and 22 women were injured. The All Manipur Students Union (AMSU) and the Revolutionary Peoples Front stated they would 'not look on silently' as 'this was [the] Army game plan for killing all womenfolk in Manipur'.[102] Women's organizations staged protests and laid roadblocks along with local committees for release of jailed AMSU leaders.[103] There are multiple Meira Paibi organizations rooted in various localities, and in many instances these groups have got caught in the various factions and groups in the Manipur conflict ('national liberation struggle', as they prefer to call it).

The Meira Paibis have used their position as 'Mother' to mediate with the armed forces and organize public meetings with them.[104] Meira Paibis participated in and organized peace rallies when riots broke out in Imphal Valley on the issue of a 'Greater Nagaland', a demand of the Naga movements in the inter-ethnic dispute. The Meira Paibis, thus, play multiple roles and their political activities are issue-based and situational. Sometimes, they support the underground groups. Sometimes, they intervene between the underground groups and civil society. In some cases, they support peace and peace negotiations, but also state that 'sometimes militancy is necessary'.[105]

Naga women's groups and voluntary associations like Leishiyar Tangkhul Women's Society and Tangkhul Shanao Long were established in the 1970s. With this, political and gender-based activism were initiated. A marker in the Naga women's movement was the March 1974 rape of a young Tangkhul girl by an army officer and her subsequent suicide. Protest against this was followed by the forming of groups like the Naga Mothers' Association (NMA) in February 1984, one of the most well-known of women's groups. It was constituted by the Naga *Ho Ho* with the aim of 'upholding womanhood' and articulating Naga women's fight 'against social evils prevailing in the state'.[106] This organization has written reports on incidents involving women. It takes up various forms of activism, drug rehabilitation, and environment concerns. The NMA initiated an enquiry into the Mokokchung incident in December 1994 where the army fired, killing many innocent civilians, and submitted a memorandum to the National Human Rights Commission on this and other such cases. The Mothers initiated a campaign on 'Shed No More Blood' and 'No More Violence' as an appeal to take up issues peacefully.[107] They came out strongly against the imposition of the AFSPA on Nagaland, and insisted that any incident involving the army, violence and women and children be referred to them. They addressed the issue of women's participation in the peace process to both their own society and the government: 'We are puzzled if this is the consensus decision of the Naga leaders. If not, the voice of the mothers/women who constitutes 50 per cent of the Naga population cannot be ignored.'[108] Such memoranda challenged patriarchal processes of decision-making at all levels.

The Naga Mothers initiated appeals, meetings with political leaders like the chief minister entering the realm of conflict and peace processes and correct enumeration of the rolls.[109] Clearly, the Naga Mothers were moving out of the purely social issues to political ones though their primary work remained with social issues. The Naga Mothers have primary concern about the militarization of children and youth since reports have shown how guns and shooting was the favorite game of children in villages like Ukhrul that have been under the Armed Forces Act.[110] The atmosphere of constant fear has meant that normal activities are carried out under stress. The Naga Mothers have stated that while the psychological and emotional scars are invisible, but the trauma that women bear is very real. They have provided solace to families by giving decent burials to unclaimed bodies.

The Naga Mothers stayed clear of the politics of revenge and retribution and stated in their resolutions and pamphlets, 'The ways in which our society is being run whether by the overground government or the underground government have become simply intolerable.'[111] They took a clear decision to remain objective in the interest of peace. The Naga Mothers Association President, Neiduonuo Angami stated that the NMA were critical of '. . . the amount of human rights violations in our society both by the Indian security force and the different factional Naga national workers'.[112] They indicated that both the state and the militant leadership 'reflect and be wise', in the absence of which peace would not be possible. The NMA was clear that peace was not just an absence of conflict, but involved justice and human rights. They had fear that 'underground factions are likely to take full advantage of the absence of security forces in all their effort to capture power by way of increased extortion and elimination'.[113] Their critique of factionalism within the Naga Movement and their strong appeals for peace and non-violence have enhanced their positions as mediators and peacemakers.

The NMA built alliances with other like-minded organizations like the Naga Women's Union, Manipur, and the Naga Peoples Movement for Human Rights, and journeyed to various towns and cities in India with their stories. The Naga Mothers met the EMMA [Eramdam Manipur Mothers Association] in March 2003, for peaceful coexistence between neighbours. The NMA sees peace as a critical aspect for survival and development of the Nagas. The Naga Mothers saw and experienced that women's agency could play mediators and proactive roles between the various factions of Naga society and between civil society and the governing authorities. They initiated peace from their homes as a purely local effort, linking the local to the national. They did not hesitate to approach both the Army and civil authorities. This was obviously an extremely difficult process.

The Naga Mothers have focussed on their role as 'objective forces' in the interest of peace. Former President of the Naga Mothers, Neiduono Angami stated: 'Our role is not to take decisions. We have left this to the NSCN.' She continually stressed that 'The decision (for peace/conflict) is theirs. We are only enabling [it].'[114] The Naga Mothers have not asserted their right to be negotiators in the peace talks. They have given up this right and remain in the background. Their argument is that their role is of 'bridging' the gap and making peace: 'It is not our role to participate in political negotiations. Those on the negotiating table represent all of us.'[115] The Naga Mothers clearly accept that the two entities that have been party to the conflict need to negotiate the terms of peace. They have accepted their traditional roles as part of the background. They believe that women's rights and 'everything' will follow if there is a political solution. Their strategy is to retain their role as transformative agencies that address social and political issues together as part of a common process.

In Nagaland and Manipur there is an increasingly strong tradition of women's activism, yet many women have argued that the liberation struggle has had no effect on the status of women. In fact, most women believe that there is no correlation between the two.[116] However, in Manipur, many women (41 per cent) felt that there have been some changes in the status of women with in the liberation struggle. This is because the underground movement here took action against polygamy and *nupi chingba* (wife kidnapping) in the 1980s, both customs that were unpopular in society, especially with women. Yet, feelings on this issue were mixed, as 18 per cent believed that the status of women in these regions had declined. Many cited instances where one militant outfit threatened to kill Meira Paibis who wanted the release of a victim. 'They call us mothers yet threaten to kill us', Meira Paibis argued.[117]

Women activists, by and large, favour the methods of peace, though they share the belief that some situations lead to militancy. For instance, 88.23 per cent of those we questioned condemned the use of militant methods by any group to achieve their goals. Instead, they recommended peaceful means. Of the respondents, 64.7 per cent felt that dialogue was the best form of exchange to bring about peace among the warring factions; 90 per cent of the respondents in Manipur believed that the AFSPA should be removed from Manipur as one of the first steps to usher peace in the state. They felt that loss of innocent lives, torture and atrocities against women by the Armed Forces could be reduced if the Act was removed. All women respondents supported the idea of removing this Act from the state of Nagaland, too, as a ceasefire was already in place. One good aspect of the extension of the ceasefire in Nagaland, other than peace, is the reduction in the rate of violence against women by the Armed Forces. Every respondent in the state felt that it had reduced drastically.

Most women, whether they were students, activists or combatants, did not believe that military action could solve the problems of the region. As one of the prerequisites to peace, 100 per cent of them supported the idea of a ceasefire between the national liberation movements and the government and among the warring factions. They felt that its absence could be a deterrent to the peace process, as was happening in Manipur at that moment.[118] All agreed that the centre should initiate peace talks with the militant outfits in the region.[119] Every respondent in both states agreed that constant engagement and dialogue was a must for peace in the region. Women felt they could play a positive role in such exchanges, as they considered themselves free from chauvinism and ego, unlike men.[120] Most women respondents felt that the government should take the initiative and create a platform where there could be exchanges: 88.23 per cent of the respondents felt they could have dialogues with the government, 76.47 per cent felt they could do so with other associations, and another 76.47 per cent felt they could have dialogues with other communities.[121]

The women's organizations of Manipur use their status as mothers to intervene at times of crisis and conflict. As killings by insurgents have increased, many women's groups like the All Manipuri Nupi Marup, and Manipur Nupi Keithal Marup have protested. At these meetings it is not uncommon to hear the women appealing as 'mothers of Manipuri society', sometimes asking for peace or that information of killers/kidnappers/rapists be given to them to 'deal with', 'as a gesture and reward for nurturing them as sons'.[122] Women get agency through the use of the mother status, and see it as an alternate method of empowerment.

Motherhood signifies peace and the suffering of war. As Sara Ruddick argues, the image of the mother who mourns the sufferings of war and loss of her sons, and holds lives together despite pain, is a mediator in civil society and between conflicting sides. This is the identity rooted in the daily lives of women, who take responsibility for violence and counter it.[123] A number of women combatants used the emotional concept of 'mother' and women's linkage with land and caring to link their relation as combatants with the underground. 'The price of revolution is very high because it constantly demands heroes and martyrs.'[124] Dr Gina Shangkham and Khatoli Khala, speaking on Naga women's role of peace state: 'The role of the Naga women, like the mother earth and like the Shakti of Hindu belief can be fundamental to the peace process.'[125] The mother of Paresh Barua, the 'commander-in-chief' of ULFA, the anti-state militant organization in Assam, stated: 'Please write that Paresh should respect me and the people of the state and come to the negotiation table immediately. . . . For me both the ULFA and the AGP (Asom Gana Parishad) are the same. Both have lost the respect of the people.'[126] In their appeals to organizations to stop factional killings they have often made emotional appeals based on such sentiment: stop 'or else turn the guns on the mothers'.[127] The mother becomes the 'mother of the nation' who pleads for justice on behalf of herself and the nation and gives up her sons for the nation. In this patriarchal bargain, she can ask for peace, or sustain the nationalism necessary for war. The mother's ability to muster emotion is then seen as an equivalent and even alternate to male power. This image conforms to the feminine 'other' of the warrior.

Given the militarized society where gender roles and distinctions remain demarcated, women used the status and position of motherhood for intervention. This gave them space for intervention, but also had limitations. Women still remain within boundaries and on margins. As Roshmi Goswami has noted, women peace negotiators take up initiatives of conflict resolution and are not always supported by the community in this difficult task. The community and the state more easily accept the task of women as healers and pacifiers rather than in more decisive roles such as speaking for democracy and undertaking peacekeeping roles. Such women are often seen as agents of either the state or the underground, and attempts are made to silence them.[128] The other reason is that while motherhood has symbolic and emotional status, it is lower in the hierarchy than manhood. Men control the status of motherhood, and can also deny it to those who do not conform to the prevailing idea of 'good women'. Further, since women's interventions are at the level of civil society, they are kept out of political society, which continues to be reserved for men. Whatever the end-result, women as peace negotiators are critical actors in civil society. They are the ones who ultimately change patriarchal structures at the grassroots level and are the agents for demilitarization of civil society. They are able to combine social, economic and security issues in a combination of human security perspectives.

WOMEN'S ORGANIZATIONS

There has been a great proliferation of various types of women's organizations and NGOs in Nagaland and Manipur. Most NGOs and activists that we interviewed have not found it easy to function, with 82 per cent stating that they had obstacles in their functioning, and 58 per cent encountered external interference primarily from the government. The major difficulty was that they were constantly being accused of being 'front organizations' of the insurgents.[129] The Army, government officials and politicians made such allegations. For example, former Minister of State for Home Affairs I.D. Swami informed the Lok Sabha that five NGOs (Manab Adhikar Sangram Samiti [MASS]; North-East Coordination Committee on Human Rights [NECOHR]; United Committee, Manipur [UCM]; Naga People's Movement for Human Rights [NPMHR]; and the Naga Students Federation [NSF]) have clandestine links with terrorist organizations in the North-East. He said these organizations reportedly maintained discreet links with terrorist outfits.[130] The BJP Youth Morcha, in a booklet entitled *Pakistan: A Fountainhead of Cross-Border Terrorism*, said that the North-East Students' Organization undergo military training with militants on the Indo-Bangladesh border.[131] They add that Pakistan's intelligence outfits like the ISI have given instructions to impart military training to the United Liberation Front of Seven Sisters (ULFOSS) near the Indo-Bangladesh border. The booklet said that the organizations which form part of ULFOSS are ULFA, NSCN, PLA, and NESO. The All Manipur Students Union and others countered these allegations.[132] Such allegations are not unusual in conflict regions, are made specially by right-wing parties that privilege national security and see dissent as being sponsored by an outside enemy state. All human rights and many civil society organizations become sympathizers of the extremists in the eyes of national security groups.

Women's groups, as we showed before, back several issues, just like other groups, including issues of militants, but advocate different methods. Thus, for instance, the NSCN (I-M) decision to boycott the January 2000 Manipur State Assembly elections, which was supported by the Naga *Ho Ho*, was backed by the Naga Women's association and the All Naga Student Union, Manipur.[133] However, women's groups have an autonomous and independent function in civil society. They have legitimacy in these societies and since they have taken up the cause of people's rights and opposed the AFSPA, risk being indicted as collaborators. At the same time, the cases of the Naga Mothers and Meira Paibis has shown that in some instances of rights violations, the Army has had to work with these women's groups and they have been able to mediate successfully between the Army and the insurgents. In instances when the army has undertaken local development projects and programmes like the construction of community halls, market hutment's, bus stands, among other things, it is the concerned local women's organization (whether the Meira Paibis or Naga Mothers) who work in tandem on these specific issues.

Women in Nagaland and Manipur have expressed faith in women's groups and organizations. For instance, 97 per cent of women interviewed felt that in order to empower women and get their rights they should join women's groups. None felt that they should join the underground or sit passively at home.[134] Large numbers of women felt that women's organizations were respected (54 per cent), while 45 per cent felt that women's organizations had equal status with men's organizations. At the same time, even though women's organizations have a strong hold in Manipuri society, their participation in decision making is virtually absent.

In Kashmir, women have spontaneously and consistently come out on the streets to protest killings, rape, disappearances and other human right abuses. Women are active members of groups like the Association of Parents of Missing Persons, and are part of the protests organized by them. They are a small part of political movements and parties, but, as Girija Dhar has stated, Kashmiri women do not have a large and organized women's movement.[135] Women play an active role in moulding children;

despite their grief, women continue to prepare their children to be 'martyrs' or peace activists. The testimony of Saira in an interview by the Women's Initiative indicates this: 'The child of a freedom fighter will be a freedom fighter.' At the same time, she adds: 'As soon as even a tiny bit of beard appears, I shave it off. I can't lose him as well.'[136] The dilemma faced by women as grieving wives who look after their children and yet mothers who have to prepare their children for conflict reveals the contradictions and difficulties of their location.

In a survey on the proposed peace talks between the Indian government and the Hurriyat Conference (the main Kashmiri political organization) carried out in April 2001, it was found that of 2,400 Kashmiris from all six districts in the Valley, 80 per cent women and 52 per cent men supported the peace talks. Interestingly, all women above the age of 36 wanted the peace talks, whereas only 62 per cent men in the same age group supported the talks. Yet, there has been little collective mobilization around this issue. The reason, as some young students stated, is that 'the only collective activity possible in Kashmir is participation in weddings or attending prayers at the mosque'.[137] Even for young students, there are no cultural activities, no students unions, and even the old Kashmiri festivals are not celebrated.

Unlike as in Nagaland and Manipur, women in Kashmir have not mobilized independently around this issue. Women NGOs have been formed that work on multiple issues, from development issues, empowering women, training and teaching, and on peace activities. But despite gradual politicization, the domain of women's concerns is linked to social concerns, to health and the well-being of the family, husband, and children. Thus, roles and domains continue to be gendered, and restricted.

Even though women are active in social and political movements in Manipur, the Legislative Assembly hardly has any women MLAs. The reasons are similar to those, elsewhere and include lack of political consciousness and social restrictions where they do not have the necessary autonomy. Further, despite their activism, women analysts have shown that women continue to be dependent on their husbands for their political views. Gender inequality continues despite political activism.[138]

Women's activism always coincides with their roles in the private spheres. The need for 'balance' between home and outside falls squarely on them, while men have the option of opting out of this. As one activist remarked: 'Our neighbours joke on us . . . whether we can run a family if both of us are going out.'[139] Women's activism begins with social concerns and moves to political action. Women's groups and actions maintain the link between the social 'family-oriented issues' and the political. Women and women's groups in conflict situations use the emotional appeal of 'motherhood' to show their link with the caring and nurturing role, and feel this gives them the right and capacity to intervene. The concept of motherhood also signifies non-partiality, and rises beyond individual notion of pain to 'motherhood to nation' or their entire 'peoples' and they extract respect because of it. For women, the question of 'respect' and 'security' is similar to the sanctity of 'honour' for men.

Women's role and agency in activism is culturally determined and varies according to the culturally accepted norms in their society. While women gradually challenge some norms, they do so while keeping into account their family position and status. This approach indicates how women can link national, local, and societal security needs in the combination that is known as human security. It also shows how women, when involved in such processes, come to such decisions.

CONCLUSION

During armed conflicts, institutional structures break down and are overtaken by militarized ones, patriarchal controls increase and gender differences are essentialized. The public language and practice of politics and the media become weapons of conflict, as terms such as 'manhood', brotherhood', 'martyrdom', 'honour', 'sacrifice for the motherland' dominate the discourse, and marginalize feminist values. In such circumstances, women's identities are constructed to intersect with the needs of militarized nationalism.

In the case of all three conflicts in Nagaland, Manipur, and Kashmir, women have been constructed as cultural symbols in conflict. They are signifiers of the 'honour' of their community, family and nation and stereotyped as the feminine 'other'. They are then either seen as subjects to be protected and confined to the private sphere (as in Kashmir), or violated as symbols of the enemy 'other'. Women's roles get bracketed in identity politics linked to either the nation or their relatives like 'mother of the nation', 'rape victim', 'martyr's mother', 'half-widow' or 'war widow' that symbolize shared victimhood and solidarity, necessary for retribution and nationalism. Women, thus, get little independent status. Women's agency is undervalued as their identity is held hostage to militarist values and they are subject to greater control then at normal times. Women are symbolic and easy victims of violence perpetrated by state agencies, factional groups, and domestic violence that intersect and sustain each other.

Women derive their identities from feminine roles and accept patriarchal hierarchies for the sake of nationalism or liberation. Women's activism is influenced by cultural and social history and this has been the backdrop to the increased activism in the North-East in contrast to Kashmiri women. Though, as conflict enters the home and daily life is politicized, women have to use activist strategies for survival and sustaining their families from within their homes. Activists 'balance' the roles of home and activism, meaning they bear all domestic responsibilities in addition to their activism, which is like juggling while walking on a tight rope.

Cultural traditions influence women's agency. Thus, the North-East has many vibrant women's groups and movements that intervene in civil society issues despite the odds. In Kashmir, women have increasingly been part of public protests and groups against human rights violations, but do not have the range of independent women's organizations and movements that the North-East has. As a consequence, women's groups have not been able to intervene in civil society independent of men. Women take on new roles and get work outside the homes in the absence of men, but these roles do not empower them as their responsibilities increase and gender structures superimpose the concept of 'good women' who continue to perform traditional roles as well as new ones.

The phenomenon of women combatants has increased in the armed conflicts of Nagaland and Manipur, where women find this a method of empowerment, retribution, and fulfilling nationalism. The structures of power and hierarchy remain similar in organizations engaged in conflict, and men are in dominant positions. Women combatants maintain the myth of male supremacy and work on the belief that power is related to force and leadership is synonymous with masculinity.

Women as activists combine questions of peace with social justice and rights, and the problems facing children and youth, because women's experience has shown that security means human security, and peace includes justice, rights, and equity. While women come to challenge patriarchal structures through their experiences of war as the case of the Naga Mothers and Meira Paibis shows, at the same time, they are not involved either with the state or the opposition since they are not considered a 'party' to the conflict. Their role, therefore, gets restricted to the 'soft option' of nurturing and working in the family, community, and civil society. Women are asked to work on issues of drug abuse, trauma, counselling, etc., while the 'hard' issues and decisions of ceasefire, political or public policy, arms, and peace are taken by men with little consultation with women.

Women are not essentially peacemakers and mothers play symbolic roles to generate nationalism, martyrdom, and militarism. Women employ the motherhood status to intervene, and motherhood combined with victimhood gives them power. This status gives them agency, but has limitations because motherhood is seen to be part of nurturing and restricted to family roles, allowing them agency in civil society and restricting them from political society. Further, this status is accorded and denied by men, who remain higher in the family hierarchy. Women, however, despite their limitations, have been able to play symbolic and real roles in peacemaking and peacekeeping. Given their experience of war, conflict, and pain, they are more prone to vote for peace. Since women have to negotiate for survival, they find it natural to negotiate for peace at the grassroots level. The ideology of militarism and its gendered practices, however, are all-pervasive and both men and women are equally susceptible to them. It remains then, the task of feminists and those interested in peace to mobilize women as a resource, not just a symbol, but as agency for peace.

Recommendations

The broadest recommendations for regions of armed conflict is to bring just peace and to demilitarize the region through a process of political negotiations. But it is precisely here that the problems lie. Since the conflict is about the sharing of political power and economic resources, the terms of peace also involve compromises for this distribution. In addition, conflicts are also about militarized and masculinized structures and ideologies, and, thus, require that women's and civil society issues be equally addressed. For this, we make some recommendations:

1. All the conflicts be viewed within their political, historical and gendered contexts. Peace negotiations cannot be enforced or depoliticized. Any attempt to resolve the conflict in a 'vacuum' and outside a political framework can result in an enforced and unjust solution that freezes rather than resolves a conflict.
2. There should be an immediate ceasefire between all sides so that civilians, women and children not involved in the conflict regain their security. There should be protection of women and girls for their rights. The armed forces must be trained for gender sensitivity and about the Geneva conventions.
3. The conflicting sides should be brought to the negotiating table, and there should be a clear framework for the talks.
4. There should be every attempt to have representatives of women and civil society in these talks, as suggested by the UN Security Council Resolution 1325. If this is not possible, a gender sub-committee should work along with the negotiators on both sides. This gender sub-committee should be informed by the women's and civil society movements and should be able to provide inputs for the talks. The negotiators should be active listeners to the views of this sub-committee.
5. The conflict region should be demilitarized. Several steps can be taken in this regard. The sale and possession of small arms should be strictly controlled and monitored.
6. Draconian legislation that has come to embody deep distrust in state institutions, especially the AFSPA, should be removed from the region.

7. Fear of militia should be addressed by having a new social contract with civil society to ensure there is no use of force in the region.
8. Women and those affected should be given relief and rehabilitation. Efforts be made to rebuild damaged schools and infrastructure.
9. Gender-friendly laws should be promoted to ensure gender equality.
10. Wherever possible, there should be gender mainstreaming in the reporting and implementation systems as suggested by the UN Security Council Resolution 1325.
11. There should be a special South Asia convention on armed conflicts and issues around it like refugees, trafficking, etc., keeping gender issues in focus.

NOTES

1. Our team interviewed 80 women activists, students, and combatants in the regions of Dimapur, Kohima, Wokha, Longleng, Ukhrul, Imphal East and West, and Vishnupur, in Nagaland and Manipur. They also filled in a questionnaire.
2. Ram Narayan Kumar and Laxmi Murthy, *Four Years of the Cease Fire Agreement Between the Government of India and the Naga Socialist Council of Nagalim: Promises and Pitfalls*, New Delhi: For Civil Society Initiative on the Naga Peace Process, and Other Media, 2002, pp. 4–5.
3. Interviews of women from the underground (Ating and others), March 2004.
4. Kamal Mitra Chenoy, 'Human Rights Violations in Jammu & Kashmir—A Report', *Social Action*, vol. 51, April–June 2001, pp. 192–209.
5. The reports of Amnesty International and the Commission on Human Rights on Kashmir bear evidence of the excesses by the Armed Forces personnel. 'Hundreds of people have over the past decade been arbitrarily detained in Jammu and Kashmir. Those arbitrarily arrested under the preventive detention law include political activists of all political hues' (India: Punitive Use of Preventive Detention Legislation in Jammu & Kashmir, Amnesty International, AI Index: ASA 20/10/00, May 2000); also, 'The authorities continued to use the lapsed TADA to detain people in Jammu and Kashmir by linking them to ongoing cases filed before 1995. Hundreds of people remained in detention under the TADA despite Supreme Court orders of the review of all cases' (Amnesty International Report, 2000); 'The arbitrary arrest and detention of those peacefully voicing dissent appears to have become

more widespread in Jammu and Kashmir with the Public Safety Act increasingly being used to punish those who speak out against the government' (Amnesty International Report, 'India: Abuse of Public Safety Act in Jammu and Kashmir', AI Index: ASA 20/13/00, 5 April 2000).

6. Gen. K.V. Krishna Rao, 'The Genesis of Insurgency in Jammu and Kashmir, and in the Northeast, and Future Prospects', USI National Security Lectures, 1997, United Service Institution of India, New Delhi, p. 22.
7. Statement by army personnel in a seminar organized by the Army, Imphal, on 23 February 2000, *Sangai Express* (Imphal, Manipur), 24 February 2000.
8. Editorial, *Sangai Express*, 26 January 2000, p. 1.
9. Chenoy, op. cit., n. 4.
10. Headlines from *Sangai Express* of 2003: 'Meira Paibis Stage Dharna' (10 October); 'Naga Bodies Condemn Rape of Girl by NSCK (K) cadre (23 October); 'Election Minister's 12-Year-Old Daughter Kidnapped (5 and 6 November); 'Kuki Mothers Appeal for Child's Release' (7 November); '10 Cadres of PREPAK Killed in Underground Clashes (8 November); 'Cold-Blooded Murder of Kidnapped Child (13 November); 'Curfew Imposed Indefinitely' (13 November); 'Women's Bodies Decry Underground Clashes, Calls for Unity . . . Students Sit In, Roads Blocked . . .' (22 November).
11. Khatoli Khala, *The Armed Forces (Special Powers) Act and its Impact on Women in Nagaland*, New Delhi: WISCOMP Perspectives, 2003, p. 33.
12. Kanglei Yawol Kanna Lup (banned) claimed responsibility for the killed chief engineer of Loktak project in January 2000, for refusing to pay those taxes.
13. Interviews conducted by our team in Nagaland and Manipur, December 2003.
14. Ibid.
15. *East India, Human Development Report*, National Council of Applied Economic Research (NCAER), New Delhi: Oxford University Press, 2004, p. 98.
16. Ibid., p. 111.
17. Interviews conducted by our team in Nagaland and Manipur, December 2003.
18. Chenoy, op. cit., n. 4; also Sushobha Barve, 'Kashmir: The Moral Dimension', *Communalism Combat*, January–February 2002, p. 24. Indian sources cite 40,000 dead, and the Hurriyat cites 100,000. In 2003 alone, 3,000 people were killed: 'Special Report Kashmir', *Economist*, 14–20 February 2004, p. 21.
19. Sarwar Kashani, Idress Kanth and Gowhar Fazili, *The Impact of*

Violence on the Student Community in Kashmir, New Delhi: Oxfam (India), 2003, p. 36.

20. Yasmin Ali, 'Victims of Violence', *Hope* (Srinagar), vol. 1, no. 2, March–April 2000, p. 3.
21. Chenoy, op. cit., n. 4.
22. Michael Cranna, ed., *The True Cost of Conflict: Seven Recent Wars and their Effects on Society*, New York: New Press, 1994, p. 61.
23. 'Special Report', op. cit., n. 18.
24. As in Anantnag in April 2000: Amnesty International, 5 April 2000; also Chenoy, op. cit., n. 4.
25. S. Gupta, 'India–Pakistan Relations: On a Short Fuse', *India Today*, 15 March 1994.
26. Chenoy, op. cit., n. 4; also Sushobha Barve, 'Kashmir: The Moral Dimension', *Communalism Combat*, January–February 2002, p. 24. Even after the ceasefire, there were over 4,000 militancy-related incidents between November 2002 and February 2004: Syed Nazakat, 'Valley Under Fire', *Sahara Times* (New Delhi), 13 March 2004.
27. Chenoy, op. cit., n. 4.
28. Ritu Dewan, Sheba Chachi et al., *The Green of the Valley is Khaki: Women's Testimonies from Kashmir*, Mumbai: Women's Initiative, 1994, pp. 2–20.
29. United Nations Development Programme, *Human Development Report, 1993*, London: Oxford University Press, 1993.
30. Asia Watch and Physicians for Human Rights, 'Rape in Kashmir: A Crime of War', May 1993; also, Cranna, op. cit., n. 22, p. 63.
31. *Hindustan Times*, New Delhi, 26 August 2002.
32. Tapan Bose, 'Kashmir: The Theatre of Militarization' in *Cannons into Ploughshares: Militarization and Prospects for Peace in South Asia*, ed. Ranabir Samaddar, Delhi: Lancer Publishers, 1995, p. 142.
33. Firdous Syed, 'Identity Formation of Indian Muslims', unpublished paper, *Hope* (Srinagar), 2003.
34. The Meitis are Hindus and believe that they are a distinct nationality. The tribals are Christians of various denominations.
35. K. Bimola Devi, 'The Educated Elite Women in Manipur', *Orient Vision* (Imphal, Manipur), August–September 2000, p. 10.
36. Sophia Rajkumari, 'Equal Status a Rhetoric', *Sangai Express*, 10 September 2003.
37. Ibid.
38. Lucy T.V. Zehol, 'The Tangkhul Women Today' in *Women in Naga Society*, ed. Lucy T.V. Zehol, New Delhi: Regency, 1997, pp. 20–9.
39. The Tangkhuls form the second-largest tribe among the Naga tribes of Manipur.
40. 'Introduction', in Zehol, op. cit., n. 38.
41. Rajkumari, op. cit., n. 36.

42. Report of Naga Mothers' Association Workshop, 6 October 1994, Documents of the Naga Mothers' Association (NMA) Sixth General Assembly, Dimapur, Nagaland, 15–16 September 1998, p. 55.
43. Kshama Kaul, 'A Pandit Story' in *Speaking Peace: Women's Voices from Kashmir*, ed. Urvashi Butalia, New Delhi: Kali for Women, 2002, pp. 185–6.
44. Aribam Sanajaobi Devi, 'Women in the Family', *Sangai Express*, 19 December 1999, p. 3.
45. Interviews conducted by our team in Nagaland and Manipur, December 2003.
46. Interview with Y.S. Salm, Chairperson of National Socialist Women's Organization of Nagaland, March 2004, Dimapur, Nagaland.
47. Roshmi Goswami, 'Reinforcing Subordination, An Analysis of Women in Armed Conflict Situations' at: <www.isiswomen.org/wia/wia399/pea00001.html >
48. Interviews conducted by our team in Nagaland and Manipur, December 2003; *Sangai Express*, 11 November 2002.
49. *Sangai Express*, ibid.
50. Ibid., 11 October 1999, p. 1.
51. Nomita Khongtabatam, interview with Chingdinliu, social worker and activist, Manipur, in *Sangai Express*, 19 December 1999, p. 6.
52. Interviews conducted by our team in Nagaland and Manipur, December 2003; *Sangai Express*, 11 November 2002.
53. Dewan, Chachi et al., op. cit., n. 28, p. 15.
54. 'Srinagar Women Defy Threats by Militants', *Hindustan Times*, 10 September 2000.
55. *Times of India*, 25 February 1999.
56. Reuters News Agency, 29 August 2001.
57. *Kashmir Times*, 20 January 2004.
58. Ibid., 16 December 2003.
59. Girija Dhar, Interview by Ashima Kaul Bhatia, *Times of India* (New Delhi), 7 July 2000.
60. Interviews conducted by our team in Nagaland and Manipur, December 2003.
61. Goswami, op. cit., n. 47.
62. 'Absolute victimhood' is when a person is deprived of any agency and is almost dead or dehumanized.
63. 'Impact of Conflict Situation on Children and Women in Kashmir', study carried out by Bashir Ahmed Dabla and Kashmir University, sponsored by Save the Children Fund, Srinagar, 1999.
64. Ibid.; also Kalpana Sharma, 'The Other Side of the Conflict', *Hindu* (New Delhi), 10 November 1999.
65. Interviews conducted by our team in Nagaland and Manipur, December 2003.
66. *Sangai Express*, 22 October 2000.

67. 'Blood in the Valley, Kashmir Behind the Propaganda Curtain: Report to the People of India on Kashmir', Committee of Organizations for Democratic Rights and Civil Liberties, Bombay [now Mumbai], 1996, p. 92.
68. Dewan, Chachi et al., op. cit., n. 28; also Rita Manchanda, 'Guns and Burqa: Women in the Kashmir Conflict', in *Women, War and Peace in South Asia*, ed. Rita Manchanda, New Delhi: Sage, pp. 42–101.
69. Jammu and Kashmir Human Rights Awareness and Documentation Centre, 'Reports on Human Rights Violations, Srinagar, 1993, 1994'; Chenoy, op. cit., n. 4, serialized in *Kashmir Times*, summary in *Seminar*, December 2000; Amnesty International Report, 2000, India: Punitive Use of Preventive Detention Legislation in Jammu and Kashmir, Amnesty International, AI Index: ASA 20/10/00, May 2000.
70. Indian Army, 'Human Rights Violations and Atrocities by Terrorists', Srinagar, 2000.
71. Dewan, Chachi et al., op. cit., n. 28, p. 13.
72. 'A Woman Must Be Covered Up for Her Own Safety', Asiya Andrabi, interview by Sudha Ramachandran, in *The Shades of Violence, Women and Kashmir*, ed. Sudha Ramachandran and Sonia Jabbar, New Delhi: WISCOMP, 2003, p. 31.
73. Interviews of women from the underground (Ating and others), March 2004.
74. Interviews conducted by our team in Nagaland and Manipur, December 2003.
75. Rajkumari, op. cit., n. 36.
76. Interviews conducted by our team, of women cadres in Nagaland and Manipur, December 2003.
77. Ibid.
78. Ibid.
79. Ibid.
80. Interviews with Meira Paibis, Manipur, December 2003.
81. Interview with Aphy, Deputy Secretary of National Socialist Women's Organization of Nagaland (NSWN), March 2004.
82. Interviews conducted by our team, of women cadres in Nagaland and Manipur, December 2003.
83. Interview with Martha and Aphy, Secretaries of the Nationalist Socialist Women's Organization of Nagaland (NSWN), March 2004.
84. Interview with Toto and Mary, Sergeant Majors of NSWN, March 2004.
85. Ibid.
86. *Revolutionary People's Front Newsletter* (Imphal, Manipur), vol. 1, issue 3, July 1998, p. 1.
87. Interviews of women from the underground (Salam et al.), Camp Hebron, March 2004.
88. Ibid.

89. This interview was conducted in a hospital, where a woman from the underground was being treated. She said she had been given electric shock treatment, beaten, and suffered gender abuse without penetration. She was incoherent, confused, and traumatized. Interviews conducted by our team, of women cadres in Nagaland and Manipur, December 2003.
90. Interviews, ibid.
91. Interview with Zuse, Vice-Chairperson of NSWN, March 2004.
92. Interviews conducted by our team, of women cadres in Nagaland and Manipur, December 2003.
93. Ibid.
94. Shiraz Sidhva, 'Dukhtaran-e-Millat: Profile of a Militant Fundamentalist Women's Organization', *Against All Odds*, ed. Kamla Bhasin, Nighat Said Khan and Ritu Menon, New Delhi: Kali for Women, 1994, pp. 123–31.
95. Ibid., p. 127.
96. Dewan, Chachi et al., op. cit., n. 28, p. 24.
97. Ashima Kaul, 'Her Master's Voice', *Hindustan Times* (New Delhi), 29 October 2003.
98. Monalisa Chankija-Longkumer, 'A General Look at Naga Society—Women's View', Naga Peoples' Movement for Human Rights, Conference on Human Rights, Official Report, Kohima, 2–3 November 1990, p. 24.
99. Interviews conducted by our team in Nagaland and Manipur, December 2003; *Sangai Express*, 12 January 2003.
100. 'Women and Conflict Situation in Manipur, for a Human Rights Approach', unpublished concept paper of Macha Leima (a voluntary women's organization in Manipur), 2002.
101. *Sangai Express*, 4 November 2002.
102. *Imphal Free Press*, 28 September 1998, p. 1.
103. *Sangai Express*, 19 February 2000, p. 2.
104. Ibid., 4 January 2003.
105. Interviews conducted by our team in Nagaland and Manipur, December 2003.
106. 'Introduction', Collection of Documents of Naga Mothers' Association (NMA) Sixth General Assembly, Nagaland, 15–16 September 1998.
107. 'Observation of NMA Mourning Day, 5 August 1994', in ibid., p. 58.
108. Memorandum submitted to the Governor of Nagaland and Lt. Gen. K.L. Seth, April 1995, in op. cit., n. 106, pp. 48–9.
109. 'Fifth General Assembly of NMA', in op. cit., n. 106, p. 62.
110. Representatives of the NMA stated, 'Childhood and the lightness of youth has been denied to this generation': Report, 'Where Peacekeepers have Declared War: Report on Violations of Democratic Rights by

Security Forces and the Armed Forces (Special Powers) Act on Civilian Life in the Seven States of the North-East', National Campaign Against Militarization, New Delhi, 1997, p. 15.

111. 'A Call from the Mothers of the Land, 25 May 1995, Kohima', in op. cit., n. 106, p. 46.
112. 'Speech of Neidonuo Angami, President, NMA, 2 October 1995', in op. cit., n. 106.
113. 'Resolution of the Executive Committee of the Naga Mothers' Association, Dimapur, 14 September 1996', in op. cit., n. 106, p. 36.
114. Interview with Neiduono Angami, former president and adviser, Naga Mother's Association, 16 June 2004.
115. Ibid.
116. Interviews conducted by our team in Nagaland and Manipur, December 2003.
117. Ibid.
118. The president and general secretary of the All Manipur Women's Development Samaj (society) expressed this view.
119. Interview with the president of Macha Léima, Imphal, December 2003.
120. Opinion of a local Meira Paibi leader in Imphal.
121. Interviews conducted by our team in Nagaland and Manipur, December 2003.
122. *Sangai Express*, 29 May 2003.
123. Sara Ruddick, 'Women of Peace, a Feminist Construction', in *The Women and War Reader*, ed. Lois Ann Lorentzen and Jennifer Turpin, New York: New York University Press, 1998, pp. 213–26. See also Anuradha M. Chenoy, *Militarism and Women in South Asia*, New Delhi: Kali for Women, 2003, p. 153.
124. Interviews of women from the underground: Zuse, Vice-Chairperson of NSWN, March 2004.
125. Zehol, op. cit., p. 1; and Khatoli Khala, 'Women and the Armed Forces Special Powers Act', unpublished research paper, WISCOMP, New Delhi, 2001.
126. *Hindustan Times*, 3 May 2001. ULFA is a militant underground organization in Assam. The AGP (Asom Gano Parishad) is the ruling political party in Assam.
127. *Sangai Express*, 22 November 2003.
128. Goswami, op. cit., n. 47.
129. Interviews conducted by our team in Nagaland and Manipur, December 2003.
130. *Sangai Express*, 18 February 2003.
131. Ibid.
132. Paula Banerjee, 'Women's Interventions for Peace in the Northeast: 1', p. 7, NSCN (I-M) official website: <www.nscnonline.org/webpage/

Articles/women's_interventions_for_peace.htm.> Banerjee says, 'An interesting phenomenon about [the] women's peace movement in Manipur relates to their close association with insurgent groups.'

133. *Sangai Express*, 26 January 2000, p. 1.
134. Interviews conducted by our team in Nagaland and Manipur, December 2003.
135. Dhar, op. cit.
136. Dewan, Chachi et al., op. cit., n. 28.
137. Kashani et al., op. cit., n. 19, p. 31.
138. Devi, op. cit., n. 35, p. 11.
139. Nomita Khongtabatam, interview with Chingdinliu, social worker and activist, Manipur, in *Sangai Express*, 19 December 1999, p. 6.

Contributors

SUNILA ABEYSEKERA is a feminist human rights activist, presently Executive Director of INFORM, a Human Rights Documentation Centre based in Colombo, Sri Lanka. She has a M.A. in Development Studies with a specialization in Women and Development from the Institute of Social Studies in The Hague. In 1998, she was one of five recipients of the UN Human Rights Prize, for her work in Sri Lanka and on women's rights worldwide.

CHANDRA BHADRA Ph.D. is an Associate Professor in Tribhuvan University, Nepal. She is mainly involved in women's/gender studies programme in the university and involved in research with women especially in rural areas. For more than a decade she has provided policy inputs on gender mainstreaming to the government, UN agencies and bilateral agencies.

ANURADHA M. CHENOY is Professor, in the School of International Studies, Jawaharlal Nehru University, New Delhi. She has been the Chairperson and Director in the Centre for Russia and Central Asian Area Studies Programme of the Centre. She has written *Militarism and Women in South Asia* (2001); *The Making of New Russia* (2001), and over a hundred articles in books and journals.

SABA GUL KHATTAK Executive Director, Sustainable Development Policy Institute, holds a Ph.D. in political science. She works on issues of peace and violence, governance, refugees, women's economic empowerment and labour rights. She actively contributes to dialogues on these themes at different fora in Pakistan and abroad.

AMENA MOHSIN is Professor, Department of International Relations, University of Dhaka. She graduated from the same department. She received her M.A. in Pacific Islands Studies from the University of Hawaii and Ph.D. from Cambridge University, UK. Her areas of interest include minority, human rights, gender and security issues. She has published a number of articles in various national and international journals. She has also authored two books on the Chittagong Hill Tracts conflict in Bangladesh. Her books are *The Politics of Nationalism: A Case Study of the CHT* and *The CHT: On the Difficult Road to Peace*.

AVA DARSHAN SHRESTHA Ph.D. is working as a Social Development/Gender Consultant in Nepal. She attained Doctor of Philosophy from University of Bath, UK in 1995 and Masters in Public Administration (MPA) from Kennedy School of Government, Harvard University, USA in 1984. She has worked for the government, UN agencies, bilateral agencies and several donors including the INGOs for the past two decades. She is also affiliated to many NGOs. Her research work primarily focuses on poverty, reproductive health, micro credit, employment and empowerment of women. More recently she has been researching on conflict/insurgency and its impact on women.

RITA THAPA a feminist activist is globally recognized for her ground-breaking work in founding Tewa, the Nepal Women's Fund. Currently she is engaged in peace-building work primarily through 'Nagarik Aawaz' which she helped found in 2001. Rita is former Chair of the Board of the Global Fund for Women and is a current board member of the Urgent Action Fund.

Index